THE ZONE OF EMERGENCE

THE ZONE OF EMERGENCE

Observations of the Lower Middle and Upper Working Class
Communities of Boston, 1905–1914

Robert A. Woods and Albert J. Kennedy

Abridged and Edited
With a Preface
by Sam Bass Warner, Jr.

Second Edition

THE M.I.T. PRESS

Massachusetts Institute of Technology
Cambridge, Massachusetts, and London, England

HN
80
B7
K4
1969

FOREWORD

Since its first abridged publication seven years ago this book has attracted growing attention because of its unique subject matter and because of the great timeliness of the issues it confronts. Now, after it has been out of print for several years, the MIT Press has responded to the book's initial reputation by bringing out an enlarged second edition. This edition gives the entire 1905-1914 manuscript in its longest form with the exception of two redundant chapters that summarize material on Swedish and Canadian immigrants already presented in the neighborhood descriptions of the book.

The subject matter of the book is the working-class and lower-middle-class districts beyond the core city of Boston. As such this is the only book I've ever seen which gives anything like a systematic coverage of these vast stretches of the American metropolis, quarters which are neither slum nor elite suburb. Put another way, this is the best social science survey I've found to accompany the early twentieth-century naturalistic novel. The concern for the life of ordinary common people took the authors directly into the problems which so trouble the American city and American nation today: mass culture versus the survival of ethnic and racial pluralism, irresponsible local government versus neighborhood power, the metropolitan economy versus local control, the family versus the street life, integration versus racial and ethnic prejudice. In short, there is hardly a topic in today's newspaper which these settlement house researchers did not uncover in their investigation of life beyond the slum.

A close reading of the book reveals that Albert J. Kennedy, more than any of the other authors, was, even before World War I, concerned with the issue we now call cultural pluralism. His chapters especially worry over the decay of ethnic ways and the unsatisfactory nature of the emerging working-class and middle-class American culture. In my interview with him in 1962 he was still interested in this theme, and he complained that most intellectuals of that era (before the blacks had raised the issue once more) had neglected this important dimension of American life.

Because of the antique tone of this book some mention

should be made of the modern reader's reaction to the racial
stereotyping found in the text. The stereotypes used by the
authors of this 1905-1914 manuscript were commonplace for the
day. They were neither kinder nor more unjust than normal
prewar collegiate discourse. When this text was read to Mr.
Kennedy in 1962, some forty years after he had last seen it, he
too was shocked by some of the statements made about immigrants and Negroes.

I'm sure that had Mr. Kennedy finished editing the manuscript he would have omitted most of the racist language as
improper and misleading. Nevertheless, since one cannot know
in 1969 what an editor would have done in 1915 or 1920, the
manuscript is published as found. Thus it stands as evidence of
the unguarded, even thoughtless, expression of young people
of good will in the years before World War I. I do ask the
reader to remember, however, that Mr. Kennedy as an author
and settlement house worker led a life of urban liberalism which
stood in direct opposition to the prejudices that appear in
this text.

Sam Bass Warner, Jr.

Ann Arbor, Michigan
February 1969

TABLE OF CONTENTS

PREFACE TO THE FIRST EDITION

By Sam Bass Warner, Jr.

Boston's first settlement house, the South End House, established a national reputation in the opening decades of this century with a series of studies of urban life. More than any other settlement group, the South End House devoted itself to systematic analysis of the city. The series began in 1898 with an examination of the slum, *The City Wilderness,* and closed in 1922 with a summary of the settlement house movement and its techniques, *The Settlement Horizon.*

Taken as a whole the series constitutes an impressive body of pioneer studies of urban poverty. It will endure as one of the most complete American records of the obstacles then confronting native and immigrant poor. *The Settlement Horizon* stands as the capstone of the series, a sophisticated discussion of the techniques which had been developed over a quarter of a century to assist individuals and families in their struggle to achieve a middle-class American life.

"The Zone of Emergence," one of the major studies, was substantially in conflict with the assumptions of the other books of the series. Supervised by Robert A. Woods (1865-1925), director of the South End House, it was written by Albert J. Kennedy (1879-1968) in collaboration with other House residents. The authors prepared an almost complete first draft during the years 1905-1914 but they never finished the work. Although editing was apparently resumed in 1920 the manuscript was never published.

Like most of the series "The Zone of Emergence" was a study of a city district, but in this case the subject was not a slum but the more prosperous residential and industrial quarters of the lower middle class and upper working class. The districts studied were Charlestown, East Boston, South Boston, and the near-in portions of Dorchester, Roxbury, and Cambridge. What the authors meant by "emergence" was emergence from the slum into the main stream of American life. The most important difference between this book and the others was its discovery that the common life of American families was of such a quality as to be in need of major reorientation. By implication this discovery challenged most of the prior assumptions of social settlement work.

The themes of the other books were poverty, tenements, bosses, and immigrants. The theme of "The Zone of Emergence" was the sterile discipline of American life. Its fictional equivalent was not Stephen Crane's *Maggie,* or Upton Sinclair's *The Jungle.* Rather the unfinished manuscript was a sort of advance demonstration of the *Studs Lonigan* trilogy written by James T. Farrell in the 1930's.

In the zone of emergence the bedroom towns were not integrated communities, but fast-changing clusters of people in one income group or another. Its churches were primarily social, not religious, institutions. Its lodges, clubs, and athletic societies more narrowed than enlarged the social horizon of their members. Its schools neither trained skilled craftsmen and technicians nor substantially enriched the culture of their pupils. Its youth were beginning to be organized into street-corner gangs. Its parents were skilled artisans, factory hands, and small tradesmen, working long hours, struggling to buy a home or move to a better district — men and women with little to give their children but a paid-up mortgage, little to give their community but a desperate demand for order and prosperity.

"The Zone of Emergence," in the incomplete form in which it comes down to us, is a confused manuscript, full of contradictions. The authors took satisfaction in the Americanization and economic progress of the population, but at the same time were troubled by the quality of the lives of their subjects. Implicit in the earlier books was a program: better housing and public health, better working conditions, protection against unemployment, and more effective teaching of the middle class attitudes of thrift, temperance, education, and hard work. Such ideas gave the writers of those books a common focus. Some of this program was also relevant to the more prosperous zone of emergence areas. But the problems which now most concerned the authors were ones of culture, not of economic welfare. The previous studies made at the South End House left the authors unprepared for this confrontation, and the result is a work that mixes description with a search for remedies.

HISTORY OF THE MANUSCRIPT

In 1958 Harold A. Richman, a Harvard senior in search of material for an honors thesis, discovered the typewritten manuscript of "The Zone of Emergence" in a coal bin of the South End House.[1] The manuscript had presumably been in dead storage since 1929 when Mr. Kennedy left Boston to become head worker at the University Settlement in New York City. In the fall of 1959 Professor John Gaus of Harvard, a former House resident, called my attention to the work. My own historical studies of the development of Roxbury and Dorchester led me to appreciate the importance of this unique analysis of old inner suburbs. A grant from the Joint Center for Urban Studies of the Massachusetts Institute of Technology and Harvard University has made possible publication of this abridgement of the manuscript.

The manuscript consists of 335 double-spaced pages, on which are many penciled editorial marks, one of which bears the date 1920. According to Mr. Kennedy, most of these marks were made by Mr. Woods, who planned to quiz the authors about the presentation of their material.[2]

Kennedy's handwritten table of contents accompanies the typescript. This table lists and identifies the authors of an introduction, six chapters on specific localities in the zone of emergence (Charlestown, Cambridgeport, East Cambridge, Roxbury and Dorchester, South Boston, East Boston), chapters on the Swedes, the Canadians, and the Negroes, and a conclusion. The last two chapters were never written. An outline for a statistical appendix also accompanies the manuscript, and according to Professor Gaus maps

---

[1] The South End House director, Charles Liddell, and a house resident, Albert Boer, have together restored the library of the South End House. The original manuscript of "The Zone of Emergence" and many old papers and records are now conveniently arranged there at the House headquarters, 20 Union Park Street, Boston.

[2] I had the pleasure of spending an afternoon with Mr. Kennedy at his home in Peekskill, New York, in July, 1961. A copy of the manuscript was sent to him before our discussions and I am indebted to him for much information concerning the background of the manuscript.

were prepared. The appendix was never finished and the maps have been lost.

The introduction, a survey of the whole work, was written by Woods and Kennedy. These two men dominated the South End House research activities. Both were graduates of theological schools and were imbued with the Social Gospel. Woods had founded the House and had directed both *The City Wilderness* and the second major study, *Americans in Process* (1902). By 1907, however, when work began on "The Zone of Emergence," Woods' many activities — as head worker and chief fund raiser for the House, and member of numerous charitable and municipal committees — forced him to give up active supervision of research. Kennedy, who had come to South End House on a Harvard – South End fellowship and was carrying on a national survey of settlement work, assumed more and more the direction of research. Over the next fifteen years the two men collaborated on three books, *Handbook of Settlements* (1911), *Young Working Girls* (1913), and *The Settlement Horizon* (1922).

Kennedy wrote more of "The Zone of Emergence" than anyone else. He was responsible for the chapters on Cambridgeport, East Boston, the Swedes, the Canadians, and a sub-chapter on Roxbury's Ward 17. His Cambridgeport essay appears to be the most finished of all the drafts. Kennedy had studied at Rochester with Raushenbush, the leader of the Social Gospel movement, and just before coming to the South End House received his S.T.B. from Harvard. From 1907 to 1928 he was director of investigations and associate head worker at the House. After Woods' death in 1925 he became head worker, but left in 1929 to direct the University Settlement in New York. From 1914 to 1934 he was secretary of the National Federation of Settlements.

William I. Cole (1859-1935), who had written parts of *The City Wilderness* and *Americans in Process*, wrote the chapter on Charlestown. Cole was a former Congregational minister from Holton, Maine, a founding member of the South End House, and its secretary until 1913 when he went to Wheaton College as a professor of sociology.

Eugene L. Sheldon (1885-1957) and Ordway Tead (1891-   ) both worked on the East Cambridge chapter. Sheldon was born in Springfield, Massachusetts, and graduated from Harvard in 1906. Between 1906 and 1908 he did a year of graduate work at

Harvard and worked as a feature writer for the *Boston Globe*. He must have written a draft of the chapter during this period. He went to the *New York World* in 1908, held a variety of newspaper jobs until 1916, and then became a professional script writer for the movies. Sheldon was ultimately a major director for Paramount Pictures.

Tead, the son of a Somerville, Massachusetts, Congregational minister, was at the South End House from 1912 to 1914 as an Amherst College Fellow. He took Sheldon's draft, did further research, and wrote the version which comes down to us. After some years in management counseling Tead became the editor of social and educational books for Harper and Brothers, New York.

The chapter on Roxbury and Dorchester has three parts. With Tead, George E. Cary (1884-) wrote the sub-chapter on Roxbury Crossing (Ward 18). The son of a missionary, Cary was an Amherst Fellow at the House from 1907 to 1909. He stayed on until 1911, serving as director of the South Bay Union community center, studying social work, and attending the Harvard Divinity School. In 1912 he was ordained a Congregational minister, and since 1919 he has held the pastorate of the First Church of Christ in Bradford, Massachusetts. Kennedy wrote the sub-chapter on Lower Roxbury (Ward 17); and Marion Booth (1887-), with Tead, wrote the essay on Dorchester (Ward 16). Miss Booth was born in Conshohocken, Pennsylvania, and graduated from Smith College in 1910. From 1912 to 1914 she held the Smith College Fellowship to the South End House. In 1914 she married Sherwood Trask. After some years of art study and school teaching, which included a year at Marietta Johnson's Organic School in Fairhope, Alabama, Mrs. Trask became a successful New York antique dealer and decorator of country inns. Since 1937 she and her husband have lived on an old Mennonite farm in Bucks County, Pennsylvania, where they have conducted experiments in agriculture.

Mrs. Eleanor H. [Bush] Woods (1873-1957) wrote the chapter on South Boston. She was born in Staten Island, New York, the daughter of an Episcopal minister. In 1896 she graduated from Smith College, and the next year did a semester of graduate work at Radcliffe. Between 1897 and 1902 she was an active worker for the Associated Charities of Boston, in the Family Welfare Society. This service led in 1901 to South Boston visiting and to an acquaintance with Mr. Woods. On September 18, 1902, she and Robert Woods married.

All the remaining chapters were written by Kennedy. John Daniels (1881-1953) was to have written a chapter on the Negroes. Daniels was Harvard Fellow to the South End House in 1905-1906, and continued in settlement work in Buffalo, Baltimore, and New York until 1921, when he became director of the English Speaking Union. He held that post until 1934. In 1914 he published *In Freedom's Birthplace*, a study of the history and status of Boston's Negroes. Presumably his chapter in "The Zone of Emergence" was to have been a selection of some of this material.

This abridgement of "The Zone of Emergence" omits the chapters on the Swedes and the Canadians. These two ethnic chapters were dropped on the grounds that they largely summarize material given throughout the book.

Two manuscript versions of the sub-chapters on Roxbury Crossing (Ward 18) and Dorchester (Ward 16) exist. The first and fuller versions are presented here. Condensations of them were written by Miss Booth, presumably at the request of Mr. Kennedy, who felt the originals were "too largely in terms of a social program."[3] I chose the first drafts because they furnish an interesting insight into the reaction of young college graduates to these old districts and because they give the most factual material. Obviously they would have been substantially rewritten before the book was published. All the chapters published here are given in their entirety without alteration except for some spelling and punctuation and the omission of a few tables. A few clarifying footnotes and explanations in brackets have been added for the reader's convenience.[4]

According to Mr. Kennedy, "The Zone of Emergence" was

---

[3] Comment in pencil in Kennedy's handwriting on the blue cover sheet to the chapter on Roxbury and Dorchester. Repeated on the cover sheet to the sub-chapter on Dorchester.

a war casualty. As the book neared completion in 1914 the South End House entered a period of crisis. At first the war in Europe brought a depression to America, thereby increasing the burden of service placed upon the settlement. At the same time the House's financial supporters shifted their attention to European causes. For the next four years the House lacked both the time and the money to complete and publish the book.

The post-war decision not to finish and publish the book must have derived from the balance of alternatives facing Woods and Kennedy. The national reputation of these two men (they were, respectively, president and secretary of the National Federation of Settlements) led to an invitation by the Russell Sage Foundation to write a survey of the American settlement movement. They could do this, or return to "The Zone of Emergence" — an incomplete manuscript no longer fresh in their minds, for which the research was already becoming out-of-date and the authors of which were dispersed. The balance of alternatives clearly favored a new work. Woods and Kennedy chose to write *The Settlement Horizon*.

In addition to the contrast between the pleasure of a new work and the drudgery of an old one, it seems likely that the discoveries of the research itself worked against the completion and publication of "The Zone of Emergence." For twenty-odd years Woods and his associates had been working to help Boston's native and immigrant poor achieve the condition and attitudes of middle class life. This almost-completed study of the more prosperous working class and lower middle class suburbs told the authors that the escape from the slum led to a place of unsatisfactory religious, educational, work, and community relations. The logical conclusion for "The Zone of Emergence" could only have been a general call for the reform of American life. The South End authors were not prepared to take this final step.

4 Xerox copies of the manuscript, complete except for the condensed versions of the Roxbury Crossing and Dorchester sub-chapters, have been deposited in each of the following libraries: Library of Congress, University of Chicago Library, and Library of the University of California at Berkeley.

Kennedy, after rereading the manuscript more than forty years later, said that the book could be characterized as the confrontation by a youthful group of Anglo-Protestants of a subject they could not handle. It seems fair to add that the book is a confrontation of subject matter which American society has as yet been unable to handle.

The chapter that was to be the conclusion was never written, nor have the answers to the questions raised by the book yet been agreed upon. They are today's problems: What should be the community life of a metropolis? What is the proper attitude toward work in a society of competitive capitalism? If American middle class culture is mediocre, drab, and empty, how should it be reoriented, and whence will its regeneration come?

The Settlement Background

The settlement movement, in which "The Zone of Emergence" had its origin, began in England and was transplanted to America in the 1880's. It was a missionary undertaking. Whether conducted by laymen or ministers, its purpose was to visit strange lands to bring new ways to the people there. The "foreign lands" were the slums of great cities.[5]

Large industrial cities were new in the world, and the poverty of so many of their citizens contradicted the popular American notion that every healthy, moral man, left to himself, could achieve economic competence. Some of the charity reformers of the 1870's had come right out and stated that the cause of personal economic failure in an urban environment often lay beyond the control of the individual. Also, the much-read English Victorian authors, though at odds in their prescriptions for reform, focused public attention upon the paradox of the

---

[5] For good surveys of the history of the settlement movement see: Jane Addams, Robert A. Woods, *et al, Philosophy and Social Progress* (New York, 1893), and Robert A. Woods and Albert J. Kennedy, *The Settlement Horizon* (New York, 1922); also, Jane Addams, *Twenty Years at Hull House* (New York, 1910); Lillian D. Wald, *The House on Henry Street* (New York, 1915); and Eleanor H. Woods, *Robert A. Woods, Champion of Democracy* (Boston, 1929).

politically free man who was yet a prisoner of his environment. Dickens, Mill, Spencer, Ruskin, and George Eliot, by stressing the link between environment and morality, led their American readers toward an awareness of what became known in the 1890's as the "social question." The social question was: how can a modern industrial society create conditions conducive to individual morality?

The agency which was to lead the attack on the social question was the urban settlement house. The principal type of settlement house was a commons, in America a residence of young, educated middle class men and women who lived together in a poor district and helped the people there cope with the problems of everyday life. Their special concerns were the care of children and the aged, the improvement of housing and sanitation, and the augmenting of public facilities for education and culture.

In England such activities were thought to be the modern equivalents of the charitable duties of the parish squire, who traditionally had been charged with overseeing the well-being of his district. In America, the placing of the college-educated elite among the poor was thought to recreate something of the conditions of the former village life in which a spirit of neighborliness gave the well-to-do the motive to assist their fellow villagers.

Both these historical analogies proved to be fruitless. In England resident squires could not be restored to London's East End; in America the prairie village spirit could not be regenerated in Chicago's South Side. The settlement movement, however, displayed a marvelous vitality. Between 1886 and 1911, in the United States alone, 392 settlement houses were established. They were scattered among 34 states.

The source of this dynamism lay in the crisis of Protestantism in both England and America. To many young people, much of the teaching of Protestantism seemed unsuited to the times, and what they valued in its message they saw to be increasingly inoperative. What was the value of a religion of personal salvation when families starved in cellars, when business and politics were often nothing but organized greed, when alcoholism, crime,

and vice seemed the most conspicuous products of urban progress? Further, the retreat of city Protestant parishes before the
inrush of foreign immigrants and native workingmen called
into question the ability of the established sects to govern the
morality of the new industrial cities. If Protestantism with its
traditional emphasis on personal rectitude, hard work and self-
improvement could not even preach to the urban masses, what
would become of the new society?

Young American men and women took up settlement work as
a new occupation that offered a moral and constructive life.
Those male college graduates who were repelled by commercial-
ism had a narrower range of occupational choice than that available to their counterparts today. Medicine, teaching, and the
ministry were almost the only professions in which a young
graduate might feel he could serve his fellow man. There was
no extensive employment in government or private social-service
organizations. The settlement movement also was able to draw
on the first generation of college-educated women. Occupational
restrictions bore severely upon them. For the men, the settlement
house was often a temporary experience of a few years; for the
women it was likely to be the work of a lifetime. These occupational conditions gave the early settlements almost a monopoly on
the service-oriented college graduates, and the energy and impact
of the beginning years of the movement were in large measure
the result of the enthusiasm and talent of the first joiners.

These young, educated, middle class crusaders were free
from the Social Darwinist philosophy of many wealthy Americans
who interpreted the condition of the poor to be the result of
inherited incapacity. But early leaders were frank in their class
orientation, seeing their task as the application of middle class
values and techniques to the problems of life in working class
slums. When Jane Addams moved her family furniture into an
old farm house on Halstead Street, Chicago, hers was not an
attempt to insinuate herself into the neighborhood mores, but
rather to offer a model of middle class home life to any who
wished to avail themselves of her hospitality and teaching. The
settlement movement's battery of child groups, night education
meetings, art shows, craft and athletic facilities was a conscious
presentation of the tools of the middle class morality. In this

pre-World War I period when millions of families aspiring to the middle class were trapped by economic forces in low income neighborhoods, these techniques in some measure achieved their end because many of the settlement's users shared the goals of their benefactors.

The movement was impatient and energetic, but not revolutionary. In England Christian Socialism was an important ingredient in the settlement movement, but in America settlement workers did not advance from Ruskin to socialism. Though often sympathetic with radicals like Debs and Heywood, Americans rarely attached themselves to the radical political parties or radical unions. Instead young settlement workers fought city hall; they badgered legislatures; they attacked specific abuses with specific measures. If the local streets were dirty, they agitated until the streets were cleaned; if a tenement was unsanitary, they forced the landlord to repair the plumbing; if parents were sending an under-age child to work, they returned the child to school. As educated men and women they kept themselves informed of legislation and techniques practiced in other cities and in Europe. There was a wealth of correspondence among them, and their writings abound with their experiences. By legislation, by group meetings, by case work, by seeking out what others neglected, by constant address to the physical and social environment of the city, they helped the cities advance toward the universal achievement of their own minimum standards for a moral life.

It was in their efforts to live out the Christian doctrine of the brotherhood of man that the settlement workers made their most important contribution. Their example of brotherhood served society at two levels — at the level of individual friendship and at the level of communication between rich and poor. America in the late nineteenth and early twentieth centuries was a highly competitive society with sharp social differentiations based on income. It badly needed mediators. The settlement workers, by their example and by their speeches and writings, educated the wealthy and the middle class to the realities of working class life. At a time when labor unions were widely thought to be instruments of revolution, settlement workers told the middle class that economic unions like the American

Federation of Labor were necessary devices for the protection of
the worker and for the preservation of capitalism. By descriptions of the welfare activities of city bosses, settlement workers
helped to teach municipal reformers that if local government
was to serve the needs of its citizens it must enlarge its functions.
In short, the settlements urged a change in the public attitude
toward the everyday problems of life. All individuals alike face
the problems of birth, work, marriage, and death. Settlement
workers asked that the institutions of the society, both public
and private, give more attention to the facts of daily living. By
so doing they helped prepare the ground for the reforms sponsored by the middle class in the Progressive and New Deal eras.

THE SOUTH END HOUSE PHILOSOPHY

When settlement workers turned to social philosophy, however, they appeared at their worst. All the conflicts and incon-
sistencies of turn-of-the-century middle class American life
hampered their attempts to propose a coherent structure for
society. In their philosophic writings, benevolence and fellowship often appeared as apologies for the fact of economic in-
equality; education appeared as a device for teaching manners;
and reform appeared as a mechanism for retarding change. Significantly, some of the best known workers like Wald and Addams
did not attempt to propose a consistent program for reform.
They wrote of their actions on a case by case basis; for them
the world was for a moment static as they faced an individual
and his personal problems. Significantly, too, today the most
dynamic descendant of the early settlement movement is the
profession of social and psychiatric case work. In the works of
Mary Richmond can be seen the unfolding logic of a life begun
in the framework of Christian charity and ended with the
establishment of the modern profession of social worker.[6]

Robert A. Woods (1865-1925) of Boston's South End House

---

[6] Mary E. Richmond, *Friendly Visiting Among the Poor* (New York,
1903); *The Good Neighbor in the Modern City* (Philadelphia, 1908);
Social Diagnosis (New York, 1917).

was the philosopher of the settlement movement, and its limitations are evident from the works he wrote and supervised, including "The Zone of Emergence." Like most settlement workers Woods was an outsider, a stranger to the city and its slums. He was middle class in thought and income. Born in a country suburb outside Pittsburgh, he was educated at Amherst College and the Andover Theological Seminary. When he moved to Rollins Street in the South End of Boston he was as exotic a resident as the latest arrival from Syria. From his similarity to the well-to-do of Boston came his strength — his capacity to raise money for projects, his ability to command the attention of middle class audiences and readers, his effectiveness before legislative committees, his confidence that his ways were the proper ones for all men, and his power as a model to those who worked with him and those who sought the services of the South End House.

In the studies prepared under Woods' administration of the South End House — especially *The City Wilderness, Americans in Process,* and "The Zone of Emergence" — all these outsider's strengths also appeared as weaknesses. There was the patronizing tone of the well-to-do in speaking of the poor; the middle class abhorrence of dirt, prostitution, gambling, and drink; the condescension of the native toward foreign ways; the amusement of the college man at the entertainments of the working class. In short, in these books, when the subject under discussion was not an individual case or a strictly factual economic description, there was frequently a complete failure of the understanding and compassion which characterized the settlement movement at its best.

To the modern reader the least excusable failure of understanding in the three books was their use of racial stereotypes. Despite a satisfactory analysis of the effect of caste restrictions upon the Negro, the South End House authors viewed the Negro as hereditarily inferior to all other Americans. The Jews, though meeting more of the requirements of good citizenship proposed by the authors — industry, intelligence, and active family, group and religious life — were, as a race, good at arithmetic, dirty, grasping, cosmopolitan, and altogether a dubious addition to the

nation. The Italians were cheerful, good cooks, colorful deco-
rators of houses, fine gardeners — a Mediterranean race; and, of
course, the Swedes were hard-working, taciturn, sexually loose,
and drank to excess — a Nordic race.

Though all of the South End House books are bound by
these racial stereotypes, "The Zone of Emergence" differed from
the earlier books in viewing the recently assimilated, not the
newly-arrived, as being the city's major problem.

Years of association with foreigners had forced Woods and
his group to change their position. The first two books, *The
City Wilderness* and *Americans in Process*, were oriented toward
the problem of making middle class Americans out of immigrants
with the greatest possible dispatch. Most of the people living
in the zone of emergence, however, were second and third
generation Irish and Canadians, or even Americans of long standing. A high percentage of the residents spoke English; many
had been to the public schools, which the settlement house
authors were accustomed to viewing as the ideal agent of
assimilation. The neighborhoods were reported as temperate,
law abiding, church-going, and in good physical condition. Yet
there was no flowering of culture or of civic ideals. Rather, life
in the zone of emergence was drab, its politics was sometimes
as corrupt as that of the poor immigrant wards, and children were
beyond the teaching and control of their parents. Under these
conditions the isolated native American citizen, not the foreigner
and his strange ways, appeared to the South End House authors
to be the major problem of the city.

In his chapter on East Boston Kennedy suggested that the
emphasis in the former books on rapid assimilation of the immigrant was wrong. He argued that the best American citizens
were those who first participated actively in ethnic societies and
who later, after this kind of community training, chose to join
the larger American community life. Kennedy proposed that
the City of Boston adopt a policy of encouraging hyphenated
American groups, and in this way promote self-education in
citizenship. In addition to this new orientation toward Americanization, "The Zone of Emergence" contained a search for useful
cultural material. Each group was scanned for qualities that
might relieve the drab and unsatisfactory aspects of common

American culture. The Swedes might improve the standards of industrial workmanship, the Germans might popularize sports and music, the Negroes might add religious fervor to Protestantism, the Italians might expand the diet and improve city architecture, and the Irish Catholic parish might be useful as an example for small-scale community control of youth and morals.

This appreciation of immigrant ways and the recognition of the cultural weaknesses of native American life led the South End House authors toward a position of cultural pluralism. In *The Settlement Horizon* Woods and Kennedy urged that the settlement preserve the unique qualities of each immigrant group. In taking this final position they were joining a general movement among American intellectuals. The immigration restriction acts of the 1920's, however, made this new position academic.

In addition to having a racialist bias, the South End House studies tended to minimize the economic causes of undesirable behavior. This failing was not due to a lack of accurate empirical data: the settlement authors wanted to know how much workingmen were paid, what food and rent cost, how many weeks in the year men worked. To gather such information all the published statistics of the day were used, and special studies were also undertaken.[7] The economic materials of *The City Wilderness*, *Americans in Process*, and "The Zone of Emergence" make them part of the long chain of nineteenth and twentieth century studies of everyday life. Unlike the ethnic observations, the economic data were accurate. This work was the basic authority which supported the reform proposals of the settlement. Thanks to this work, when Woods testified on housing, working conditions, unemployment, and relief, he knew what he was talking about.

Today it is clear that many of the problems of both the slums and the relatively more prosperous neighborhoods were the consequence of low income. One of the ways nineteenth century America purchased its new cities and its new machines was to underpay the clerk, the factory hand, the carpenter, and the laborer. The settlement program urged economic unionism,

---

[7] The amount of early South End House research was extensive. A complete bibliography of this work is Woods and Kennedy, eds., *Handbook of Settlements* (New York, 1911), 128-130.

housing code enforcement, better police protection, and temperance as devices for meliorating the lot of the underpaid. More, however, was required. In Boston the rapid exodus of families from the poor sections of the city during the prosperity that followed the two World Wars, and the raised standard of living of even those who remained, together have ended many of the social problems which concerned the authors of *The City Wilderness* and *Americans in Process.* To have achieved the control of economic affairs necessary even to approach the conditions of 1950 in 1912 would have taken a degree of re-orientation of American economic thought that only the pre-war Socialists were willing to contemplate. The leaders of the settlement movement were economic moderates.

Above all else Woods and his associates were social moralists. To modern readers trained by sociological analyses like William F. Whyte's *Street Corner Society* the South End community studies have an antique and often unacceptable tone. Their very moralism, however, prepared the South End House group for the discoveries of "The Zone of Emergence."

The method of these old books is no longer popular with sociologists, but well handled it was a method completely compatible with the use of empirical material for the construction of ideal systems. A series of questions were asked: first, what are the minima of environment and personal habits necessary to sustain a moral life? second, to what extent does life in the areas studied meet these criteria? third, given the description of actual conditions, what can be done to bring the community up to the minimum levels of performance?

Many of the confusions and contradictions of the book stemmed from the authors' failure to see that they were proceeding by measurement to absolute standards. Kennedy's editorial notes in "The Zone of Emergence" in which he objected to a chapter as "too largely in terms of a social program" show his desire to work within the terms of the material itself. Woods regarded these books as dispassionate scientific research. The formal structure of the books, their limitation of the explicitly programmatic chapters to the introduction and the conclusion, and their careful attention to first hand observation and statistical evidence, all witness the scientific intent of the authors. One generation's social science, however, is another's sermons, and today it is apparent that moralizing fills every chapter.

Instead of scientific accuracy, instead of standards given by the subject under study, the South End House authors measured with a sense of fair play. They viewed society in the structure of a moral contract: society owed a man an environment sufficient to allow him to be moral without requiring him to be a hero; given that environment, society had the right to expect conformity to its minimum standards.

In the studies of the slums the problems confronted were so striking as to render irrelevant any questions of the adequacy of the minimum standards. Was the workingman intemperate, saloons tempted him at every turn; was the shop girl brazen and loose, hers was a lodging house neighborhood of single men, and the red light district of the metropolis; was family life torn apart, poverty forced the mother and father to work long hours; was the boy unskilled and ignorant, he had to leave school to take odd jobs; was the Irish ward politician corrupt and self-seeking, politics was one of the few paths to wealth open to him; did the widow cheat the charity board, adequate assistance was otherwise unobtainable. The environment seemed to excuse every failure of individuals to meet the minimum standards of middle class morality.

In the first two books the drama of city life was the struggle and triumph of individuals against their environment. The hopeful conclusions of both books rested upon Woods' observation that thousands of immigrants and poor Americans were winning this struggle — educating their children, improving their own skills and their jobs, putting by capital, making their way up and out into the middle class mainstream. Woods, an outsider to the city slum, took confidence in feeling that many of the slum's residents shared his values, and he took further confidence in the knowledge that he and his fellow settlement workers could help speed the process. They could help by reassuring the rest of America that in Babel things were much as in Springfield; they could help by urging the city and the state to undertake remedial legislation in housing, welfare, and working conditions; and they could help by raising money for family aid and special educational facilities.

In the rise of families from slum conditions, and in the reorganization of slum community life, Woods saw the promise of urban democracy. Woods' hopeful conclusions to *The City Wilderness* and *Americans in Process* were built upon his faith that the large forces of society could be contained and moulded by a revival of America's traditional small-scale institutions. In his view the voluntary associations of church and club must be revitalized, and the direct government institutions of the town meeting and the public school must become the models for the agencies of permanent urban reform.

This program of urban regeneration through the creation of a metropolitan social structure of hundreds of democratic villages was an extreme statement of the settlement idea. Jane Addams once called it "geographical salvation."[8] A committee of local landladies could not prevent the continued deterioration of the housing of central Boston; nor could an evening economic study group or a union relief committee stop the recurrence of the depressions that pressed so hard upon them. At most, such groups could improve the performance of their local ward boss, and, for their little district, they could achieve better law enforcement and better municipal services. Perhaps most important for their members' sense of well being, such groups could replace the feeling of isolation and helplessness with the pleasures of group life and activity.

Woods never seemed to realize to what degree his hopeful program for neighborhood revival was in direct conflict with his observations of Americanization. If for Boston's families the meaning of America was the chance for each individual and each family to make as much money as they could, if the family's most pressing social duty was to rise from poverty, what source would feed the regeneration of community life and morals?

Woods did not, however, ignore what he saw. In "The Zone

---

[8]In a letter to me December 3, 1962, Mr. Kennedy wrote that he was present at a meeting at Hull House in Chicago at which Mr. Woods "was expounding his doctrine of 'neighborhood in nation building' to which Miss Addams snapped back, 'Mr. Woods I do not believe in geographical salvation.'" This same incident is referred to by Kennedy in an address delivered at the National Conference of Social Work, June 4, 1953.

of Emergence" he chose to continue his studies of Americanization by following the movement of rising families out of the
crowded central city into the nearby residential quarters. The
fine title, "The Zone of Emergence," neatly condensed the theme
of Americanization. The very scale of the study, however, jeop-
ardized the neighborhood orientation. The former two books
had examined districts of a square mile in area; "The Zone
of Emergence" covered a whole ring of cities and towns around
central Boston — East Boston, South Boston, Roxbury, inner Dorchester, half of Cambridge, and Charlestown.

Kennedy, the principal author of "The Zone of Emergence,"
today regards as one of the most important contributions of the
book its destruction of the concept of the city as being made of
a series of semi-autonomous neighborhoods. Woods, himself,
never abandoned his hope that the model of the village could
be used to build city neighborhoods, and thereby bring about
the regeneration of American urban society. Two years before
his death he reiterated this theme in his book, *The Neighborhood
in Nation-Building*. A year later at the urging of his Amherst
College friends Woods went so far as to write a campaign
biography of Calvin Coolidge. He saw Coolidge as the example
of the best ways of the old rural America, and he hoped that
Coolidge's presidency would serve to revive the respect for and
use of these ways.

The village orientation toward the city neighborhood accounted for the detailed treatment in "The Zone of Emergence"
of clubs, churches, and small social and political groups. This
same orientation caused the authors to look carefully at the
patterns of everyday life within each area. The principal modern
value of the book stems from the authors' discoveries in this
smallest scale of city life.

LIFE IN THE ZONE OF EMERGENCE

Within the communities of the zone of emergence the
South End House observers found conflict and confusion at all
levels of society. Of first importance, the forces that created the
environment were beyond the control of those living in it. With
some care the authors demonstrated that transportation and

industry were the twin agents that moulded the local communities of the Boston metropolis. A new bridge, a horsecar line, or a cheap ferry brought thousands of new families to live in a district.

Each change in transportation often made possible new industrial development. This industrial pattern in turn determined the class of people who came to live in a district. The wharves of East Boston brought skilled artisans, native Americans and Canadians. These same wharves also brought immigrant Irish longshoremen. Kennedy predicted that the recent construction of a textile mill would degrade the district as a residential area by encouraging the influx of ill-paid help. He wrote: "In East Boston as in other localities similarly placed there has been much rejoicing over the establishment of new industries . . . Under present conditions a high class locality ought to send out invitations for a plague about as quickly as a cotton mill." The history of Ward 18, Roxbury, was told largely in economic terms: the failure of a piano company and its replacement by low-paying service and distribution firms was destroying the district's lower middle class character.

The commuting habit also undermined established forms of community life. The coincidence of place of work and place of residence, so characteristic of the former village life, was an exception in the new metropolis. Many of the residents of the zone of emergence worked outside their town boundaries. The new work and residence patterns meant that many towns lacked citizens who were interested in local affairs. Furthermore, the well-to-do and educated who traditionally took an interest in civic life were distributed very unevenly.

The interaction of the industrial and traffic patterns of Greater Boston caused each district to be successively occupied by ever lower income groups. Since the nineteenth century was the century not only of industrial change, but also of European immigration, the shift from one income group to the next lower one was often associated with a radical change in ethnic composition. The newcomers built cheaper houses than their predecessors; their structures crowded the land. The conflict of physical occupation became one aspect of a larger conflict among various habits of life. Strange languages, strange people, strange

churches impinged upon the ways of the former suburban villages. Most frequently the old families left the town, or, at the
very least, prosperous native Americans of long standing ceased
building in these inner industrial and residential areas. The
families that remained, rather than actively transmitting the old
New England ways to the newcomers, shut themselves up in their
established churches and clubs. The expansive democratic element in the New England heritage, which could have facilitated
communication between the old and the new, as it often did in
the case of the settlement workers, was abandoned by old residents in favor of defensive solidarity. The village churches
and the village government, formerly the symbols of a united
community, became bastions of minority interest.

Under such circumstances the local merchants were one of
the few groups which had an active interest in promoting local
community feeling. They supported weekly newspapers and
sponsored fairs and pageants, but the South End House observers found these to be weak efforts, incapable of generating strong
localism.

The politicians were representatives of ethnic minorities
whose task it was to put together coalitions of the minority
clusters of their districts. In Cambridgeport and Dorchester the
Protestant middle class held power; in East Boston, South Boston, and Roxbury, Irish Catholic combinations dominated. Political mores ranged from the more or less traditionally correct
procedures of Cambridgeport to the notoriously corrupt practice
of the Curley brothers in Roxbury's Ward 18. Whatever the style
of politics, local government in the zone of emergence was
largely ineffectual, and unable to exert much positive influence
upon the fate of the community.

The description of the character of community life in "The
Zone of Emergence" challenged the analysis of the previous
books. In the former studies, transience, new immigrants, poverty, and a politics of personal welfare were identified as factors
preventing the growth of an active and detached citizenship —
one that would be willing both to follow legal procedures and
to serve the interests of the whole community. In the zone of
emergence, by contrast, few were poverty-stricken, employment
was comparatively regular and often well paid, there was a high

proportion of home-ownership, most spoke English, and many
had at least an American grammar school education. An informed and detached citizenry, however, did not develop. In
the case of the slum, settlement house workers hoped to be the
agents for the creation of community life. In the inner residential and industrial suburbs, they faced, by contrast, the problem of reforming the habits of the major portion of America's
urban population. How could settlement houses reform a mass
whose income and place of residence showed that it had already
met the society's minimum standards of knowledge and morality?

The South End House investigators found, in addition to a
failure of community life, that Boston's median income group
was leading a life in which traditional ways were twisted or
destroyed. Conflicts and confusion characterized such adjust-
ments as the group had so far made to metropolitan living. The
life of the common citizen compared badly to some of the past
styles of American history; it lacked either the rigor of the Puri-
tans or the easy going sense of pleasure of the Revolutionary
bourgeoisie. The investigators' aesthetic judgment of neighborhoods in the zone of emergence summarized their assessment of
the new ways: they were "drab," "monotonous," "inadequate,"
and "deadly commonplace."

Bars, movie houses, social and athletic clubs, lodges, and
church groups served the people at play. The City of Boston
and neighboring towns had begun to provide recreation facilities
for residential neighborhoods, and the authors evaluated these
facilities in detail. For example, the Wood Island Park of East
Boston was in their view excellent, the Columbus Avenue Playground in Roxbury was too small and too far from the crowded
district it was to serve. The recreation program was, however,
largely one for children, and even if it had not been, it is
doubtful that municipal recreation activities could have materi-
ally advanced the cultural revival necessary to meet the settlement observers' criticisms.

"The Zone of Emergence" described a kind of desert in the
middle of American society. Lack of wealth prevented the
variety of modes then open to the rich, while Americanization
had dulled the color of the immigrant slum. The second and third
generations no longer respected and carried on the arts, crafts,

and festivals of the parents and grandparents. The young Jewish housewife of East Boston went to the movies; the West Indian son or grandson no longer played cricket in the public park; the old Irish literary societies of East Cambridge and Charlestown had ceased production. Members of later generations who wished to keep in touch with the old ways had to travel into the declining neighborhoods of the central city where the old people, the first ethnic church, and the social hall remained. No new folk music, art, literature, or religion sprang from the daily life of the Americanized residents of the zone of emergence. These citizens had become the majority; their amusements, like their work, made them part of the general culture of a large American metropolis; they were now members of a society that covered half a continent; yet how far were the dances at the social and athletic club, the annual lodge banquet, the parish jealousies, and the atomized local politics from the scale of life which governed their fate.

Under these conditions, the public school, one of the great hopes of the former books, ceased to seem a hero to the settlement house authors. The youth of the zone of emergence still needed at least a grammar school education, and the local schools were shown to be one of the principal means whereby immigrant and lower class children moved up the occupational scale. Irish school teachers, politicians, and journalists, Canadian dentists, Jewish lawyers and doctors, all frequently reached their professions through the route of the public school. The book did not, however, strike a theme of satisfaction with the schools, but rather demanded that the curriculum be expanded to include industrial training. Though most of the children of the zone of emergence would not become professionals, no public school system then offered adequate commercial or industrial training for the future working force. The settlement workers' demand for practical training was motivated, however, by more than a desire to improve workers' efficiency; they were seeking a solution for the unsatisfactory attitude toward work which they had observed.

Young people in the zone of emergence sought neither crafts nor factory work. The child of the skilled mechanic chose an office job; the laborer's daughter preferred to work among the riches of the department store rather than make the same or better pay in a factory; a carpenter's son went to school only to become a clerk. He never married. The pattern of such choices threatened some of the major premises of the society from which these young people sprang. How could the citizens of Roxbury and Cambridge be happy if work became to them but the labor necessary for wages, offering neither the satisfactions of craftsmanship nor the chance for wealth? How could democratic society be made a fellowship if the work of its lower classes was despised? What would be the future source of the nation's dynamism if its youth chose comfortable, easy jobs instead of the hazards of economic conflict? The second generation's choice of a routine, secure life marked an unheroic end to the drama of Americanization which was the hopeful theme of the earlier South End House books. Could it be that the parents' struggle from the slum tenement to the small suburban house ended there?

Former American middle class patterns of family life also seemed in jeopardy. Many parents did not even require the children's regular attendance at meals, a traditional minimum device of child supervision. Because the mothers often worked, children were separated at an early age from adult care. They played unsupervised on the front steps and street. Among immigrants the conflict between the generations divided children from parents. In the urban residential districts the lounging men and boys of rural Main Street appeared in the form of the modern juvenile gang. In many places the "malicious mischief" of these gangs had become a problem to homeowners, tradesmen, and unpopular minorities. The miles of city streets, the crowding of urban lands, and the new habit of apartment living made impossible the free play of the former village. Despite kindergartens, schools, and public playgrounds the raising of children in the city remained an unsolved problem. Among the older boys and girls, those beginning regular work, the new habits of city life threatened to undermine middle class sexual customs. The young people were no longer apprentices living with a family or clerks boarding with relatives; increasingly, they were anonymous lodging house residents whose only outside supervision was the discipline of large industrial and commercial establishments.

That a high proportion of residents of the zone of emergence were church members suggested to the South End House observers that a religious revival might become the agent for creation of a new morality which could order community life. The active interest of Protestant and Catholic churches in temperance led the authors to hope that this reform might mark the beginning of a revival. The subsequent Prohibition debacle today mocks their hopes. But it is not surprising that the crusade against alcohol could mislead an American moralist who was casting about for a medium with which to begin the reorganization of society.

Successful temperance required an act of individual will. It was a voluntary assertion of morality, and its proximate cause was either individual conviction or pressure from a small group. The predominance of temperate habits in an urban district could be interpreted as the promise of further moral progress. If a man, or a small group, could successfully renounce alcohol, was it not reasonable to expect an increased interest in family and community life, more regular work habits, and a search for new entertainments in sports, hobbies, and art? Even if the life of a small district seemed to contain no ideas or institutions sufficient to create new and satisfactory habits of work, family, and community life, at least such residents could be taught. The renunciation of alcohol was surely a demonstration of a quickened moral sense; such men and women must be educable.

The success of municipal prohibition movements could likewise be considered a token of moral progress. The no-license votes of Cambridge and the informal controls of Dorchester showed the presence of many enlightened citizens. Local prohibition demonstrated, further, that despite the strong pressure of breweries, liquor dealers and corrupt politicians, a democratic majority could still take effective action against community evils. Taking place in sections of the city that had big Catholic proportions, these votes also offered the additional encouragement of a show of united action by all creeds.

Heartened by what they thought were signs of promise in the anti-alcohol campaign, the South End House observers ignored some of their own evidence. They found, for instance, that residents of the no-license districts were heavy users of

Boston's saloons and purchasers of local drugstore liquor. Local temperance activity was largely a defense by middle class families against the most glaring evils of public alcohol consumption. Homeowners wanted to keep the saloon off *their* street, away from *their* house. The churches of the zone of emergence were not in fact leading their parishioners toward a new morality.

The authors also found that young people in the zone of emergence were losing interest in church affairs. This growing indifference, which characterized both native and foreign youth, promised ill for the future of established middle class religions. Most damaging, however, to the authors' hopes for a religious revival was the domination of the churches by a social, rather than a religious, purpose. Each class and each ethnic group had its own churches. The old Protestant families held the early nineteenth century parishes, which were separated from the new Baptist, Methodist, and Presbyterian congregations of the Canadian and native American newcomers to the city. The Catholic Church, too, was divided both into specialized ethnic parishes and into congregations of the poor and the well-to-do. The Jews did not escape fragmentation either, and in their case the new Reform movement added a doctrinal division to the economic ones. All churches were actively expanding their social functions — parochial schools, sodalities, young people's groups, even benefit associations and recreational facilities were being added to the ancient duties of the service and the minister's parish visitations. Except for some remarks by Kennedy on the citizen training benefits of these church functions, none of the many parishes of the zone of emergence was cited as being the source of a new pattern of morality and behavior. None was leading its parishioners toward a new attitude toward work, a new pattern of family life, a new educational orientation, or a general cultural revival.

In summary, "The Zone of Emergence" was a confused and contradictory book. The authors' desire to find a satisfactory source for moral change led them to be overly hopeful for the possibilities of the anti-liquor movement; their racialism caused them to misjudge immigrant life; their economic moderateness caused them to seek social solutions for what were often economic problems; their moralism confused their application of absolute standards with their careful empirical work; and their hope of perpetuating the small scale democracy of the pre-industrial era led them to think of localism in the no longer appropriate terms of the old village.

Despite these serious shortcomings, "The Zone of Emergence" remains an important book. Local historians, if they read with care, will find a description of the inner residential quarters and towns that surround Boston. No such survey has ever been made before or since. Social historians should seek out this book for similar reasons; descriptions of lower middle class and working class life are rare for any city in any period and this book is an important addition to the small list.

Above all, "The Zone of Emergence" is an interrogation of common life. With all their now-apparent confusions and prejudices the South End House authors valued accuracy enough to seek empirical data, to walk the streets, to count the churches, schools, and clubs, to talk to neighbors, to go to local politicians. Today one would like to send them back, armed with the techniques of modern social science, but most of the questions they asked of the material are the questions for which we still seek the answers. Just because these 1912 authors were working with the middle class Protestant orientation of the settlement movement they observed a central crisis in twentieth century American life. They demonstrated that the slum was but a dramatic manifestation of the revolutionary power of the industrialization of work and its associated urbanization of society. Like so many of the works of the post-World War I novelists, "The Zone of Emergence" is a declaration of moral disintegration. In the new urban situation the former patterns of sexual behavior, family life, work, play, and community life were changing rapidly, but the patterns were still confused and frequently in conflict with one another, often maintained because, lacking any other ways, men sought order by perpetuating what had gone before. Despite many changes, the old ways had not yet generated a new religion, a new art, a new economics, or a new government which would be able to order up the vast scale of life in which the common people now lived.

THE ZONE OF EMERGENCE

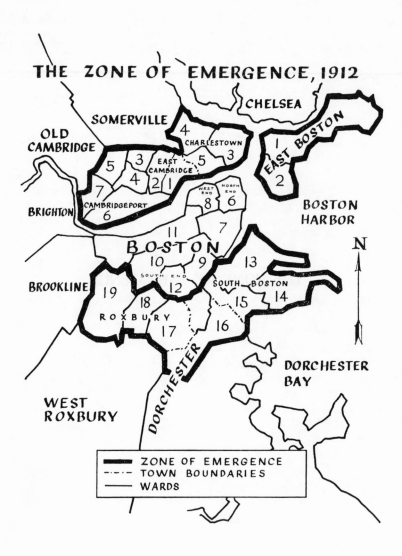

THE ZONE OF EMERGENCE, 1912

I

INTRODUCTION

A city is naturally round. In the Anglo Saxon world its nucleus is the "market," a downtown commercial and manufacturing quarter about which zone after zone is circlingly added as the population increases. The belt immediately about the business section, hemming it in, is given over to a circle of poor and crowded neighborhoods broken in one place by a downtown residential quarter illustrating wealth and social power. The outer edge of this inner belt usually marks the confines of the "old city." As additional territory is needed, the farms "beyond the walls" are invaded and disintegrated, or the adjacent towns are annexed. It sometimes happens that the land between the city proper and the suburbs, avoided in the outward movement, is neither city nor country, but gradually, by forward, sidewise, and even refluent pressure, intervening spaces are filled in, and the city completes its characteristic outline.

An oval peninsula, the town of Boston looks out over the water upon five jutting angles of land which run in toward it as a center: East and South Boston facing the outer harbor; Charlestown and Cambridge within; and Roxbury, with which it was once connected by an often overflowed isthmus or "neck," at the rear. As the city grew the downtown business quarter requisitioned the residential streets of the old town, and was itself later hemmed in by a series of congested tenement districts, broken only by the Back Bay. Beyond this inner belt, commonly known as the North, West, and South Ends, and the Back Bay, lie the ring of districts whose neglected story throws a deal of light upon the degree and method of progress which the city's immigrant peoples have been making.

A series of interlacing wave lines may be set forth to indicate the broad general and economic character of the belt as a whole. From the State House, which is the city's convenient geographical point of departure, the distance to the active center of each of these communities is nearly the same. Their downtown parts are near enough so that a considerable number of inhabitants walk to and from their work each day. Here runs the fire limit, the outer margin of tenement congestion within which wooden construction is not allowed, and beyond which the three-flat house is making rapid headway against the detached cottage. Here is the latitude of the standard wage of trade unionism. These various lines suggest a sort of beach up which people are struggling.

It is natural that public concern for urban conditions should first concentrate upon the need of the innermost tenement districts. Their situation brings them more or less continuously under the eye of the resourceful citizen, and their swarms of newly arrived immigrants continuously recreate the great drama of the building of the nation. Their colorful and dramatically staged misery makes a clear appeal to the city as a whole. This immediate and compelling challenge finally makes them a classic land of poverty. Unfortunately, in the minds of many citizens the clearly fixed field of civic responsibility and vision ends with these innermost tenement neighborhoods. Beyond is penumbra, in whose dim distance somewhere the average man believes the mass of the people live wholesomely in modified village isolation. The present volume represents an approach to a study which would widen the radius of concentrated social concern to a more appropriate and more effectual bound. It is hoped that these pages will show that from an economic, a political, and a cultural point of view, the districts immediately between the old city and the suburbs constitute a single sociological fact with a sharply defined significance and appeal.

Two main causes have contributed to give the zone its special character. One of these is the development of rapid transit, the other is the growth and the changed character of the local industries. The chief concern of the people of these districts during many years, was the vital one of getting into Boston. The main highways were laid out to this end, and in each community there was a time when the question of ferries and bridges most engaged the interest of the citizens. Once these improvements were secured the always vital problem of popular transportation came to the front. Each community rejoiced in its "hourlies" as the old stages were called. These were followed by the railways during the first half of the nineteenth century and each district was on the first station out of Boston. Horse cars were next provided, changing to the trolley and leading within the past decade to rapid transit by means of the elevated and the tunnel. The Elevated between Roxbury and Boston, the East Boston Tunnel, the Cambridge Tunnel, the East Cambridge Viaduct, and the projected tunnel[1] through the upper end of South Boston and into Dorchester emphasizes the emergence character of each community.

As the growth of commerce and industry makes increasing demands on the innermost portion of the city, those factories which require a considerable amount of space for their processes seek cheaper land on the outskirts of the city, and the older and more well-to-do inhabitants move away. The neighborhoods thus requisitioned naturally change character. It is this very tearing down of the community, however, which frees its more liberal conditions for the workers. Each of the districts under consideration was at one time a high-grade residential community. The American population retired before the inroads of the transportation companies and the factories, on the one hand, and the proximity of unskilled foreigners which the new industries called for on the other. Already, however, this same process is again being repeated. Further encroachments on the part of industry are now driving the Irish away, and their places are taken by more recent immigrants. The struggle for control shows itself plainly and dramatically in the assessors figures where a rise in population is generally accompanied with a decided fall in taxable personal property, and, in certain cases, of land and real estate as well.

Except in the case of the purely residential suburb close to a large city the local industries usually place the tone of the community. High grade industries attract and create a high grade population; and *vice versa*. Therefore the industrial fortunes of the communities we are considering are of the utmost importance. To a surprising degree, the industrial development of each one has proceeded on practically parallel lines. A period of rapid industrial growth based on peculiar local advantages of situation or on local enterprise; followed by a period of

---

[1] The subway tunnel from the South Station in downtown Boston to Andrew Square on the Dorchester-South Boston boundary was built between December 1916 and June 1918.

arrested development or even of industrial decline, lasting until
1900; followed again by a period of generous growth and upbuilding. The middle period of depression was brought on by
a series of causes which affected the industry of the entire city.
The decline of the iron and machine trades, the changes brought
about by the formation of trust[s] and combines, and a series
of labor difficulties together with a normal amount of poor
organization and administration, and the failure of managerial
ability in times of crisis, have all had their effect in changing
the industrial character of the belt.

The present revival of industry within the zone is thoroughly
sound, being based on nearness to the heart of Boston, on relatively cheap land, and on ease of transportation both by water
and railways. The zone is peculiarly well situated for factories
which carry on those services most necessary to maintain the
physical well-being of the population, being strategically close
to the down-town districts on the one hand, to the suburbs and
the outlying country on the other. The characteristic industries
include the railroad terminal service, the distribution of coal,
wood, ice, milk; the preparation and manufacture of meat products, bread, crackers, soap; and the delivery of these goods and
services over a wide range of territory. In addition to these most
characteristic industries there is a wide variety of manufacture
carried on in foundries, machine shops, piano factories, rubber
works, cabinet making establishments and stone yards. Charlestown, East Boston, and South Boston, provide in their docks for
a large seagoing and coast trade, and Roxbury and East Cambridge are reached from the harbor by schooner traffic in coal and
lumber which struggles for its right of way against a series of
drawbridges.

Though there are some exceptions, the neighborhoods of the
Zone of Emergence impress one familiar with the downtown
tenement communities as distinctly more habitable. The air is
brighter, cleaner, and more vibrant; sunshine falls in floods
rather than in narrow shafts; there is not so much dust and
smoke; the streets are quieter; there is less congestion and more
evident freedom of movement. These strikingly valuable advantages are found even in the worse portions of the community
where the housing is in itself sometimes worse than that which

is found in the downtown tenements. On the whole the housing of the zone is very much better than that of the inner belt. While there is a definite proportion of large tenements and poorly built houses, the majority of dwellings are three-family tenements or cottages, and practically all are detached with openings to the air in each room.

The total population of the zone (including Cambridge) was 297,772 in 1905 and 316,946 in 1910. The population of the Boston Wards 1 to 5; 13 to 15; 16 to 19 numbered 247,164 (1910) as over against 109,528 persons in Wards 6, 7, 8 and 9. The average density per acre in the zone is 56.24 as against 113.11 in the inner belt.[2] Some notion of the growth of population will be seen from the fact that during the years 1901-1907, 105 new buildings of the first and second class (valued at $2,265,-026) and 162 buildings of the third class (valued at $441,068) were erected yearly.[3] In addition a very considerable amount of remodelling goes on constantly, whereby cottages and small dwellings are unfortunately turned into apartments for two and three families.

The men over twenty years of age are more than half unskilled or semi-skilled and their numbers, moreover, are nearly balanced by those of the skilled workmen and the clerks. Over sixty-five percent of the residence property of the zone is owned by those who reside on it, and this is the best possible index that can be given of the end that holds the imagination and galvanizes the powers of a large proportion of the population. Doubtless the greater share of this property is encumbered with mortgage, but it is an index of striving and accomplishment.

In national affiliation 73,755 or 24 percent of the population is American or third generation through foreign ancestry. 182,905

[2] The authors are contrasting here Boston's zone of emergence districts (East Boston, Wards 1-2; Charlestown, Wards 3-5; South Boston, Wards 13-15; inner Dorchester and Roxbury, Wards 16-19) — with the inner low income sections of the city — the North End, Ward 6, the downtown and wholesale district, Ward 7; the West End, Ward 8, the lower South End, Ward 9.

[3] Buildings of masonry and masonry with timber floors were classified as first and second class construction, and wooden frame houses as third class.

or 61 percent is English speaking immigrant (including provincials); 40,243 or 13 percent are non-English speaking immigrants of the first and second generation; 3,500 or 1 percent are Negroes. Eighty-six percent of the population uses English as its native tongue, and this great body of the population gives tone to the entire locality. Whatever may be true of the inner belt of the city, certainly the zone of emergence is predominantly Anglo Saxon.

On the side of the zone which touches the city, a few struggling relics of the native American forces remain. The rear guard of the city's American population is to be found on the suburban side of the zone.

Mingled with this American remnant and advancing on the whole with a more substantial momentum is a considerable body of Irish, Provincials, Italians, and Russian Jews. The Irish dominate; indeed the zone of emergence is the great Irish belt of the city. They entered the zone on the wake of the industries which drove out the American population. The departing Americans sold their property to the newcomers, who, at a single stroke, often thus secured living accommodations that represented a decided advance over any they had dreamt of previously. These cases where the environment served to advance family life are more than offset, however, by other cases in which the conditions presented in tenements remodeled from private dwellings tore it down. In its conditions of living, its social and political organization, and all those subtle qualities which give the tone of the community, the zone is second-generation Irish.

Acquaintance with the Irish in these districts leaves one with a distinct sense of admiration for the accomplishment of the nationality. They are the ranking national group. Their institutions are at once the largest, strongest, and best managed that one comes upon. It seems necessary to emphasize the obvious fact, because so many people who should realize it have failed to do so. This is particularly the case of the average church-going Protestant who resides in or on the edge of the zone itself and who holds to the assurance that his own religion and social organizations are in some special manner the chief and only forces in existence.

Strategically located through the Zone of Emergence is a great series of parishes, with well built and often beautiful churches. Many of these parishes support schools, which in the aggregate care for a number of thousand children. Whatever one's attitude toward the vexed question of religious instruction in the schools, this visible evidence that a great body of relatively poor people support an expensive institution for conscience' sake is, to say the least, inspiring. The superficial rejoicing of certain over the fact that other Catholic immigrants are not building up such schools leaves out of consideration the far from admirable consideration that they are not possessed of a degree of spiritual idealism that would lead them to do so. In one aspect, at any rate, the parochial school represents a revolt in the same direction as that of the founders of the nation itself. Perhaps it shows also a greater degree of spiritual vitality than is likely to be found in Protestantism today.

In addition to the church and the school, many parishes support clubs for young men and boys and in a number of instances there are special houses given to recreation and entertainment, where social work of a high order is carried on. Further still there are the sodalities and societies of the church, all of which combine the social with the religious exercises. Very generally also the picnics, outings, and other large affairs of the churches constitute the ranking social events of the neighborhood.

One public service of the church deserves special mention, namely, its assistance to the cause of temperance and clean speech. Most of the churches have strong temperance organizations which have already rendered good service in the movement to control the liquor traffic. In Cambridge especially the church has been the backbone of the movement which has kept the city in the no-license column. The Holy Name Society, with its large roll of members, represents present achievement of a high order and holds great promise for the future as its interest broadens.

The fact that the Irish are now being pushed by other immigrants is turning out to be to the advantage of that race. It was of course to be expected that there would be laggards among the Irish as among other peoples. Just as the rear detachment of Americans fifty years ago were forced ahead by the pressure of the Irish, or worsted forever, so the Italian and

Portuguese and the Jew are helping the Irish. This works out with much significance in certain schools in which the children of backward Irish families have been notoriously lazy and difficult, but who have been stimulated by the incoming of other races.

Within the borders of the zone are also found certain racial types which in the main have been able to skip a grade in their Americanizing progress. Even the immigrants of this group do not settle in the downtown districts, but seek their first footing among the relatively favorable conditions of the zone. Provincials, Swedes and other Scandinavians are found in considerable numbers in each of the districts. The Negroes have been pushed out of their downtown strongholds in a body and are now massed chiefly in Roxbury, secondarily in Cambridgeport. This forcing the Negro upward into a better environment is one of the unwitting good turns which the community has done as against its many deliberate shoves in the opposite direction.

An exception which not only proves the rule, but is not really an exception, is the lodger who in so great numbers nomadizes through the upper South End. He has not sufficient enthusiasm to strike out into new economic and social enterprise, but is strongly dominated by the social standards of the family and neighborhood life out of which he has come. So much is this the case that he or she often gives over all personal family and neighborhood ties in order to be loyal to a different one set by superficial social conventions. Here, as at many points of the zone of emergence, one finds the tragedy of a standard which is sadly out of focus with the actual producing power of the individual. The art of living a suitably proportioned life on the income of the regularly employed clerk or mechanic amid the alluring disturbance of human values which the city precipitates might perhaps be called the high desideratum of the zone.

Jews, Italians and Poles are found in each of the districts in the zone, and their colonies are an earnest of what may be expected of their fellows in the North and West Ends. The accomplishment of these peoples within a limited time has been very great, and argues much for their future as citizens.

A noticeable thing about the zone is the amount of property in the hands of immigrant peoples. Nearly fifty percent of the small dwellings and three-family tenements are in the hands of one-time immigrant families in relatively humble circumstance. This real estate is mortgaged in a large share of its value but it stands as a symbol that the newcomers are "taking possession of the land." Ownership of property is one of the surest indications that emergence is an emergence indeed. The lust for land and building constitutes a stage through which all newcomers go. A house is large enough to signalize achievement in the most forceful way. It has a quality that bolsters a man with his neighbors as no other small ownership does. It furnishes an extremely valuable training in acquisition, and has great utility as automatically interesting the owner in government, neighborhood, and the general community situation as nothing else does. Indeed analysis would show that this custom of buying a house constitutes one of the great educational forces in American life.

The public health of the zone is encouragingly good considering some of the handicaps. The tenement property in practically all of the district has been erected on what was once tide-water flats. The fact that a considerable proportion of each community is built up on made land unavoidably creates a problem. Cottages do not easily lend themselves to remodeling as three family tenements, and the question of sanitation is peculiarly vital in such reorganization of housing. These districts have also been neglected, compared with other portions of the city, in the amount of public and private effort devoted specifically to building up the health of the citizens. Dividing the city's death rate into four classes of which the first class shall be the very low one of thirteen or fourteen deaths per thousand, Ward 8 [the West End] of the inner belt stands alone, there being no district in the zone of emergence in this classification. A second grouping, that of fifteen or sixteen deaths per thousand, includes Wards 1 and 15 [East and South Boston]. A third classification, that of seventeen or eighteen deaths per thousand, includes Ward 9 [lower South End] of the inner belt, Wards 2, 3, 4, 16 and 18 of the zone [East Boston, Charlestown, inner Dorchester and Roxbury]. A fourth grouping of more than nineteen deaths a thousand includes Wards 6 and 7 [North

End and Downtown] of the inner belt and 5 and 13 [Charles-
town and South Boston] of the zone of emergence.

One advantage of the much indented configuration of Boston is that most local sections of the city have at least in part a
natural boundary. This is particularly true of the districts that
make up the zone. Set off geographically like towns by themselves it is easy for them to retain something like town spirit.
East Boston and South Boston in particular have the atmosphere
of small separate cities. The other districts of the belt have a
harder struggle to maintain their individuality as against the
great traffic with which they are plowed through. Most local
districts have interesting and much prized inheritances of local
importance in their own individual right, and two of them have
suggestive annual observances of public holidays: Charlestown,
the Battle of Bunker Hill, and South Boston, that of Evacuation
Day. These stir local loyalty and bring people from other parts
of the city to stand in its radiance.

In the lower parts there is an approximation to the relatively
inarticulate and chaotic social status which is found in the
crowded neighborhoods lying next to the business section, but
a little farther out one finds the cultivation of real society with
larger reality to it in some sense on account of the overflow of
the city in these neighborhoods. Practically each community
in the zone has its own banks, department stores, small shops and
other business enterprises which are able to compete successfully
with similar institutions in the city. Indeed some of them succeed
in drawing a city trade away from the inner belt. These business
interests naturally do everything possible to foster local spirit
and are improvement agencies in keeping up the local social
life.

Within the past few years there has been a notable increase
of interest among the immigrants of the zone in politics. Heretofore political power has been almost wholly in the hands of
the Irish. The growth in numbers among other nationalities, the
eagerness of the young people to have a share in the honors and
rewards of public life, and the hard work that has been put into
efforts of these leaders to secure the naturalization of their fellow
countrymen is bringing about a growing interest in public affairs.
In another place we shall endeavor to forecast the implication

of this new interest.

The Protestant churches in the belt are far from vigorous, and, with one or two exceptions, are holding out against inevitable disintegration. The difficulty of keeping alive tends on the whole to make them uncooperative, and hence of less public influence than they might very reasonably be expected to have.

The recreation of the people is largely in the hands of commercial institutions. The Boston theatres and other amusement resorts attract large numbers of people in town. Each district of the zone has anywhere from one to half a dozen moving picture shows, and there are usually one or two halls for dances and parties. The public playgrounds care for a certain proportion of the children. It is interesting and significant that the school center movement [4] finds its most successful exemplification in these localities.

It is not too much to say that the zone is essentially law-abiding as befits communities where the citizens have so much of a stake both in the property and living conditions. There is relatively little serious crime and much of that comes from outside. There is no commercialized prostitution such as exists in town. Sexual looseness there is, but this is no worse, and in many respects not so bad, as in what are considered upper-class districts. One of the more serious, and by far the most irritating, evils is juvenile delinquency. This is due to a number of interacting causes which are discussed in the course of the present volume. Certainly the situation argues serious difficulty in home, neighborhood, and community life. The worst fault of the zone is drunkenness. Fortunately saloons are not as numerous as in the inner belt. Thus in East Boston there is one saloon to 1,500 population or to 460 polls,[5] in Charlestown one saloon to every 680 of population or one to 215 polls, in South Boston

---

[4] In Boston the school center movement established informal evening classes in sewing, mechanical drawing, and crafts. Between 1899 and 1907 New York, Boston, and Rochester began pioneer programs for neighborhood evening use of the schools. All the programs were mixes of social clubs, education, and athletics. Paul Monroe, A Cyclopedia of Education (New York, 1913), V, 260-261.

[5] A poll in Massachusetts was a male, twenty-one or over, upon whom the poll, or head, tax was levied. In theory the polls should equal all adult males. In fact, an indeterminate number escaped listing.

one saloon to every 1,032 population or 320 polls. These figures are of course bad enough and demonstrate a very wide use of intoxicants. Indeed the over-use of drink is the very great fault of the zone, which may be said to be the area of all others in the city distinguished by a large use of intoxicants.

II

CHARLESTOWN: WHERE BOSTON BEGAN

The settlement of Charlestown antedates that of Boston by at least one year, for on this peninsula the vanguard of the colonists sent out from England to settle the region around the head of Massachusetts Bay first established themselves. The scarcity of running water, which alone was thought to be wholesome, soon caused the breaking up of the community and the scattering of the people. One of the last to leave was the leader himself, John Winthrop, who with a large following crossed the Charles and settled on the Peninsula of the Three Hills, which later received the name of Boston. Thus the beginning of Boston may be said to have been at Charlestown.

With this dispersion, the history of Charlestown properly begins; for the householders who "stayed and became inhabitants" were the real founders. After the manner of the times in New England, admission to the community was gained only by a consenting vote of the town meeting; even a householder wishing to entertain a stranger over night was required under penalty of fine or imprisonment to obtain permission from the selectmen.

After the Revolution, the town, partially burned by the British at the time of the battle of Bunker Hill, was rebuilt, and the new houses and other structures were in general larger and finer than any previously erected. An era of prosperity began that continued without special interruption until the outbreak of the Civil War. This period of seventy years comprises the beginning, development, and decline of old Charlestown, as the preceding one hundred and fifty years comprised the history of early Charlestown.

From the earliest days Charlestown has been more or less a center for the distribution of merchandise. When the town was laid out, the present City Square was set apart as a market place after the English custom. To this market, a road brought buyer and seller from the upper country, and during the last part of the period the Middlesex Canal provided a waterway to Boston from Lowell. Once the bridges were built, their tolls served to preserve if not actually to build up this local out-of-door exchange, after the manner of a protective tariff. Here for nearly two hundred years an open-air market was carried on. Shipbuilding, soap boiling, the manufacture of morocco leather, and market gardening ("Charlestown pears" and "Charlestown grapes" appearing in the menus of the leading Boston hotels) flourished.

Charlestown has always been the home of the middle and lower classes. Even in the days of its greatest prosperity it was predominantly bourgeois, although bourgeois at its best. Progressiveness in educational matters was to be expected in a town whose first pastor was John Harvard, a name identified forever with that of the pioneer college in the New World. A young ladies' seminary, one of the first institutions of its kind to be established in this country, was widely and favorably known. Its more than two hundred pupils included the daughters of many families outside of Charlestown. The tradition reappeared in comparatively recent years when one of its citizens made provision for the establishment of Tufts College as an institution in which both sexes might have equal opportunities. Eminent citizens were not lacking. Among them may be mentioned Loammi Baldwin, the "father of civil engineers"; Thomas Ball, whose equestrian statue of Washington adorns the Public Gardens; and Samuel F. B. Morse, the inventor of the electric telegraph, whose birthplace, a fine old colonial house, is still standing on Main Street. Other well-known residents are Edward Everett, the statesman and a governor of Massachusetts; John A. Andrews, another governor; and Charlotte Cushman. Here lived also for a while Oliver Holden, the composer of *Coronation*, and Starr King, whose eloquence did so much to keep California in the Union.

To the social life of the district a peculiar quality was given by the proximity of the Navy Yard and the intermingling of citizen and soldier. The officers at the Yard lived at the local hotels or in houses of the town which they rented. Many of them found their wives in Charlestown. Thus a semimilitary society grew up, and social rating came to be fixed according to one's rank in the Yard. The naval social influence was seen also in the type of men's club which flourished, a type wholly social in character and distinguished by general if not excessive drinking.

One of the most forceful examples of the typical bourgeois temper of early Charlestown is found in the burning of the Ursuline Convent at Mt. Benedict. Although the direct cause of this tragic event was supposed to be religious prejudice, underneath was an equally bitter feeling of antagonism toward the Irish laborer who was supplanting native-born workmen. Religious intolerance was reinforced by economic fear. For more than half a century the blackened ruins of the convent were left untouched, a silent but eloquent witness of persecution. For many years, one devout Irish woman visited the ruins every Sunday afternoon to recite her prayers, never forgetting the petition for the enemies of her faith. In the back of her prayer book were written the names of the leaders in this riot, for whom especially prayers were said. Long afterward the twice-burned bricks from the ruins were built into the foundations of the Cathedral of the Holy Cross in the South End.

It was the freight traffic, however, that produced modern Charlestown. When the Boston and Lowell road was laid, it was carried through what was then the westerly part of the town at some distance from the deep water. To connect the railroad and the water front the Charlestown Branch Railroad Company came into existence, and a spur track was built from the main line directly across the peninsula to the wharves about a mile away. The Charlestown Wharf Company was incorporated to supplement this branch road.

In time the Fitchburg Railroad Company appeared and acquired both the Branch and the land of the Wharf Company. Later, with other railroads and dock companies, it was absorbed in its turn as part of the Boston and Maine system. With the terminal freight stations of the entire system on the peninsula Charlestown became a vast center for handling merchandise. At the Hoosac Tunnel and Mystic Docks, the great oceangoing steamships of a dozen different lines received and discharged their cargoes; and at the long rows of railroad freight sheds trains, almost without number, are loaded and unloaded.

One result of the extension of the freight traffic appeared in the early sixties when the Irish began to come into Charlestown in rapidly increasing numbers. The multiplication of railroad tracks, storage sheds, and docks, combined with the smoke and noise of the trains made the peninsula a less and less desirable place to live. Consequently, the better-to-do families began to move away, and houses and land depreciated in value. Also, until very recently freight handlers were obliged to live near the scene of their labor in order to be within call whenever a freight arrived, whether at noon or at midnight.

On the other hand, the Irish in Boston were ready to take advantage of the chances thus offered to settle across the Charles. The North End and the neighborhood of Fort Hill had become crowded as fresh arrivals poured in from the old country. An outbreak of cholera in the late fifties, and a series of turbulent and bloody riots at the North End, caused by the drafting of men for the Civil War, hastened the exodus. Dissensions in St. Mary's Church as to whether the priest should be a man from the North or the South of Ireland also, if rumor is to be believed, served to influence the departure of certain among the Irish from the North End.

These newcomers to Charlestown were hard-working, thrifty, and ambitious. Most of them had been in this country for some time, and not a few were well started on the road to prosperity. As a rule they bought the houses in which they lived. They settled at first around the edges of the residential district, especially near the docks, but soon began to make their way up the hill, buying the homes thrown upon the market by the outgoing families. Economic changes among the old native stock facilitated this process. The fortunes of many of the long-established families had begun to decay. In not a few cases possessions had so far dwindled away that little was left but the homestead. Thus it happened during the war that the necessity of raising money to provide substitutes for the army brought home after home into the market. The failure of the Atchinson, Topeka, and Santa Fe Railroad a dozen years later had much the same effect, leaving many families with practically nothing. The buying of houses by the Irish was often for investment and in many cases laid the foundation for a substantial fortune.

The district is primarily the home of the wage earner. Out of every 100 men 43 are unskilled workers, freight handlers, teamsters, etc., 27 are engaged in skilled crafts, and 26 are clerks and small shopkeepers, while only 2 are doctors, lawyers, ministers, or members of other professions.

The largest employer of all in the district is the Navy Yard, which in its various shops gives work to between 2,000 and

2,500. Next in size of its payroll comes the Boston and Maine with 2,100 men in its freight yards and approximately 800 long-shoremen and other employees on its docks. The Harvard Manufacturing Company, the National Biscuit Company, two breweries, an establishment where breakfast foods are prepared, two plants for making furniture, and a spice mill call for hands ranging in number from 15 or 20 to 200 each. The wharves along the Mystic, lumber yards, coal pockets, and grain elevators require in the aggregate the services of several thousand men.

Those who work in the district may or may not have their homes here. Of the 200 employees of a firm of milk distributors 160, or four fifths of the whole, live outside of the district — for instance, 82 in Somerville, 16 in Cambridge, and 15 in Everett. The factory hands with comparatively few exceptions live in this area, usually near their work. Very few of the men in the Navy Yard reside in the district, most of them coming from all over greater Boston. A very large part of the population finds employment outside the district. Every morning throngs may be seen leaving the peninsula for their work across the Charles. A pathetic sight, to one astir early enough to see it, is the straggling procession of scrubwomen long before light in the winter, making their way over the bridges to clean the great office buildings in the center of the city.

This separation between the home and the scene of one's work, so characteristic of Charlestown, is made possible by the facilities for getting about afforded by the street cars. Surface lines extend along two of the principal thoroughfares the entire length of the district, connecting at City Square with tracks to Boston and Chelsea and at Sullivan Square with tracks to the cities and towns beyond. The overhead structure, crossing from Boston to City Square, continues along Main Street to Sullivan Square with one intervening station at Thompson Square. Probably the local traffic of these lines represents, on an average, 25,000 people every day of the year, including Sunday. This is an estimate based on the number of cash fares, tickets, and transfers taken at City Square and Thompson Square, which lie well within the district, and an estimated proportion of similar receipts at Sullivan Square, where the bulk of the traffic is from outside the district.

The census returns of 1905 give the number of people living in Charlestown as 40,000. This is nearly three times what it was in 1847, although the area available for living purposes has decreased rather than increased through the encroachments of business. For the past four decades, however, the number of people in Charlestown has not varied greatly. At present it is only 6 or 7,000 more than it was 40 years ago. This comparative fixity in numbers is due to the limits imposed by the present types of housing accommodations. If many more people are to be provided for, dwellings of another sort must be put up. Under present conditions the district, with regard to its population, is "completed."

Where once a single family had the freedom of an entire house, two, three, or even more families are to be found today, each occupying a floor or part of a floor. Apartment houses, usually three stories in height, have displaced the fruit trees and shrubbery of former times in gardens and backyards. A large tenement district has sprung up at the "Point" on the site of the tan pits where the manufacture of morocco once was carried on. When viewed from a height, the housing portions of the district present the appearance of a mosaic of roofs, so closely do the dwellings seem to be to one another. Hardly an open space is visible, with the exception of streets and squares. There is also a marked absence of trees or greenery of any sort — sad evidence of the obliteration of the old gardens. So compactly are these sections built over that the onlooker shudders at the thought of the dire consequences should a serious fire break out. The wooden construction that predominates, together with the proximity of house to house, would invite rather than resist the flames. Little short of a miracle could prevent complete destruction. Internal housing conditions have undergone a change correspondingly great.

Of the 40,000 persons in this district, 28,000, or 70 percent, were born of foreign parents. Of this 28,000, nearly 16,000 were born in this country and a few more than 12,000 outside the United States. These figures, it should be observed, do not take into account the children of native-born parents whose fathers and mothers were immigrants. Of the entire number of foreign-descended, both native and foreign-born, almost one half, or

19,000, are Irish — 7,000 representing the first generation and 12,000 the second. These figures are close approximations. Those of foreign extraction other than the Irish approximate 9,000 — 5,000 of whom were born outside this country. Of the latter number the British Provinces including Newfoundland furnish three fifths and Italy, Russia, Germany, and other countries the remaining two fifths.

The fifteen or twenty years immediately following the annexation of Charlestown to Boston, in 1874, may be said to have constituted the best days of the Irish regime on the peninsula. Irish families were living in Monument Square, Winthrop Square, and other sections that had been the home of the elite of old Charlestown, and they had developed a social life that was comparable with the best life of the past. St. Mary's church, the first Roman Catholic Church in the district and one of the first in Boston, had built a large and imposing house of worship, and another Roman Catholic Church, the third here, had been organized. Roman Catholic societies, partly religious and partly social and educational in their purpose, had come or were coming into existence. Among them was the Catholic Literary Union, an organization of leading laymen, which from the first has been a strong influence for the higher life of the community.

But the causes that had operated to start the movements of population described had not ceased to be active. Before the end of this period the Irish themselves began to leave. Thus in the outgoing procession representatives of the old native stock and those of the comparatively recent alien stock were mingled. A new impulse to this leaving was given by the building of the overhead track of the elevated railway through the very center of the district from end to end. The excessive noise of the trains made living on the adjoining streets almost intolerable. Families that had held out against all other influences to move retreated before this nerve-racking noise.

The Church of St. Francis de Sales leads in organizing the life of those who remain. Its parochial school was the first in Charlestown, and today it has an enrollment, in the two divisions, one for boys and one for girls, of about 1,000. From its last grade, which corresponds to the last grade of the public grammar school, pupils pass directly into the high schools of the city. A men's club, with rooms of its own, is a flourishing organization, and a corresponding organization of young men and boys is under the personal leadership of the pastor. The more conservative type of Roman Catholic church is represented by St. Catherine's. With the exception of the purchasing of a block of tenements to be remodeled at some future time into a school building, this church has followed rather closely the ordinary routine of parochial activities.

Of the general societies of Roman Catholics, the Catholic Literary Union, occupying a fine old house in Monument Square, is the most important. Its annual banquet on the eve of the anniversary of the Battle of Bunker Hill is an event of more than local interest and importance, because of the size and character of the gathering and the prominence of the speakers. Here Roman Catholics and Protestants sit down together, meeting on the basis of a common interest in the community and a desire for its welfare. A corresponding organization of women has been formed within a few years with similar purposes. The Union is the first example of the type of club introduced by the Catholic Church, a club whose social side is subordinated to some serious purpose, usually religious or literary. The out-and-out social club that flourished a generation ago has wholly disappeared, partly because most of the natural constituency of such a club has moved away and partly because of the withdrawal of the officers of the Navy Yard from association with the citizens. The last club of this kind closed its doors a few months ago.

Protestantism survives in two Congregational churches, two Baptist churches, and one each of the Episcopal, Methodist, and Universalist denominations. A Unitarian church went out of existence a few months ago. All together the number of families ministered to would not exceed fifteen hundred. The First Parish Church, organized directly after the first dispersion from Charlestown, was the sole church there until the beginning of the last century when a Baptist church was founded. It enjoys the distinction of having retained the original site of its meeting house and of worshiping today where it first met for worship 275 years ago. These facts probably have much to do with its continuance as its membership has dwindled almost to the vanishing point. There is some drawing together of the Baptist churches as a result of diminishing numbers and resources, and without doubt the two will soon unite. St. John's Episcopal Church has suffered a smaller net loss than the others, but this has been due to the incoming of people from the British Provinces, who have taken the places of many who have left. The very struggle in which they are severally engaged to hold their own in numbers and influence has served to bring these five churches together in a more than usual degree. Protestantism is presenting here a more united front than is often seen except perhaps in missionary fields. Between the Protestant and Roman Catholic bodies a good degree of friendliness exists, and cooperative efforts in local reform are not uncommon.

Those coming into Charlestown today are no longer solely or predominantly Irish. Jews, Italians, and Armenians are establishing themselves here in gradually increasing numbers. In the case of the Italians and Armenians, business openings, actual or potential, furnished the original motive for coming. The pioneer Italians moved here to start fruit stands or bootblacking parlors. The colony thus began to draw other people of the same race, although the occupations of the later comers were often out of the district. Hence an Italian community has been built up that is still receiving families from the North and West Ends.

The Armenians, like many of the Italians, come at first to engage in trade. Instead of setting up fruit stands, however, they open places for the sale of provisions. Beginning in an exceedingly small way, they have developed, by industry and persistence, a number of good-sized stores and before long will control a considerable part of the provision trade of the district. In the case of the Jews, the chance to buy houses at bargain rates as homes for themselves or for investment furnishes the primary inducement to settle here. The Irish coming in at the present time are of a distinctly different type from those of this race who started the influx fifty years ago. They lack the thrift and ambition of those early comers. For the most part they are ordinary laborers, whose removal here means no special rise in the social scale.

Bunker Hill Monument, rising to a height of 221 feet, overtops all other structures on the peninsula, and about it centers a great local tradition that holds the old and new citizen alike.

Bunker Hill Monument and the celebration of the 17th of June serve not only to keep freshly in mind an important historical event but also to call attention to the district in a special way, the monument bringing visitors here from all parts of the world. The celebration lifts the peninsula, for one day at least, into public view, where its rich historical associations are seen and duly recognized, and local pride, a valuable asset to any community, is thereby increased. Processions, band concerts, and fireworks enter prominently in the program. The clubs and other social organizations keep open house, and the people entertain generously. A reflection of the present character of the population appears in the civic parade. Among the organizations taking part are the A.O.H. [Ancient Order of Hibernians], Knights of Columbus, the Clanna-Gael, and the O'Reilly Cadets, the last-mentioned taking its name from John Boyle O'Reilly, long a citizen here. With these Irish bodies are usually joined, singularly enough, a company of uniformed Russian Jews, two orders of Italians, and two or three organizations of Portuguese from the North End.

Two playgrounds, one at the Neck, the other at the Point, and a beach bath equipped with dressing booths, constitute the public means for out-of-door recreation. The playgrounds, which are fairly well supplied with apparatus, are under the direct control of the Boston School Committee, and the beach bath is one of those maintained by the city. These agencies, however, are insufficient for a population of such a size and character, and this relative lack of means for making life more interesting and raising it to a higher level is reflected in the spirit of lawlessness to which reference will be made.

A branch of the Public Library, with 20,000 or more books, and a well-equipped reading room open to child and adult alike is an important factor in the intellectual life of the district. Its average daily circulation of books is about 150. The Bunker Hill Boys' Club has its headquarters in the heart of the district in a large old house, formerly a private residence. Aside from its spiritual activities — which include reading and recreation rooms open every evening, classes in industrial and fine arts, entertainments of various sorts, and a camp — the Club renders an important public service in bringing together on the plane of common interests boys of different races, religions, and walks in life. There must of necessity follow a lessening of racial and factional differences among them and in the community at large and an increase of mutual effort in measures for the good of all.

The Sailors' Haven on Water Street, which is under the auspices of the Protestant Episcopal Church, has a religious as well as a social side and is primarily for seafaring men, although longshoremen are included within its scope. In its commodious building there are lounging rooms, with special facilities for writing letters, besides a general assembly hall, and various offices. About 30,000 men pass through the doors of this building every year. A similar center of helpful influences for those who follow the sea is maintained a few doors away. This is connected with the Roman Catholic Church and is known as the Catholic Sailors' Mission. The Charlestown Improvement Association, an organization of the more responsible and public-spirited business and professional men, is aimed, as its name implies, to promote measures relating to the general good.

In a district such as Charlestown, a great number of saloons is to be expected. Ninety-six liquor licenses of all kinds are held in this part of the city. Of these, 67 — the equivalent of 1 to every 600 of the population, are the first victualler (the license of the ordinary barroom). The remaining licenses are innholder, 2; brewers, 2; bottlers, 6; grocers, 6; and druggists, 13. It is not surprising that, with so many saloons and other places where liquor can be had, there should be a large amount of excessive drinking. The number of arrests in the district for drunkenness during the year ending November 30, 1907, was 2,765, and during the preceding year it was 2,227. Of these, however, fully one half were of persons living outside the district.

Each town on the traction lines running from Charlestown that votes no-license adds to the number of arrests for drunkenness in this district. It is doubtful whether any of these towns would be able to maintain a prohibitive law were it not for the proximity of such places as this where saloons abound. The abolition of the canteen in the Navy Yard also has increased the number of arrests for excessive drinking.

A partial list of other offenses for which arrests have been made during 1907 follows:

Murder	1
Robbery	3
Larceny from Persons	17
Delinquent Children	224
Assault and Battery	149
Larceny	98
Breaking and Entering Bldgs	13
Violation of City Ordinances	278
Buying and Receiving Stolen Goods	6

This includes the more serious offenses and those for which any considerable number of persons have been arrested. The total number of arrests for the year was 3,858, of which 2,765, as has been said, or almost exactly three fourths, were for drunkenness.

This table, of course, gives only a partial view of the district from the point of view of law and order. The number of serious crimes committed is very small, and there is a marked lack of prostitution and gambling, but a spirit of lawlessness is widely prevalent, especially among young people. It will be observed that 224 children were arrested for delinquency during the year for which the figures are given. Asked what was the most urgent social problem in the district today, several keen observers among the citizens mentioned that of the wayward boys and girls. In its extreme form of hoodlumism as well as in its more usual form of mischievous idleness, this waywardness seems to arise rather from the lack of wholesome and vital interests than from any evil purpose. Hoodlumism, when it appears, is seldom organized. Gangs of young roughs, making a pastime of annoying passers-by and resorting to theft or worse crimes when a suitable opportunity is presented, are rather infrequent. This is due in no small degree to the vigilance of the police in breaking up any incipient organizations for mischief by arresting the leaders and securing their punishment in the district court.

An index of the extent of poverty in this part of the city is furnished by the figures of the two local conferences of Associated Charities. The total number of families dealt with in any way, including mere investigation, by these two bodies during the year ending May 1, 1908, was 263, or less than three out of every hundred families in the district. These 263, it should be said, include the families that have sunk the farthest below the poverty line, the extremely poor. Above them in various gradations are other families who have been caught by special funds or private benevolence before reaching the offices of the Associated Charities, or who are receiving such aid as they need from the churches. But if the figures given are a trustworthy index, the number of dependent or partially dependent families is relatively small, a conclusion that finds support in the marked absence of outward signs of widespread or extreme poverty.

The population is destined to become more and more mixed as time goes on, for the changes still taking place will create opportunity for new classes and conditions of people. The opening of small provision stores (to which reference has been made) furnishes a recent illustration. A few years ago, when most of the larger stores had a fairly well defined constituency generally known to the proprietor and more or less catered to by him, these little places of business would have received no patronage. Now, however, the population has become so disintegrated that purchasers seldom have a personal relation with those from whom they buy, and they go where they can buy the most conveniently and cheaply. The encroachments of large-scale business upon the housing areas will result undoubtedly in the occupancy of all the level territory with tracks, warehouses and factories, the portions of the district left for living purposes being restricted to the hills. In the future as well as the present, the population will be limited in size only by the housing accommodations, for the nearness of the district to the center of the city will continue to make it a more convenient section in which to live. But whatever the picture of the future may be, it will be painted against the background of an interesting and honorable past, a past that has witnessed both the founding and development of a New England community of a high type, and the transition of that community into a section of the tenement-house frontier of a great city.

III

CAMBRIDGEPORT

Cambridgeport is a condition of life midway between East Cambridge and Old Cambridge. A few spiritual representatives of Old Cambridge linger on the eastern slope of Dana Hill though they scornfully repudiate the Port; but the northern and eastern borders of the district have been captured by a group of more recent immigrants; and these the common sentiment would relegate to East Cambridge as their proper station and habitat. The port is predominantly Anglo-Saxon, English speaking, thoroughly American and as homogeneous as the existence of powerful groups of northern New Englanders, Provincials and second generation Irish, each tenacious of certain of its own loyalties, will permit. Industrially the population ranges through all grades of the craftsmen-clerk-shopkeeping classes. Intellectually and socially the Port is bourgeois; its hope in its children for whom it sacrifices all else. Spiritually the section has changed little in the course of a hundred years.

Going a Journey to Boston

Cambridge was ordered established in 1630 by Governor Winthrop to provide a safer and more defendable seat of government than the sea-board towns of Boston and Charlestown. This fiat settlement was not successful; and the real founding came two years later when the General Court assigned the newly arrived Braintree Company to "New Town." The community grew slowly, and with growth became confronted with the first characteristic Cambridge problem — communication with Boston. The one available route was by way of Charlestown and the ferry at Copp's Hill. In 1635 the town made public provision for a ferry at the foot of the present Brighton Street [now Boylston Street], which offered a way through Brookline and Roxbury. The Charlestown route was shorter, but the Cambridge way insured an easy ferriage and quiet water. The increasing inconvenience of the ferry led the townspeople in 1656 to vote £200 out of the rates to build a bridge. The structure was completed in 1662, when it was formally opened and named "The Great Bridge"; the largest structure of the kind so far erected in the commonwealth. This bridge furnished the first wagon road to the city; but it still left Charlestown the advantage, as it was seven miles by way of the bridge and only four by ferry. And thereupon Cambridge became confronted with her second characteristic problem of keeping in repair the roads and bridges over which her neighboring townspeople travelled to Boston.

The century following the building of the Bridge was one of great activity in the Colonies. Lands were cleared, roads laid, ferries established, bridges built, and the interior opened to trade; and this general growth promoted the importance of Boston as a commercial center. The need of communication became more pressing and the question of routes a live one. In 1750 it became increasingly evident that a bridge must needs be built from some point on the mainland to the city. Charlestown looked on itself as the logical place for such an enterprise, but certain proprietors in Cambridge saw the availability of their own land for such a purpose and had a vision of a Cambridge graduated from "a little place inhabited by students, professors and the small number of servants they employ" to a commercial village that should outrival Charlestown as a trade center. During the years following 1750 frequent petitions were presented to the General Court by both Charlestown and Cambridge Bridge Companies. The victory finally went to a Charlestown company and the Charles River Bridge was erected in 1786. Cambridge was stimulated anew by failure and in 1792 secured permission "to construct a bridge from the westerly part of Boston near the Pest House to Pelham's Island in the town of Cambridge, with a good road from Pelham's Island to the aforesaid in the most direct and practicable line to the nearest part of the Cambridge road." In November, 1793 the West Boston Bridge was opened to the public amid great rejoicing and very justifiable local pride.

The bridge shortened the route to Boston from eight miles to three miles and a quarter and saved a mile and a quarter over the Charlestown route. For a few years the bridge had an easy supremacy in attracting travel from the North and West; but the success of the Charlestown and Cambridge ventures aroused the investing public to the value of bridge property, and such corporations began to be multiplied. Among these was the Craigie Bridge Company, which proposed to connect East Cambridge and Boston. Competition hastened the building of new roads and turnpikes, and within a few years practically all of the main thoroughfares of the Port were laid out. Main Street, the present Massachusetts Avenue east of Main Street, Broadway, Harvard Street, Hampshire Street and Webster Avenue in the North; and River Street and Western Avenue in the South were built. These highways fixed the city plan of the Port and caused all avenues to converge on the [West Boston] Bridge.

CAMBRIDGEPORT: THE FIRST SPECULATIVE SUBURB

The first effect of the bridge was to strengthen Old Cambridge. "The erection of the bridge has very perceptibly influenced the trade of Cambridge, which formerly was very inconsiderable. By bringing the travel from the westward and northward through the town it has greatly invigorated business there." — Holmes.[6]

This advantage was short-lived, for the bridge had opened an opportunity for trade at one end which was not long neglected. Topographically the Port did not invite settlement. The land to the east and south of the bridge was largely marshes flooded by tide water, and the high lands in the west were some distance from the bridge entrance. But the strategic position at the end of the bridge was too good to be lost and a store was shortly built by Vose and Makepeace, two young men who had been engaged in the sale of "East India goods" in the south end of Boston. Two years later a tavern was erected, additional stores and houses located, and dikes constructed to drain the land. By 1800 the colony numbered one hundred people. The proprietors of the bridge who held large tracts of land now entered upon a plan to develop the Port. Among those who became interested was Rufus Davenport, a commission merchant, of Long Wharf, who,

---

[6] The phrasing in the original is slightly different from that quoted in the text. From Abiel Holmes, "The History of Cambridge," *Collections of the Mass. Historical Society for the Year 1800*, VII (Boston, 1801), 4.

taken with the possibilities of speculation in the Port, entered upon a plan to make Cambridge a second Boston. He saw the district as the natural port of entrance and departure for all the north and west trade of Massachusetts, Vermont and New Hampshire. To increase the somewhat meagre advantages of the Port an elaborate system of waterways and dikes was projected and largely executed. Canals of sufficient depth and width for coasting vessels were dug; whose combined length averaged well over a mile; new streets were laid out; building lots were marked off; and in 1805 Congress passed an act making Cambridge "a port of delivery to be annexed to the district of Charlestown and Boston."

Dock lots sold as high as $1.50 a square foot. A small shipyard was established and a coasting schooner launched from it. Trade began to come to the Port and a good sized lumber business developed. In 1807 the parish numbered one thousand people. But at the very flood tide of prosperity failure appeared. The Embargo of 1807 brought all business to a standstill. Almost overnight property that had sold for twenty cents a square foot became worthless, and many people lost their all. By 1812 when war was declared the wharves were already rotting and grass was growing in the streets. The feeling of the town toward the national administration was very bitter, and the blame for failure was laid on the Embargo and the war. But the project failed because it was inherently unsound. It is hardly possible to imagine shipping leaving the deep water docks of Boston for the mud-scooped canals of the Charles. The venture was also the first of a line of speculations which began after the depression caused by the Revolution had passed away; and its seeming success stimulated many like improvements. South Boston [Bridge opened 1805] Canal Bridge [or Craigie's Bridge, 1809], and the Mill Dam [1821] followed hard on the Port. These enterprises also hoped to profit by attracting trade and selling their lands. The multiplication of ways of entering Boston tended to bring into the city much of the business which had hitherto been carried on outside. The Embargo Act undoubtedly tended to hasten the work of these natural causes for decline.

THE PORT AS A TRADING VILLAGE AND A SUBURB TO BOSTON

After the War of 1812 the Port settled into the lethargy of failure. Many persons who had bought property continued to live there, but always the Port remained a place through which one passed to Boston. Roads continued to be built; great inns grew up and prospered; and runners from Boston came out to intercept the heavily laden wagons from the country and to buy their produce. Industries began in a small way; soap making developed, cabinet making shops, and a car and carriage factory were established; and other small suburban industries developed in time.

About 1835 railway building began and the Port once more looked forward to greatness. It even hoped for terminal facilities or a station at the least. But one by one the roads were built and the claims of Cambridge passed by. The Worcester Road went through Brighton and cut off travel from the southwest [1835]. The Lowell Road cut off travel from the north [1835]; and the Fitchburg Road instead of going through Cambridge to Waltham went by way of Charlestown [1845]. The first city directory, published in 1847, complains "This section (Cambridgeport) of the city is the principal place of business, though the opening of the Quincy Market in Boston and the construction of numerous railroads running from Boston, all of which by some fatality seem to avoid Cambridge, have almost annihilated the extensive trade which was formerly carried on between the Port and the country towns, even as far back as the borders of Vermont and New Hampshire." The traffic over the highways ceased; forestallers came out no more; one by one the five great inns closed and the stores followed.

By rare good fortune a statistical picture of the Port is available for this period. The directory of 1848 divided the city into three sections and treated each separately. The population given under the head of "Householders and Adult Boarders" lists 1,065 such persons. This would argue a population of close on six thousand. The characteristic industry of the Port was soap-making of which there were thirteen firms. In addition there were two bacon works, three confectionery establishments, three furniture-making firms, four cabinet makers, two carriage builders, one car manufacturing plant, three box-making firms and a few shops making cigars, also a few shops for the sale of foodstuffs, drugs, etc.

Of the 1,065 householders 265, or one fifth, had their place of business in Boston; 45 were professional people, and 139 were widows or retired. In the labor forces 204 were craftsmen in the building trades, of which number 123 were carpenters. There were twenty-seven woodworkers and carvers; twenty blacksmiths; thirty-two soap makers; thirty-eight leather and shoe workers, thirty-five engaged in transportation; sixty-nine handled provisions; forty-six engaged in making clothing and doing personal service; and fourteen clerks. Of laborers there were eighty-three, and one hundred and thirty-nine were engaged in miscellaneous forms of service.

Nationally the Port was a homogeneous New England community. Of its 1,065 householders only eighteen bore Irish and four other names of foreign sound. There was no industrial quarter and the mansions of successful businessmen and the cottages of carpenters and craftsmen stood cheek by jowl. The Port in 1848 was still a country town despite the fact that two years previously Cambridge had taken out a city charter.

THE RISE OF THE MODERN PERIOD

Though for long years the strength of Cambridge seemed fated to drain into Boston, a new era was at hand. The rise of Boston as a manufacturing center began about 1850, and the Port was soon recognized as a highly available industrial suburb. The grant in 1852 of the long desired charter for the construction of the Grand Junction Railway connecting the B. & M. [Boston and Maine R.R.] with the B. & A. [Boston and Albany R.R.] and the filling in of the swamp lands along the river were the forerunners of growth.

The old industries took on new life and new groups developed. Table A makes evident their essentially suburban character.

TABLE A

Industry	1855 Capital	1855 Employees	1865 Capital	1865 Employees	1880 Capital	1880 Employees	1890 Employees
Metals	$ 1,000	25	$290,000	222	$139,000	231	1,075
Mus. Instr.	14,000	20	14,000	34	600,000	660	894
Soap		147	262,000	137	375,000	250	292
Bakery	11,800	39	26,000	67	121,600	300	506
Confec.	30,000	18	48,000	25	76,000	90	347
Printing	41,000	120	216,500	584			

The metal, musical instrument, and printing groups demand abundant floor or yard space; convenient railway facilities, and nearness to a generous and efficient labor force. The food producing groups also desired cheap land; a location within easy delivery reach of city consumers; and a low priced labor supply. Soap making, too noisome to be tolerated under city conditions, is still saddled on the Port. All of these industries were well developed by 1880 — in which year the city added to its desirability as a manufacturing quarter by passing a no[liquor]-license law.

Coincident with this industrial expansion came a decided increase of population through immigration. The directory of 1848 listed only twenty-five persons with foreign sounding names. The Census of 1855 tabulated 1,410 Irish and 587 Scotch. The city felt itself overwhelmed; the Poor House officials and the City physician were specially affected, and the public documents pour out continuous complaints. The latter official attended thirty-six Irish in 1850 and forty-two in 1852 — largely laborers, domestics, or women in childbirth. The prevalent disease was "ship's fever." A report for 1859 notes 642 paupers "all foreigners," and another in 1861 tabulated 507 paupers "nine-tenths of them Irish and English and only 76 with a legal settlement." In the end the city profited by these strangers, and the early industries owe much to the hard working and efficient labor force on whose muscles it moved toward success. Later the Provincials came, and the even more efficient Swedes, and the Russian peoples.

Since 1855 the Port has maintained a continuous ratio of just one half of the total population of the city, and has increased in numbers at the nearly uniform rate of 10,000 persons a decade.

	Cambridge	Cambridgeport
1800	2,453	100
1855	20,473	10,724
1865	29,112	14,053
1875	47,838	24,016
1885	59,658	31,052
1895	81,643	41,313
1905	97,434	51,285

THE INDUSTRY OF THE PORT

A district ultimately takes on individuality according to the labor of its population. Nationality, local custom, tradition, and education may lend elements of color, distinction, even of artistry to its life; but its characteristic lineaments are fixed by the work in which its population engages. A high type of industry demands a corresponding type of labor; and such labor, with wonderful prophylaxis, recreates even a low grade population into a body of forceful, worthy moral people. A low-grade industry calls for a low-grade labor force; its processes plunge its operatives even deeper into the slough of inefficiency; and complete their degradation by chaining them twenty-four hours a day in the filth laden moral and physical atmosphere of its own being.

Cambridgeport has always been a residential as well as an industrial suburb; yet it is this latter function which is fast fixing its character. Nearness to Boston combined with cheap land; railway and spur track facilities; easy hauls (several firms give cartage at one percent of the cost of production); nearness to the metropolitan supply of both skilled and cheap labor; and no-license provision (specially valued by industries using great heat in production): these advantages make the Port an industrial quarter of increasing importance.

The metal industry employs the largest force, though it has grown to its present dimensions since 1880. It has a heavy capitalization and an annual pay roll of close to one million dollars. The musical instrument business dates from 1850, though it was not until 1875 that it began to assume generous proportions. The making of confectionery has become important since 1880, which year dates the rise of the soft candy and chocolate habit. Printing and binding concerns have grown steadily since

1840. Laundries and bakeries though long established are of recent growth. Wood working firms developed in the forties and show a slow, steady growth. The soap industry is the oldest and early came to good size. In late years it has not grown. The industries in the miscellaneous group are generally of recent origin.

The printing and binding, metal and musical instrument group of industries are of a high grade and develop a capable type of operative. Less favorable conditions and a consequently lower though skilled type of operative is developed in the woodworking and some other industries of the miscellaneous group. The confectionery, laundry — and to some extent the food producing — groups are in general low grade industries. Largely semi-parasitic, they either exploit their operatives or put a part of the burden of production on the shoulders of parents or other supporters.

The Port generally has a high type of employer; and the feeling between employers and employees is good. As always there are a few men too mean to have the direction of any fellow creature. With other suburbs the Port has been largely deprived of the residence of persons of its employing class, many of whom at one time lived in Cambridge. The establishment of large corporations and the tendency of men of wealth to colonize is responsible for this state of affairs. Absenteeism here works the usual disadvantages. The employer tends to become careless of all else in the community save the size of its tax rate, the quality of its police and fire protection, and the state of the paving in the industrial quarter.

The physical condition of the factories is good. There are many buildings of recent erection, some of which are model plants of their kind, and the supply of light and air is above the average. The equipment of the printing and binding, musical instrument, baking, and rubber concerns is of exceptional merit. Hours of labor and wages are fixed by law and the general state of business and have little relation to the purely local conditions. One or two exceptions to this rule are too peculiar to require consideration.

Nationally the labor force is divided into several well defined groups. The printing and binding industry which offers good wages and conditions of labor has a heavy percentage of American employees. Persons of American ancestry hold the more responsible and better paid positions in a large share of the other industries. Americans, Swedes and a small portion of Irish-American, Provincials and Letts furnish the bulk of the skilled labor. Irish, Irish-American and Provincials also furnish a large part of the semi or muscularly skilled workers. Italians, French, Poles, Lithuanians, and Jews furnish some of the less responsible operatives and carry on the hard and dirty forms of work.

The Port is a poor union district. "The air of Cambridge," said one man, "is antagonistic to organization." The building trades and the city laborers have the only strong unions. In addition there is a central labor bureau, and a dozen or more disheartened or half-hearted locals. Strike after strike in the past has been lost. The union movement suffers not only from the Port atmosphere, but also from divergent nationalities in industry, the nearness of Boston labor market, the tendency of many men to belong to Boston locals, and the deepseated hostility of manufacturers to the union. "The thing that makes the Port at all available," said one manufacturer, "is the marginal railway and its character as a non-union town." It is a significant thing that there are no Cambridge locals of any strength in the great group of industries which we have considered.

Perhaps 75% to 85% of the working force resides in the district. The men are distributed over a wider area than the women, most of whom live near enough to their work to go home to luncheon. Those who do not live in the Port generally reside in East Cambridge and Somerville, and there is a sprinkling from greater Boston. Long-established, and medium and low grade industries paying small wages, tend to concentrate their employees within a walking distance of their plants. Highly skilled, well paid or newly established industries tend to draw their employees from a wide circle. Most unskilled factory men live in the Port, with the exception of certain Syrians and Italians who walk back and forth in order to live in their colonies. Building and other mechanics and highly skilled operatives tend to scatter within a three mile radius. Newly established industries draw even less skilled employees from a considerable area for some time. Employees remain in the Port because it is a desirable industrial residence. Somerville is merely an echo of the Port, and acts as an extension of the suburban industrial-residential conditions exemplified by the Port.

The average male employee earns between twelve and eighteen dollars a week. There is a moderate percentage which earns more; and a small group falling below this wage. The female labor force earns from five dollars to ten dollars a week; the average wage being about five dollars and a half.

The labor force of the Port approximates 8,000 male and 4,000 female operatives; to which must be added about 100 men for industries not noted above; 400 men in the city employ; 400 male and 600 female clerks; 500 business men and 200 women — a total of 10,000 men and 4,800 women.

The total Cambridgeport labor force, according to the census of 1905, consisted of: —

Vocation	Males	Females
Government	463	47
Professional	496	470
Personal Service	823	1,187
Trade	3,349	1,102
Transportation	1,802	8
Manufacture	7,137	2,621
Labor	1,350	
TOTALS	15,420	5,435

We can by comparison with our known labor force come to some conclusions as to the number of Cambridge men employed in Boston. A good share of those listed under government work in the Port though there are some who go to Boston. Perhaps half of the professional class has its work in Boston. A very large share of those engaged in personal service work in Boston, this classification including the major portion of the Negro labor force. Under trade we shall list 2,600 persons at work in Boston — 1,700 males and 900 females — the largest grouping outside the Port. These are clerks, stenographers, and business people. The group devoted to transportation is engaged in the metropolitan area. Of the group devoted to manufacture perhaps 1,500 men work in industries without the Port and 700 laborers move about within the metropolitan area as they are called.

Economically those who work in Boston are divided into several groups. There is a small class of peripatetic half-skilled workmen and unskilled laborers attracted by cheap rents. Next a group of skilled workmen who have selected the Port for its better living conditions as compared with the closely built tenements of Boston. There is a growing group of home-owning mechanics and clerks, who have invested their savings in a small cottage, or a two or three family apartment; workers who retain their residence in the Port despite vicissitudes of employment. Beyond these is a rapidly growing group of highly paid clerks, salesmen, commercial travellers and small business men who wish to live in a suburb and yet escape the cares of a house. This class is increasing with the growing number of large apartments continually being erected. Further there is a growing group of unattached young people who select the Port as a boarding place in preference to the West and South Ends. This group is located within a dozen blocks about Central Square. Lastly those young people who live at home and go to Boston to work.

Apart from the small group of property owners and a somewhat larger body of householders the value of this Boston labor force is a doubtful one for the Port. It tends largely to spend its conscious hours away. The peripatetic working group is constantly in flux, an index of which is found in the listing of public school pupils. In the industrial wards the shifting reaches about one-third of the enrollment.

Apartment house dwellers also tend to form few if any local ties. They do not join the churches, and they take little interest in the local civic life. They happen to live in the community, and like or dislike it as their apartment suits them.

In this, of course, the Port has encountered only the average suburban problem. Modern industry demands mobility in its force, and the worker feels that there must be no ties not easily cut. This, with the congestion of the city, has brought the tenement or apartment house, built in such fashion as to need the minimum of effort to be immediately habitable. The workers have become habituated to change, and caprice acts with the industrial tendency to promote peripatetic family life. The roots of responsibility to church and state are dying; and the family is suffering in this weakening of reciprocal need and obligation. The householder, with long residence and of sure position in social affairs, looks with suspicion and disfavor on these nomads; and the speaking tube, with its disembodied voice, makes it additionally easy to disregard the newcomers. The result is that in a section of the city retaining all the characteristics of a country town, next door neighbors maintain that unnatural and studied aloofness which is bred within city blocks. One woman, living in a pretty lane of half a dozen houses, said, "I've lived here five years, and I don't know a person on the street." The difficulty came in the fact that the houses were apartments for two and three families. To this suburban class Cambridgeport is all too apt to become a bedroom of Boston.

Industrially then the Port is a community whose characteristic labor force ranges from the semi-skilled workman through the clerk and small tradesman class. Our table [never completed, fragment omitted] shows the dominant group as the mechanic-clerk class. To this grouping should be added an additional thousand of such as receive a premium for city work or for special muscular skill. The community therefore takes its industrial tone from the $15.00 to $30.00 a week group of workers, and the Port must therefore be ranked as a stronghold of the great and powerful social grouping known as the "middle class."

POPULATION

Chart C [omitted] gives the present national composition of the Port. The native and third generation from immigrants number 13,560; about one-fourth of the population. One half of the entire population (26,455) descends from English stock. One half of this group is Irish; the remainder is Provincial and British. The Negroes number 3,500; somewhat less than four percent of the population. The non-English speaking immigrants and their children number 7,709 persons; about one seventh of the population. About 85% of the population is descended from English speaking stock, which accounts for the essentially American character of the district despite the composition of its population.

The seven years between 1848 and 1855 saw Cambridgeport pass from a homogeneous New England village to the beginnings of a highly cosmopolitan industrial area. By 1855 there were 1,410 Irish, 587 Scotch, 146 Germans, and 105 persons of other nationalities. Despite the depression caused by the war, the Port continued to grow, and by 1865 housed 2,119 Irish, 480 Canadians, and 475 English. The Scotch fell away to 143; the Germans held their own; and the pioneers of the Swedish and French colonies came into sight.

During the decade (1865-1875) the Irish increased 1,600 and the Canadians 1,000. The Swedes grew from 17 to 126. The forerunners of the Spanish, Portugese, Italian and Russian peoples appeared. There are no figures available for the period 1895-1905, but during these years the Irish grew from 3,892 to 5,126 (only 1,200 in thirty years); the Canadians increased to 6,074; and the English, Scotch and Welsh held their own. Swedish immigration remained stationary until 1890, but in the following five years grew with great rapidity. In 1905 they numbered 1,645 persons. Portugese immigration began in 1895 as an overflow from East Cambridge, and numbers 560. The Russian peoples began to appear about 1900, and almost overnight they increased to 1,645, and will probably number close to 5,000 in 1910. The Greek-Syrian-Armenian immigration began about 1904, and while it numbered only 168 in 1905 will show a considerable increase within the decade.

Immigration into the Port can be roughly divided into three periods. First, a period dating from 1850 to 1890, during which the immigration came from the British Isles and Canada; a second period, 1890 to 1900, which witnessed the rise and growth of the Swedes and Portugese; and the third period, 1900 following, characterized by an increasing inflow of Russian peoples from the Baltic, and the beginnings of immigration from the Eastern Mediterranean region.

The American population of 13,000 is only partly of local origin. There are 3,626 persons who come from New England states other than Massachusetts; 1,549 from Middle Atlantic states; and 464 from Western states. Maine sends the largest quota, made up of carpenters, builders, factory foremen, operatives and businessmen. Many Maine people who have come from the same portion of the state hold family and town reunions, which add a picturesque element to their social life.

English Speaking Immigrants from the British Empire

In 1905 the Irish of the first and second generations were approximately 14,000 strong. Since 1885 the increase has consisted largely of the American born. The early comers settled on the low swamp lands between East Cambridge and the Port, and on the edges of the great marsh in the southern and eastern part of the district. Colonies were established in the Jefferson Street region, still known as the "tin village"; and in the district south of Massachusetts Avenue and west of Central Square, still locally known as "Paddy's Hollow." As the lowlands were filled in the old shacks have been replaced with tenements, which are largely owned by Irishmen and their descendants. An examination of the assessor's list of the Jefferson Street and Franklin Street region shows such landholders on a large percentage of property.

This body of Irishmen soon found itself industrially, and many firms which date back before 1880 are still partly manned with these immigrants. They work on the streets, in the city works, in the soap, iron, candy, baking, and some other industries, where through long years of service they have become industrially wise. Many employers sigh for the old laborer of these years.

Irish-Americans of the second generation number 8,779, and there are perhaps 1,000 or more to be credited to the third generation. The second generation is doing a great deal of excellent work. Native social qualities; capacity for leadership, and responsiveness to a given situation are psychical qualities of great value in factory work. A number of young Irish people have become foremen. Many more are prevented from assuming responsible positions of this kind through lack of skill. This generation also supplies many machinists and operatives, a portion of the building laborers, and unskilled iron workers, and a very considerable part of the clerk and office force of the Port, in addition to those who go to Boston. The young people also supply from 60 to 80% of all the Port female factory help.

The third generation is often in the High School. Its members are becoming clerks, skilled office help, managers and professional men, but not to the extent that they should. The Catholic Church attracts the more capable type of children to its parochial schools, and the difficulty of making the journey to the Catholic High School [Harrison Avenue, Boston] and the official discouragement of the use of the public High Schools undoubtedly holds back many young people from higher education.

The better portion of the Port must increasingly belong to the second generation Irish. The early comers lived on the marshes; but with the passage of years the more successful have driven back the American people from their previous residential districts, and year by year encroachments are made upon the sacred precincts of Dana Hill. When East Cambridge began to be crowded with arrivals from the West End [of Boston], the more capable Irish families of that district moved out along Cambridge Street and the Inman Square region. These two lines of attack upon the very citadel of Cambridge conservatism have practically resulted in the surrender of that region.

Social life centers about the Catholic Church. There are two parishes; one founded in 1866 with 10,000 souls [St. Mary's]; and a second parish [Blessed Sacrament] founded in 1905 numbering perhaps 2,500 souls. St. Mary's maintains a parochial school with 1,800 pupils and provides in addition a large and finely equipped gymnasium and a very good hall for secular entertainments. There are the usual sodalities and societies, among which are strong temperance organizations. The Church has been of inestimable value in the struggle to keep Cambridge no-license. In addition to the church societies are a number of well established lodges, political and social clubs, and many ephemeral social and outing groups organized among the young men and women.

The Irish of the Port are in process of assimilation; but it is an assimilation by means of ideals. They are not intermarrying with people of other nationalities or religions, but they are surely making the best American standards their own. No one can study the life of the better class and not understand that this vanguard of school teachers, foremen, stenographers and shopkeepers are all Americans to the core of their being. They love and understand American political and social ideals; and even at the present they measure up to the best in population that the Port has ever had. In the end the rear guard of their people will follow them.

The English immigrants number 1,004, and there are 1,410 of the second generation. They are largely skilled craftsmen, many of whom came here to work in the printing and binding trades. There is still a small colony scattered through the southern section of the Port. These families fall easily into the social life of the district and are no longer to be distinguished.

The Scotch number 407 of the first, and 825 of the second generation. They are fore-people, mechanics, builders, and tradesmen. Many of them own their own houses, and in the good district of the Southern Port one frequently sees Scotch names on the door plates of small cottages tucked cosily into well-kept door yards. The second generation number many high school and college graduates, and are found in banks, offices, and commercial positions of responsibility.

The Canadians total 6,074 of the first, and 2,735 of the second generation, the major portion of whom come from Ontario and Nova Scotia. The Irish and Scotch Catholic group ally themselves with Catholic churches; and the Irish easily amalgamate with their brethren from overseas. They are unusual in that they become naturalized and take an active part in politics and organized labor.

The French Canadians are settled in family groups and live mainly in the sixth ward. They do the lighter work in woodworking, candy, box, and rubber factories. Their social life centers either in Boston or North Cambridge, both of which places have a French church and a large colony.

The great majority of the thousand immigrants from Newfoundland live in the third ward, in family groups. They do hard coarse labor, mostly in the East Cambridge industries, though a few engage in the rough work of the Port. Their social life centers in East Cambridge.

In the more strictly residential wards, 5, 6, and 7, there are 3,348 women and 1,374 men who are Canadian born. Some of the women are domestic helpers, and a very large proportion do some form of office work in Boston or Cambridge. There are a number of students who come from the Provinces for commercial education, and who board with friends. The men are largely clerks, building craftsmen of one kind or another, streetcar conductors, and to a small extent operatives in the woodworking and machine shops.

The two Presbyterian churches, which are largely made up
of Canadians, and the Baptist and Methodist churches number
many among their membership. There is also a decided tendency
to go to Boston to church, especially among girls working in
families, and for those who board in the Port. There are no
distinct Canadian social institutions; but there is a strong clannish
feeling among them, and their social life tends to center within
their own groups.

SWEDES

The Swedes number 1,645 foreign born and 890 of American
birth. The colony is scattered through Wards 4 and 6, the two
better class industrial wards. Though this immigration started
in 1895, there was little increase until 1890 [sic]. Industrially
more skilled than the Irish they have always tended — even in the
first generation — to keep pace with the successful Irish-Americans and Provincials. The Swedish community is made up of
craftsmen. Clergymen excepted, they have no professional men
and practically no businessmen in the Port. This makes the
group nationally and industrially homogeneous but monotonous.
They furnish Cambridge with some of the best craftsmanship
that it possesses. About 150 men are employed in the metal
trades, 100 in the wood-working industry, 50 in baking, and a
score or more in the building trades. The remainder work in
East Cambridge and in the metropolitan area.

The younger generation is taking advantage of the high
schools and colleges, and many of them are turning to the professions. The young women are becoming clerks, stenographers,
nurses and school teachers.

The assessor's lists show 225 pieces of property listed under
Swedish names, and more could be added by any one familiar
with those who have Anglicized their names. The favorite type
of property is the two and three family tenement, partly occupied by the owner; although the lists note properties valued
from $30,000 to $50,000.

Three churches have a total membership of about 800 persons, some of whom come from Boston and the outlying suburbs.
Three lodges, a gymnastic club, a singing society, and a temperance order minister to the social needs of the community. A

large number of persons have memberships in Boston organizations. Some of the less responsible of these lodges give dances in Cambridgeport halls, but such dances are considered provincial and not to be compared with the more fashionable Boston events. The Swedes of the Port manifest the same social peculiarities that have been noticed in the general consideration of the race.

THE RUSSIAN PEOPLES

This immigration is the last wave to overflow into the Port, and it is new enough to be still novel. Among nations as among individuals Fate makes strange bedfellows. Four distinct peoples and three distinct groups are the Jews, Lithuanians and Poles, and the Letts. They represent three religions, three degrees of culture and three types of mind. The Jews, most alien in religion, are traders; the Poles and Lithuanians are Catholics, countrymen, primitive in habits, and industrially untrained; the Letts are Lutheran Protestants, largely city dwellers and craftsmen, simple but not primitive.

The Jews in the Port are in three groups, namely, the Americanized Jew, who has changed his name after having acquired the language, and does all he can to conceal his race; the English Jew, bearing such English names as Burnett, Miller, Phillips, Pollock, etc.; and the Russian Jews of recent arrival. While the first two classes number but a few hundred persons, they have become a distinct factor in the commercial life of the Port.

The Russian Jews came into the district by way of East Cambridge, and in the wake of other Russian peoples to whom they catered by their knowledge of their language. The great influx began about 1902, when their numbers trebled within a year. There are now close to 2,000 in the Port, which is on the way to become a center through the erection of synagogues. At present there are two Jewish colonies; one in the north in the Cambridge-Columbia Street district, and another in the southern part of Western Avenue. The northern colony is composed of those who have moved from the North and West Ends of Boston. The southern colony tends to be largely made up of more recent arrivals from the Russias. The families are as yet scattered in small groups some distance apart, but an examination of the assessor's lists shows a decided tendency to close in. Settlements have been made in some of the worser Irish districts to the disgust of that nation, whose representatives are moving out. At their first coming public sentiment was so outraged that it was physically dangerous for a Jew to use certain streets; children were persecuted on their way to school. This became so serious that a Jewish protective organization was formed, since which time most of the dislike has taken less violent form.

Industrially the Jew continues to be a trader and keeps various kinds of small shops. Several Jewish mills and factories making clothing have been started. The rag and junk dealers abound, and the Cambridge Street district is dotted with barns and buildings wherein this filthy and dangerous business is carried on. Many among them also go to Boston to their work as cigar makers, clothiers, cabinet makers, etc. There are a number of building craftsmen and a score or so who do ornamental iron, copper and tin work. Perhaps there are one hundred Jews employed in the industries of the Port. The women are beginning to work in the factories, and are found in the low-paid industries like candy and rubber.

The assessor's office showed 360 pieces of property listed by Jews (a gross under-estimate owing to the impossibility of recognizing Anglicized and English Jewish names). There are several such whose holdings of Port real estate are very large.

As usual the social life of the people is already rich and varied. Two synagogues at loggerheads with one another over matters of doctrine minister to the religious life of the community; there are two relief societies which concern themselves with Passover indulgences [help to poor]; a Protective and Political Association; two young men's clubs, and several more or less successful social clubs among the young people organized after the pattern of the Irish social clubs. In addition there are Jewish schools, and a night school has been maintained for teaching English. The Jews attend the city night schools and take all courses except the mechanical. Their children are rapidly filling the primary schools and kindergartens, where they are characterized as chiefly dirty, ignorant of the language, brilliant at figures, slow at other things, but with one or two representatives almost always well up toward the head of their class.

The Jew in the Port is . . . dirty, hard-working and successful — and without doubt will in the near future almost wholly preempt a large portion of the Cambridge Street quarter to his uses. So far, however, his impression on the Port has been largely to the disadvantage of the district.

The Poles and Lithuanians can be treated together because their problem is practically the same. The Pole is keener than the Lithuanian, who is simple, ingenuous, and unsuspicious. As nearly as one can tell there are about 1,000 Poles in Cambridge, three-fourths of whom live in East Cambridge; and 1,200 Lithuanians, most of whom live in the Port. The Port is the Lithuanian, and East Cambridge the Polish center.

Lithuanian immigration began in 1901, and came first from South Boston. It has increased each year, partly by South Boston recruits, and even more largely from abroad. The colony is located in the Rogers and Brooks blocks [large wooden tenements at Main and Burleigh Streets. Now torn down.], and Burleigh — Portland — Jefferson and Warren Streets region.

Both the Poles and Lithuanians are unskilled, and do rough work in the packing, boiler, machine, and rubber shops. A few carry on some of the lesser skilled processes in the woodworking factories. They are not good shopkeepers and have few stores. For a time the Lithuanians in the Port attempted a cooperative shop, but it failed for want of competent management. They are poor unionists, being doubly handicapped by language and lack of skill, and willing to surrender to injustice rather than lose their weekly wage.

They are saving and thrifty; but of late years the cost of living has become too high and their savings accumulate too slowly to admit of large showings. There is one Lithuanian, however, who has property valued at $11,000. A well informed Lithuanian knew of only twelve persons in Cambridge who owned houses. Much of their present savings goes into transportation for relations and friends [to America], and in preparing for marriage. The women of the colony are outnumbered several to one by the men; and single women are in great demand in marriage. They recognize their advantage and make the most of it, looking forward to marriage unabashed. "I came here," said one, "in order to get married. Many poor girls in Lithuania come here to be married. There the father must pay to get the girl married — here it is not so." The girl works for a time in the factory, picks over her suitors, and finally marries.

Once married the couple take a house, and run a boarding establishment, as the woman's part of the contribution to the income. The "house" is from four to seven rooms in a tenement, and the boarders are unmarried young men. Each room of the apartment save the kitchen will harbor two people. The boarders pay $1.00 weekly, which sum provides the room, care, personal washing, the cooking of the food together with milk, tea, coffee, and "the onion." The boarder provides the housewife with a pass-book to the store, and she buys at his command. One sees these women going to the shop in the morning with from four to a dozen pass-books.

The menu of the Lithuanian consists of an unending round of bread, pork scraps, and tea and coffee. The shop sells only pork; when beef and mutton are called for the proprietor sends out to other stores. Vegetables are eaten only when they are very cheap. When the boarder arrives from work, his articles are cooked and served to him, and he jealously guards his interests in the pass-book. The female immigrant if she assists in the work is often boarded for fifty cents a week.

Lithuanian girls do not like the factory, and they much prefer their housework. They complain that factory hours are long, and the treatment unfair. In the Rubber Works they are given the roughest work, with the least pay, and in the bakery the forewoman tends to discriminate. "Sure she's a big, husky furriner, put her up nixt the furnace." Thick set and heavy witted they are no match for the keen and nimble Irish in the matter of turning out work.

The social life of the colony centers in South Boston, where churches, stores, societies, and friends are located. The Port has one Lithuanian benefit association of the ordinary type, highly prosperous because the membership is all young. The Poles of the Port have a good deal of social life in East Cambridge, where there is a new Polish church, several clubs and societies.

Both the Lithuanians and the Poles are naturally light-hearted and fond of gaiety. They love dances and festivities; and the newly arrived immigrants cling to the old customs. But this soon changes in the American atmosphere; the day's work leaves them too worn out for the old diversions, and they become increasingly quiet, even to sullenness. Drink is secured — whiskey from the drug stores, and beer from Boston — and times of debauchery follow. There is a strong movement for temperance emanating from the churches, and the people are being affected by it, how strongly it is hard as yet to tell.

When they learn English they are proud of it, and some of the more successful break away from the colony, and try to ally themselves with the English speaking population. This is especially true of the second generation who are ashamed of the dress, manners and speech of the immigrant. Such live in lonely isolation knowing only Lithuanians of similar taste, and largely refused that fellowship they would like among the Irish and other English speaking people.

The children go both to the public school and the parochial school. They are not bright and are additionally handicapped by their home life. As a rule they are taken out of school at the first opportunity and sent to the most convenient factory.

As a whole the Lithuanians are a primitive and childlike people, but worthy and capable under proper leadership. They have been unduly made prominent through certain crimes, and the public has an entirely false impression of their true character.

The Latvians are few in number, the total colony consisting of only four hundred persons, of which number ninety are children under working age. They are scattered through the fifth and sixth wards on Washington, Clarke, Winsor Streets; Pearl, Brookline and Douglas Streets. The first Latvian immigrants came to this country seventeen years ago, but there was no Latvian minister until after 1896. The immigration has been greatly stimulated by Russian persecution, and the latter immigration is far inferior to that of ten years ago. The Latvians in the port are fairly well educated and trained when they come here, and are craftsmen of some skill. They work in the piano shops as cabinet makers and polishers; and machinists in some of the metal industries. Their women go out to service until they marry, and while they have the boarder system it is often on a very decent plan.

Their church and society life centers in Roxbury, and they have meetings, dances, etc. in Kensseble and Putnum Halls. They have a prayer service with the Baptist church on Thursday nights, which averages fifty to sixty people. A Boston Latvian Benefit Society to which many of the Port colony belong; and a Young Men's Club meeting weekly in the Port to discuss political economics and literary matters, constitute organized social effort.

Latvian children are bright and well up to the average. They seem an admirable people and of great value to the community.

THE NEGRO

Next to the native stock the Negroes are longest resident in the Port. The colony numbered about 100 until 1865 when it increased to 371; to 921 in 1875; and to approximately 3,500 in 1910. There are two Negro centers; one immediately about Burleigh Street and the other on Howard Street. The Burleigh Street colony, one time situated on the swamp, is very old, and the houses are small, two-story shacks. The Howard Street colony began to grow about 1890, and is much more desirable in housing and surroundings. There are 2,500 persons living in the Burleigh Street district and its surrounding colonies, and 1,000 in the Howard Street quarter.

The population is organized on state lines. Of 1,649 born south, 554 came from N. Carolina and 528 from Virginia. The female population from N. Carolina and Virginia is from ten to thirty percent higher than the male, which shows a settled family life that permits of sending south for relatives and friends. The two colonies also run on state lines, the Burleigh Street region being predominantly North Carolinian, and the Howard Street center Virginian. Churches, lodges, etc., are affected by state divisions.

There is also a growing group of Negroes from Nova Scotia and the West Indies. The former are from the same stock as the Southern Negro, and such immigrants mix easily with the native stock. The West Indian Negro has been coming to Cambridge since 1903, working his passage on boats plying between the Islands and Canada, and coming through the Provinces; but some come directly. This immigration has been stimulated by the American invasion of the West Indies and the stories circulated concerning high wages and the superior conditions of living in the States. West Indians are often well educated, and have a directness of manner and felicity of speech which is most attractive. They are skilled workmen and have been printers, cabinet makers, wood workers, carpenters, etc. They remain British and take little part in American life; living in hope of an ultimate return. A few attend the Episcopal and the Catholic churches. They do not intermarry with the Southern stock, preferring to send back for wives. Their social life centers in Boston, but there are several cricket clubs and a good literary club in Cambridgeport.

The majority of the Negroes of the Port work in Boston as waiters, porters, hotel and personal servants. In the Port a few are teamsters, porters, and a very few work in the factories. There are no places open to them in the industries; the sentiment among the operatives being overwhelmingly against them as fellow workmen. The colony has a few professional and business men, and one newspaper. There are no distinctly colored stores, largely because the Negro lacks initiative, and partly because of the impossibility of organizing racial buying sentiment. A number of them own their own homes, and a few are well off. The majority live close to the margin, partly through lack of industry and foresight, and partly because of industrial conditions. There is much friendly and neighborly aid and they do not call on organized charity more than other peoples.

Their social life is very luxuriant. They have a childish delight in multiplicity of organization, and every normal Negro at some time forms an organization or association. Even the humblest seem pressed to fulfill their social obligations. Boston sets the standard for Cambridgeport life. The ranking families, churches, business, professional, trade and social organizations are over the river. Many Cambridgeport Negroes belong to Boston organizations, especially lodges; and to Company L of the 6th Regiment. In the Port the chief social force is the church, which numbers about one thousand communicants, and raises in the vicinity of $7,000 a year. The course of church life is not smooth, as money comes with difficulty and there are many calls for denominational aid. The clergy are ill-paid, and the work beset with personal difficulties. The charity of the church goes to its own members or South.

The Port supports a number of lodges and benefit orders. There is a certain fluorescence about the names, — Good Samaritans, Galilean Fishermen, Love and Charity, Household of Ruth, Heroines of Jericho. The lodge center is a hall on Main Street near Windsor Street: [sic] recognized as a social center. Most lodges charge six dollars a year for dues and pay sick benefits of five dollars weekly for twelve weeks and from fifty to one hundred dollars as a death benefit. The lodges have perhaps one thousand members and are of great importance, both socially and economically. Their financial life is unstable, however, and there are generally one or two of them on the verge of bankruptcy. The Masons and the Odd Fellows are the ranking lodges, and the others fade off in the social scale.

In addition to the lodges there are a number of philanthropic and social clubs, and a dozen or more cultural clubs. The "Forum" is notable with two hundred members, and it has secured capable speakers, both white and black, for its Sunday afternoon meeting. There are various Alumni associations of High Schools and Institutes, dancing classes and small group clubs.

The Negro has to bear up in his relations to whites under the double handicap of racial incapacity (measured by white standards) and racial discrimination. The latter difficulty causes the race constant irritation and soreness. This comes out most plainly in the Negro attitude to the public school. The punishment of a colored child or a failure in promotion is felt to be discrimination of race. Yet the colored child is not the equal of the white child in comprehension, execution and order. He gravitates toward the end of the class, and is suspicious, quarrelsome, and hard to handle. There are a few Negro children who are excellent scholars, and two cases may be instanced where Negroes outdistanced white children of good families. They attend the evening grammar schools in limited numbers, but do not use manual training courses of the Rindge School. A few attend the High School. On the whole there is a deepseated feeling that it is useless to attend school because of the impossibility of using commercially such education as one may secure.

THE PHYSICAL CONDITIONS

The Port started out under great physical disadvantages. That part of the district nearest Boston was bordered altogether by low-lying swamp lands, which made it at once unattractive and unhealthful. Within the past twenty years through the energy and good leadership of a few men, this low land was filled in, and the city provided with an attractive river line, and a parkway of exceptional promise [Charles River Parkway, now Memorial Drive].

On the whole the present sanitary condition of the Port is good. Three of its sides are bordered by the River. The Back Bay borders its most congested section, and does much to keep the air good. The worst evil of the Port is the soap factories, which are malodorous and wholly unsuited to an urban community. The main thoroughfares of the Port are straight, broad, and well lighted, although not altogether well paved. There are a few streets and alleys in the congested district north of Main Street, which are narrow, insufficiently lighted, and badly kept. After a rain they become noisome alike to sight and smell. There are parts of the Port which need attention to the matter of surface drainage, and the problem of interior sanitation is not yet wholly met. The lighting in the Port is good and calls for no criticism. Parks, playgrounds, and open spaces are now adequately provided; though with a few exceptions much in the way of development is yet to be done. Large areas of unoccupied land still provide open spaces within easy reach of every part of the district.

HOUSING

The Port in 1850 had only the regular housing conditions of the average New England village, when it was confronted by a mass of newly arrived immigrants to provide for. Since that year it has had to provide for from 500 to 1,000 additional persons yearly. For some years housing conditions in the Port were not what they should be, and its housing law was too lax for public welfare and safety. The new provision of [?] has remedied this defect. In the hurry to put up houses many cheap tenements were built in the swamps, or on poorly filled land. For years a dry cellar was a very irregular thing in parts of the Port. As the people continued to increase houses were built in front and back yards. During the years any kind of a dwelling that could be converted into a three family apartment underwent that transformation. A number of large barrack-like tenements reproduce the worst Boston conditions. The Port uses a large number of horses, stables for which are often tucked away in back yards. The growth of the rag industry and the coming of the filthy peoples is going to do much to increase the problem. There are already the germs of some good slums in the district off Main Street and Cambridge Street.

In the districts given over to the better class mechanics, clerks, and small businessmen there has been a very noticeable increase in the growth of the apartment house. Several score of such buildings have been erected within the past few years; and more are continually being built. Streets like Massachusetts Avenue (beyond Prospect Street), Magazine Street, Harvard Street, Broadway, once the heart and citadel of old Cambridgeport family life, are being given over to this class of dwellings. Some of these apartments obtain high rentals, but they presage none the less the fall of the district. They make room for the nomadic family, and the family whose life was rooted in the city's life and growth is already disappearing. The subway will accent this tendency and the Port can be expected to increase its numbers of apartment dwellers enormously.

At the present Cambridgeport housing is equally divided between the single family cottages and the two or three family tenements; though there is a steady decrease of the first class and a rise in the number of the second class. The large apartment group is steadily increasing and is going to give the tone to the community.

The moral effect of this movement in housing is now beginning to be felt. The two and three family house is not condemned as is the apartment. It has come into being because of the cost of building. It is no fault of the working man that he lives in a section of a house. He lives that way, because his work demands mobility and the price of the tenement is what he can afford. He is not in a position to be fastidious.

The steam heated apartments are the double outgrowth of economic conditions and desire. They cost as much as an ordinary dwelling of equal size and consequence, but they do away with a great deal of the work of running a house. And for this reason they are desired. All observers argue that measured by the old standards the apartment dweller shows a loosening of moral fibre. It fosters lack of civic and household responsibility; and if the apartment is inevitable its occupants are yet in a transitional state wherein they have lost the old moralities of the independent household without having developed a new code of civic and social morality to take its place.

SOCIAL CLASSES

The passage of the Port from village to city organization is nowhere more apparent than in its social life. Physically the district is an overgrown country industrial town. It has vacant land in abundance, detached houses over a good share of its area, quiet little streets and lanes that might well seem some miles distant from the State House. Two weekly newspapers distribute local gossip; and a representative man can know a good portion of the "knowable" people. On the other hand its population is becoming increasingly cosmopolitan, its interests are cityward, its amusements and social life are increasingly beyond its bridges in the metropolitan area. It no longer has much neighborhood life; next door neighbors tend to live in stony city indifference. These tendencies are vastly on the increase.

The drain of Boston on the Port is enormous. A considerable portion of the population goes cityward to work and feels itself far more at home there than in the Port. The housewives go to Boston for purchases of all kinds; partly because the stores are more attractive, and partly for the pleasure and excitement. The provision shops alone flourish. Theatres, entertainments, sports and amusements center in Boston. Dances and parties held in Boston halls are considered more fashionable than similar events held in the halls of the Port. And there is yet the call of friends, and the very heavy liquor drain.

Social classes group themselves into several well defined divisions. A remnant of families born and brought up in the traditions of the Port has affiliated itself with the Old Cambridge group in ideals and spirit, and is no longer typical of the Port. Another remnant of this class holds to the older tradition and constitutes itself a more or less exclusive society to set the tone of the social life of its district.

A portion of the renting householders and the apartment dwellers are fairly permanent; and identify themselves with the interests of their neighborhood. This section is small, and the larger part of the group is made of peripatetic families who move frequently and form few local ties. If the income is good their social life centers in Boston. Failing this a few easy neighborhood acquaintances are sought, and the group ekes out a miserable half-starved, envious and dissatisfied social life.

The boarding-house group is growing in importance and the district has its own lodging-house problem. At present it numbers one thousand persons, nearly all of whom are located in the neighborhood of Central Square. The group is composed of teachers, office and business workers, clerks and to some small extent factory operatives. This population is made up partly of persons working in the Port and partly of those who desire a more open environment than the South or West Ends afford. They develop the same difficulties about finding places to eat; the same tendency to move from one place to another; and the same lack of social opportunity that distinguishes the Boston lodger. Because of the village-like character of the city, however, the lodging houses are of higher moral character than those in Boston. There are few transient roomers. Supervision is closer. A number of families take a larger apartment than they need, with the purpose of earning enough from the letting of rooms to live near the center of the town and closer to Boston. Lodgers in these houses have opportunity for semi-private life which sometimes proves delightful for all concerned. But the lodger is a stranger and a sojourner. He becomes a religious taster, going from church to church; and lives in the city as a casual onlooker.

The bulk of the Port is made up of middle grade work people, more or less permanent, in national groups with their characteristic national life. Thus the Irish center about their two churches and special organizations; the Negroes, Swedes, French, Portugese, etc., all have their own exclusively national life; meeting other peoples only incidentally in the streets, at the moving picture shows, or in the factories. There is a well defined and explicit social life in each of these nationalities. Below these groups is a drifting class of workers, men skilled and unskilled, without the stability to hold a place any length of time. They go restlessly from one job to another, moving their families eternally — the despair of landlords, school-teachers, churches, politicians, everyone. They are the modern industrial gypsies, and their symbol is the moving van.

And last the final submerged tenth of working people, who are physically and mentally so inefficient that they make an outcast class by themselves. They are frequent visitors at the offices of the Overseer of the Poor and the Associated Charities, and the Relief Committees of the churches know them.

Religious Institutions

The religious life of the Port falls easily into a nationalistic mould. The most obvious are the churches of the non-English speaking group; the three Swedish churches; and the Portugese Catholic church. The English speaking churches fall into six groups: two Irish Catholic churches, two Scotch-Canadian-Presbyterian bodies; the Baptist, Methodist bodies of the Canadians and American stock; the Unitarian, Universalist, Congregational, and Episcopal group of the American peoples; the five Methodist-Baptist churches of the Negro; and two synagogues of the Jews.

The individual churches in the Port are not in a flourishing condition. This is due to several causes, the first of which is the constant shifting industrial class. A glance at the map shows the few blocks about Central Square as the church center of the town; within a dozen city squares there are a dozen churches. The Unitarian church on Austin Street was thirty-five years ago the logical center of its constituents. Today it draws its congregation from far west of Prospect Street. The same is true of the Universalist Church on Inman Street, and of the Congregational Church of St. Paul's. These bodies once attracted the "solid people" of the Port, but their constituents have moved over into Old Cambridge, or out of the city. Within the last thirty years the Catholic, Methodist, and Baptist churches have been the growing bodies.

The section of the Port north of Massachusetts Avenue and east of Prospect Street is Catholic. On Norfolk and Harvard Streets is the great Catholic center of St. Mary's, with the parochial residence, the parochial schools, the Hospice of the Sisters, St. Aquinas Hall, and the gymnasium. To the east is the Portuguese Catholic Church, and over in East Cambridge the Polish Church. This district itself is Catholic in complexion. The parish of St. Mary's numbers 10,000 persons beside the large number of Poles, Lithuanians, and French, who go to South Boston and East Cambridge. The Parish of the south numbers 2,500 persons which makes the Catholic Church the strongest religious body in the district. St. Mary's has developed a very complete life of its own, including boys' clubs; gymnasium; parties and entertainments, as well as the religious clubs. Its temperance work has been most commendable, and is invaluable in the no-license cause. The Catholic sentiment of the Port is liberal and cooperative within the limits allowed by the doctrines of the church.

The white Baptist-Methodist bodies make up the strong Protestant churches, and their constituency centers in the southern section of the Port. This will not be so for long, and the decay of the Protestant churches is not far away. The center of religious dominance is beginning to shift from Protestant to Catholic.

SOCIAL INSTITUTIONS

The Port is also well supplied with lodges having almost all the popular bodies represented in some way; carrying out their usual activities. Clubs, etc., have been spoken of in connection with the characterization of separate nationalities.

Taken all in all the type of Cambridgeport life is deadly commonplace. It is a craftsman-clerk district with the drab life of that group. The Catholic, Methodist, Baptist churches represent it religiously; the Catholic and Protestant fraternal and benefit orders, and the multitude of small ephemeral social clubs represent it socially. Two or three moving picture shows furnish its organized amusement. For wider or more varied activity it goes to Boston.

POLITICS

Cambridge, although within a metropolitan area, has been able to hold to the village idea in politics. The majority of office holders are Americans, because the roots of political power are still in Old Cambridge and Magazine Street. A certain set of people have fought long and hard for no-license and non-partisanship in city elections, and these two causes are looked on with a considerable degree of favor by the better citizens. The churches have been drawn into the struggle, and a common cause has done much to unify sectarian differences.

The important opposition factor has been the Irish. Had they been properly organized and officered they might have played a considerable part in public affairs. But the quality of its leadership has been poor and organization has consistently failed of its purpose.

Only once did the city have an Irish mayor, and that case was in the nature of an accident. The dominant party has been able to control the Irish vote, through the street cleaning department splitting the factors in such a way as to deprive them of national significance. But Irish influence in politics is constantly increasing. The second generation is becoming more and more clamorous for influence, and they are tending to fill offices open to civil service competition.

The Canadian vote has never been of a great deal of importance, largely because the men have refused to become naturalized. Naturalized Canadian citizens, however, have tended to support the good citizenship machine.

The Negro vote has been growing steadily and is now about six hundred strong. For the past several years leaders have been organizing political clubs in the hope of securing political favor for the race. These organizations have fed on promises and secured little of performance. The forgetfulness and perennial hopefulness of the Negro makes him an easy object for political manipulation, and each year these renew their hopes. A city official and a few very minor jobs have been portioned as a result of Negro political activity. The colored political situation is rather more a political opera bouffe than a reality.

The Swedes are slow in becoming naturalized, and it takes overmuch urging to secure their interest in political affairs; and they have had very much less part in politics than their numbers gave them opportunity to exercise. Latterly there has been an awakening of political interest and an effort is being made to systematically stimulate them to become naturalized and vote. National political parties are being organized, and there is every indication that the Swedish vote will become larger. The movement has its roots in national self-interest and second generation ambition. It is felt that the young men of the race should have backing in their aspirations for city positions.

The Jews have started political organizations but they are still too small to play much of a part in civic life. They are strong enough to have secured recognition from party dealers; and before long the Jew will have to be reckoned with politically.

The roots of Portugese political power center in East Cambridge; and the Poles, Lithuanians and other late arrivals do not as yet play any part in the political life of the city.

There is a small socialist club in the Port, and a number of very tiny socialistic cliques among certain non-English speaking peoples. Some Swedes, Letts, Lithuanians and Poles attend the national socialistic clubs in Boston, but fall away as they prosper and become naturalized.

The political situation in the Port is finely balanced, and could be easily disturbed. The coming years will undoubtedly bring many changes. The young Irish element will demand increasing recognition, and the Swedish, Jewish, and Negro parties can be expected to increase in numbers and influence. In time the growth among the Poles, Letts and Lithuanian peoples will mean new factions to be considered, and the no-license, nonpartisan party must expect to win its struggles many times over in the coming years. What is needed is some initiation or leadership that will begin now to awaken the voting strength of the non-voting nationalities and give them that training in the duties and responsibilities of citizenship that is often so sorely needed by aliens.

THE MORAL PROBLEM

The Port differs from most industrial cities in its nearness to a metropolitan center and its character as a prohibition district. For thirty years Cambridge has gone no-license and no further proof is needed to confirm the fact that the city itself finds the system good. The Port also approves, for, though it does not vote "no-license" by any overwhelming majority, it does vote for it. And the Port has benefited by the no-license. Even liquor users admit the passing of the disgraceful scenes, the pauperized population, the underclothed and underfed children of the license days. When license reigned teachers found it necessary to maintain stores of cast-off clothing to dole out to half-frozen and half starved children. Shortly after the saloons disappeared this changed, and within a year there was no longer the need for such service.

The business and manufacturing interests are glad of no-license. It results in a more efficient labor force during working hours; a decrease in industrial accidents and the consequent charges to both employer and employee; a more generally efficient type of worker; relief from mental stress; and better conditions of work. That employers do appreciate the value of no-license is seen by the fact that in several cases, they have taken pains to complain against saloons just over the river, and to have their location changed.

The police also testify to the increased orderliness and tractability of the Port since the no-license order, and the better level of life and morality. Charity workers and clergymen testify to the same end, and there are no responsible dissenting voices from this testimony.

This does not mean that there is no drinking going on. Liquor is still to be procured in many ways, and it is procured. Many drug stores are regular purveyors, and it is practically possible for any person familiar with local conditions and able to walk to secure from them such liquors as he may wish. A drug store with a coterie of men about it is not an infrequent sight, and anyone familiar with a particular neighborhood can point out the passage of drinkables. There are a certain number of freak clubs meeting in odd and out of the way places which make a specialty of a private stock of liquor. Kitchen barrooms spring up from time to time, flourish for a little and then disappear. Frequently they are captured by the police, more frequently they are not. Expressmen play their part in evading the law, and the numerous teamsters of the city purvey liquors for their friends.

And it is always possible to go to Boston, which is within walking distance of a large share of the population of the Port. On the other side of both the Craigie and West Boston Bridges are extensive colonies of saloons, all of them with a hospitable door toward the Port, and it is sometimes reported that these keepers contribute to the Cambridge no-license campaign.

The total city arrests for the year 1907 were 3,334, of which number 1,306 were of persons within the Port. Of these 774 were for drunkenness, which number includes repeated arrests of the confirmed alcoholics. The number of individuals arrested would fall considerably below the number given. This figure on the other hand would be greatly increased, perhaps doubled, if one could tabulate all the Boston arrests of Cambridgeport persons. As the figures stand they make an exceptionally good showing for the district.

Commendation of no-license is not altogether universal within the Port. There is a pro-license section of the community that objects to enforced abstinence, and makes strenuous pleas for "personal freedom." They point out the fact that Cambridgeport trade suffers severely at the hands of the moderate drinker, who after investing five cents in a single glass of nourishing beer squanders the rest of his substance on Boston groceries, etc. It is further argued that Cambridgeport ought, rather than Boston, to have the benefits of the license fees for the sale to Cambridge people; and these critics attribute the tax rate of the Port to the liquor situation.

Critics of no-license confuse the retail situation with the liquor traffic. Cambridgeport will never be a prosperous retail city because of its nearness to Boston. So long as Boston furnishes large and attractive stores, bargain sales, and excitement as a part of purchasing, a great deal of Cambridgeport buying will be done across the river. It is the women, not the men, who do the buying. The loss to Cambridgeport business is negligible when compared to the resulting saving in industrial efficiency and decent living.

It has to be admitted, however, that the no-license of the Port succeeds not of itself, but because of the accident of its nearness to Boston. Cambridge goes no-license by only a narrow margin, and if it were certain that liquor could not be easily secured across the river, the vote would change. A working class population, like that of the Port, demands at least the opportunity of occasionally tippling. As it is, Boston has become a liquor cesspool, into which the drinking element of Cambridge-port drains. And it is this fact that has caused the no-license situation to continue as many years as it has.

The excellently clean bill of moral health that the Port undoubtedly has is due to its nearness to the large city. The confirmed, the degraded, and the hardest drinkers go over the bridge for their carousals. And as a rule the larger share of other crime follows the liquor route. It is a significant thing that there are no flagrantly public houses of prostitution in the Port. In some of the foreign colonies there are occasional flats frequented by "strange young men" and there are boarding houses which are "loose" in tendency; but there is no organization of this social evil — for it, too, goes to Boston.

In 1907 there were 3,334 arrests in Cambridge, of which number 1,306 were of persons living in the Port. They may be divided as follows:

Drunk	774
Disturbing Peace	135
Crime:	
vs. Person	99
vs. City Ordinances	90
vs. Chastity and Family	87
vs. Property	85
Misdemeanors	22

Drunkenness accounts for more than one half the arrests and disturbing the peace for 135. The next group of assaults, violations of city order, crimes against chastity and property range from 85 to 100 each. This is an amazingly good showing. Nationally the arrests are as follows: [table omitted]. The Irish lead with 624 arrests, divided into 287 for the first and 337 for the second generations. Some 71 of the second generation arrests were of Irish-American boys under sixteen years of age. The curse of the Irish is drink, which accounts for 387 of the arrests. Crimes against property increase in the second generation, which is a bad sign. The Swedes and the Portugese are very orderly; the Lithuanians and Poles are arrested for drunkenness and assaults. The Jews offend mainly against property, such Jewish arrests amounting to about one half of the total arrests for such offences. Almost all the cases of violation of health laws are Jewish. The Nova Scotians tend to drunkenness and crimes against property. The Negro tends toward drunkenness and crimes against chastity. But the number of arrests among other peoples than the Irish is small. This race with one-third of the population, furnishes about one-half of the crime, the major portion of which, however, consists of drunkenness. In unarrested crimes the Irish again furnish the bulk of the drinking and fighting, and the Jews are complained of for violation against property. Among the young people there is a great deal of looseness of that unorganized but none the less vital sort that tends to pull down the moral reactions of the total population.

Crime among children seems on the increase, and there is a spirit of lawlessness among the American born children of immigrants which argues badly for the future. That malicious mischief of many of these boys is on the increase is a view substantiated by the police, school authorities, and public service corporations. There should be some means of making punishment to be feared and dreaded, a state which does not now exist.

IV

EAST CAMBRIDGE

Prior to the farsighted activities of one Andrew Craigie, who in 1807 acquired the whole of what is now East Cambridge, the greater part of that island was devoted to pasturing the cows of the town. From the time of its grant to Atherton Hough in 1632 the land passed through several hands, being divided, sold, and consolidated again. An indication of its attractive location is seen from the fact that in 1750 Governor Phipps built a mansion on the hill which is still the highest nearby point and which in that day commanded a sweeping view of the Charles River from Brighton to Boston Harbor. Indeed, a realization of the strategic situation of East Cambridge is a necessary preliminary to understanding what has transpired there, from the bridgebuilding work of Craigie to the latest expansion in manufacturing.

East Cambridge was at the outset, much more so than today, a well-defined physical unit. It was separated from Cambridgeport on the west and south by the Great Marsh, from Somerville and Charlestown by Miller's River on the north, and from Boston on the east by the Charles. At high tide the river overspread the marshland to the depth of a foot or more, and in this way the upland became a complete island twice each day. The eminence known as Putnam Hill (so called because it was fortified by General Putnam during the Revolutionary War) is the highest point in Cambridge, and this area, which originally amounted to about half a square mile, has since been nearly doubled by filling in the marshes and the canals. These canals in the heyday of early commercial ambition encircled the district. Miller's River extended into the North Canal, which flowed where the Grand Junction Branch Railroad now runs, and this in turn met the Broad Canal, which reached back into the Charles. By East Cambridge then we mean the territory that is so bounded. By 1853 the railroad had displaced the North Canal, and Miller's River had been shortened and narrowed. There remain the Broad and Lechmere Canals, which with the riverfront form the water approaches of the present time. With the filling of the tide marshes and the building of the Charles River Embankment (1889) the land assumed the general outline it now presents, although the building of the Charles River Dam has since added a small park area.

The advantages of this locality for industrial sites as well as for suburban homes were apparently appreciated by General Craigie only after Francis Dana and his associates had begun a promoting scheme in the part of Cambridge to the southwest which became known as the Port. The original impetus to utilize Cambridge came from the desire to shorten the journey to Boston, and Craigie quickly saw that the most direct road from Cambridge Common into Boston lay through his land in East Cambridge. Taking his cue from these developments of the Port, he quietly bought up all the land to the east of the marshes and by 1807 was preparing to compete with Cambridgeport for traffic, trade, and population. He secured a charter to organize a company to build the necessary approaches and in 1809 had the satisfaction of opening Canal Bridge — later known as the Craigie Bridge. The Lechmere Point Corporation, as his company was called, also carried out his ideas by building the Prison Point Bridge into Charlestown in order that its population might spread in his direction. Craigie's next and most astute move was to get the county in 1816 to accept as a gift the land and the building that the corporation had erected for the County Jail. This came as a final exasperation to the promoters of the Port. Thus began a contest that ripened into a bitter conflict of long standing wherein the best energies of both companies were weakened and from which the Port never completely recovered.

Meanwhile Craigie had persuaded the Boston Porcelain and Glass Company to come to East Cambridge in 1814, and another glass bottle concern presently came in from Salem. This marks the real industrial beginnings of the district. The factories brought their workers, who settled about the base of the hill, while the prison officers and lawyers settled in the center of the new village. Thus early there arose that feeling of discrimination and aloofness between the two classes of residents which continues to the present although the inrush of population is obliterating it. In 1818 a school was started, and the First Methodist Church was organized, though on account of its poverty it had to postpone the erection of a building until 1825.

The two succeeding decades, the twenties and thirties, were

periods of brisk growth in industry and population. Two more glass and bottle manufactories, two brush factories, and the largest soap factory in the country throve and called for the labor of approximately 350 workmen. Three other churches organized in the twenties, and another grammar school was needed in the thirties. No mean stimulus came from the life that passed through on its way cityward. Two large taverns, the Mansion and Lechmere Houses, were centers at which the truck farmers gathered on their way to market. Cattle, hogs, and turkeys were driven down Cambridge Street, and the white covered wagons that put up overnight created business for liverymen, blacksmiths, and harness-makers. And by no means the least contribution was the inception of the Boston and Lowell Railroad, which literally ran through some of the factories in East Cambridge and upon the prosperity of which the ultimate effect was of course wholesome.

The last vestiges of the animosity among the three towns that compose Cambridge over the bridges, roads, and corporation charters cropped out in the eagerness of Old Cambridge to incorporate itself as a separate city in 1842, but wisdom prevailed, and the three parts were united under one city government in 1846. We may note in passing that the first two mayors were East Cambridge men. By this time the region was on a solid and prosperous economic footing, and the population had increased to 4,000 people. There were three grammar schools, six churches, and from ten to a dozen factories. In 1847 an attempt was made to fill some of the marsh lands, indeed, a new company was organized for this purpose more or less ineffectually every decade until the permanent retaining wall was finished in 1889. The railroad from East Boston to Cottage Farms was put through in 1853, and had no small share in stimulating industrial advance.

The decade from 1855 to 1865 marks a transition in the character of the industries and of the people. Glassmaking was already declining in the face of western competition, and although two concerns lingered as late as 1875, their period of highest prosperity passed in the decade under consideration. The soap factories were giving way to those in the Port, and the manufacture of brushes also ceased. The pork-packing, casket-making, and oil clothing manufacturing industries, which flourish today, were beginning. Another attempt to reclaim the lowlands was made by the East Cambridge Land Company in 1861. The movement out of East Cambridge among the older Yankee inhabitants also began at this time. East Cambridge today gives no suggestion of the high quality of citizen that once lived on Putnam Hill. But add to the fact of increased means and business success the incoming of numbers of uncongenial people to work in the factories, and the reason for the exodus from this attractive hilltop on the part of earlier inhabitants is not difficult to understand.

After the Civil War expansion began again, and in the succeeding fifteen years most of the factories and houses that we see at the present time were built. In these years operations either were begun or became firmly established in the woodworking concerns, pump and bridge manufactories, rubber works, sugar refinery, publishing house, and gasworks. The firms that deal in the bulky commodities received by water — coal, lumber, and stone — were also started in this period or even earlier. Structurally, therefore, until very recently, the district has undergone little change, except in the deterioration of property. The character of the people in these years became more uniformly working-class and more uniformly Irish — with the exception, of course, of the Portuguese, whose colony forms a distinct feature of the social structure here. And finally before reviewing the changes, the waves, and the nature of the population we should understand the comtemporary industrial conditions, for the life here has always depended intimately upon the economic forces at work.

Today there are about thirty corporations in East Cambridge, each of which employs over twenty-five persons. These may be classed under several large divisions. There are six woodworking, four metalworking, and two printing establishments. Three factories prepare pork products, sugar, and syrups. The eight coal or lumber dealers and the marble, granite, and freestone workers are brought here by the economy of water transportation. Several other large concerns that handle oil and ice have selected East Cambridge as a center for distributing these commodities.

For all these as well as for the other miscellaneous industries, East Cambridge offers exceptional locational advantages.

The community is only a mile from the State House. Land is cheaper than in any other place of like proximity. The tunnel to Park Street and (eventually to the South Station) on the west and the viaduct to the North Station and subway from Cambridge Street make the business sections of Boston only five minutes away. Connections with the suburbs on the other side of the city are easy. On its one front, ships can unload raw material; on its other, spur tracks that connect with both the Boston and Albany and the Boston and Maine systems can bear away finished products.

Four of the factories employ more than 800 men apiece, and there are nine where from 100 to 400 are engaged. There are about 2,900 men and 700 women who are doing unskilled machine work with wages averaging, for the former, $12, and for the latter, $6.50 a week. For the 560 men in positions of skill, the wage approximates $17, and for the 750 women, $9 a week. In nationality the unskilled workers are Irish, Portuguese, and Polish, of the first or second generation; this also holds true of the women and girls. The skilled men — the machinists, woodcarvers, upholsterers, typesetters, etc. — include Americans, the older Irish, Swedes, Germans, and a few Portuguese. About 75 percent of the unskilled men and 85 percent of all the women make their homes either in the district or nearby in the Port. But the artisans, the clerks, and those who do the light, clean work come almost without exception from out of town. As far as the working conditions go, there is nothing to indicate that they are any worse or much better than the average. Factories are not built to minister to the physical or aesthetic well-being of the workers, and those of East Cambridge are no exception. East Cambridge, then, harbors a population about 70 percent of which is engaged in unskilled work of a kind that offers little opportunity or incentive to live or think on anything but the most mediocre and dispiriting of levels.

Having now gained some hint as to the industrial character, we may return to discover what sort of people compose the workers. The first settlers were English tradesmen and artisans who found a near market for their wares across the Charles. The glassworks of the early days, and later the woodworking concerns, brought German craftsmen as well as Scotch and English of a superior type. This with the fact of its then suburban situation gave a distinct tone of superiority and social standing to residence here. The more rapidly the factories multiplied, the more rapidly did East Cambridge take on the complexion of a true industrial community. Through the thirties the Irish began to arrive both from Boston and directly from the old country; by the forties the influx was well under way. By 1841 enough had arrived to warrant the building of the St. John's Catholic Church. In connection with it the St. John's Literary Institute was formed to give instruction in English and to encourage debates, general mental improvement, and recreation. Its members boast that this society had the first crew that rowed on the Charles River. The coming of Father Mathew in 1849 resulted in the formation of the Father Mathew Total Abstinence Society among a group of young Irishmen. The power and influence of this organization as it grew and waxed strong cannot be ignored in a discussion of the liquor situation here. When the war came, a whole Irish company, composed largely, it is said, of men from the glassworks, went to the Front from East Cambridge. This immigration, then spread as it was over twenty-five years, has entrenched itself so firmly in the life of the place that its influence on the human history has been the preponderant one. At present out of a population of approximately 12,000, about 60 percent are of Irish parentage.

From the point of view of the descendents of the English, however, this influx was an intrusion and a disaster. The aristocracy of Quality Row, as a portion of Third Street was called, eventually began to leave. As the second-generation Irish prospered and moved higher up the slope, the holders of the hill fell away before them. Today there remain at most a very few of the Yankee stock — those upon whom the burdens of old age, real estate, or both have fallen too heavily. The Protestant churches have one by one given up the ghost. The Methodists and Episcopalians survive only by calling back those who have moved away, and it is only a matter of time until their Canadian constituency will also leave. The sons of Ireland have become the aristocracy, and practically all the substantial homes are in their hands.

Apparently, however, the drama is to be played again. Already the Polish leaders have moved hillward, and for their church they own a sightly spot on Otis Street which was formerly used by the Universalists. Moreover, since 1905 there has been a marked movement among the older Irish families into North Cambridge, Belmont, Medford Hillside, and Somerville. The young people of this class are, generally speaking, in office work in Boston, and for them marriage means removal as East Cambridge affords no modern two-family houses or apartments with the up-to-date appurtenances that the onward march of civilization seems to demand. Another ten years will find the district deserted of these better-grade Irish homes. It is this progress of the Irish from the hard, poorly paid, manual labor to a firmer economic base and more intelligent occupations that constitutes a visible sign of that invisible grace which it is the nation's hope will bring salvation to the other peoples as well. From ignorance and passive observation to desire to participate but inability to get a footing, and hostility on the part of those of longer residence, to a growing comprehension of common concerns and an active cooperation with the best forces at work — this is the hard but royal road that has been traveled by the Irish and that must be traveled by every other race that would become a component of the nation.

All this is also true to some extent of the Portuguese, although as a group they have not yet established themselves as firmly or as powerfully as have the Irish. They are handicapped, of course, by an ignorance of our language which often seems to denote a degree of diffidence and unaggressiveness that is easily mistaken for lack of energy, acuteness, and ambition. For this reason also their life has remained slightly distinct and colonized. They entered East Cambridge soon after the Civil War, but whether the first comer was a barber or a cabinetmaker is not clear. However, we do know that the first dozen families came from Boston — a beginning of the dispersion that has now emptied the North End of this nationality. A furniture factory that was the means of support for an increasing number of Portuguese — cabinetmakers, carvers, polishers, varnishers, and unskilled laborers — was destroyed by fire about the year 1871, and on rebuilding the increased number of workers needed was supplied by incoming Portuguese. Subsequent immigration has been partly through New Bedford, which harbors the largest and most prosperous colony in the state, and partly direct from the Azores and from the St. Michael's Islands. The field of employment has widened so that both men and girls are in the rubber shops, oil clothing manufactory, and pork-packing industries. Until 1902 many of the faithful were communicants of the Portuguese church in the North End. In that year a parish was organized in Cambridge, and the building on Portland Street just over the line into the Port, that had been built by the Portuguese Fraternity in 1897 was purchased for a church. When the Boston edifice was sold about two years ago, the proceeds were divided between this parish and the one in East Boston, as it was into these two districts, particularly the latter, that its constituency had gone. At present with its rebuilt front and new parish house the church gives a fairly accurate indication of the prosperity of its members. The Portuguese are now scattering from East Cambridge to the extent that a considerable number of the older church people come from the upper parts of Cambridge and from all over Somerville.

For the Portuguese colony it can be safely affirmed that life here is a real step forward. For those from Boston there is more room and air, and as houses are smaller and cheaper, the thrifty ones become property owners in a short time. For those from abroad there is offered a wider horizon and a broader field of endeavor, if not for the adults at least for their children. But it still remains true that the qualities and traits of the Portuguese are not such that their advance or achievement is at all spectacular, brilliant, or in any way exceptional.

A few scattered Polish families arrived over thirty years ago, but the real movement among the Slavs dates from the last fifteen years. Since that time the changes in population have been going on much more rapidly.[1] The Poles, Armenians, and a very few Jews comprise the newcomers. And they, together with the less energetic Irish and Portuguese, are doing the rough, unskilled factory labor. It is these also who occupy the con-

[1] A rough approximation of present figures of population would be: Irish, 7,000; Polish, 1,200; Italian, 200; Portuguese, 3,000; American, 400; Armenian, 200.

course of cheap wooden houses with which Putnam Hill is surrounded. Nevertheless, the Polish people exhibit a happy and hopeful front. Many of them are young people of fine physical parts, a trifle stolid perhaps but willing and ambitious. These men have now married — there were thirty-seven Polish weddings in 1911 in these two wards[2] alone — and there are many families starting thus on the long road toward a better standard of life. As with the Irish and Portuguese, their children will go to school, learn American ways, get better wages, and establish their families on a more healthy economic scale, for at present they are not so established. It is hard to say whether these unskilled Portuguese, Poles, and Armenians are more victims of unduly low wages or of their own ignorance of better standards. Certain it is that the recompense they receive is insufficient for the support of an adequate, normal, healthy family life. Men lodge with families at one dollar a week, and women at fifty cents a week, this being the cheapest way to get a bed; or families rent their rooms to lodgers, this being the cheapest way to pay rent. In either case both are led to these undesirable expedients for the sake of economy. Certain it is also that a fair number of these people save money — a fact that in no way controverts the truth of the previous statement. If one could see where and how they live, and what they eat and wear, it would become clear that their thrift is only a measure of their ignorance concerning matters of housing, health and general culture. The fact remains that if wages were higher, values in rentals more adequate, work more regular, and hours shorter, the seemingly imperative call to lay by every spare cent would lose much of its urgency.

Unlike the Polish colony, the Armenian group seems to be remaining small. Here, too, there are numbers of young men living in crowded boarding houses, with as yet a much smaller complement of women. For this reason they have not settled down as home builders to any considerable extent, although more and more of their women will be brought over in the next five years. Where work is to be found, there they shift. And as they seem to have started in working with rubber, they

[2]East Cambridge, formerly Ward III, is now divided into Wards I and II.

scatter from here to the rubber shops of Watertown or Malden as the chance affords.

But this movement is not confined to the Armenians. It is difficult but vital to grasp the constant flux of all this population. Back and forth within the district and the Port, into Somerville and back, or into the upper parts of the city, families come and go to the extent that in one of the schools a quarter of the pupils are discharged to some other school every year to be replaced by a similar number who move in. The loss of neighborhood attachments, domestic stability, and educational continuity that results is a considerable one from the point of view of the maintenance and upbuilding of the family life.

The actual physical conditions of living are not discouraging, but are in fact an advance, if compared with the congested parts of Boston. Streets are wider and cleaner; houses are less crowded and are never more than three stories high; there is a freer sweep of fresh air through the district — save when the wind blows from the direction of the slaughterhouse. But taken by themselves the surroundings do seem to form a background in which the life of the children is too relentlessly determined. With the exception of the houses on Putnam Hill, some of which are of brick and most of which are single, the buildings in East Cambridge are of wood, built very close together — a frightful fire hazard — and for two or more families. Almost all the building was done prior to 1880, with the consequence that many one-family houses have been made to accommodate two; the water closets and sinks have been put in wherever there was room, regardless of light or air. Among the later immigrants there is undoubtedly overcrowding at night. Home life under such conditions inevitably disintegrates. The children are on the streets at all hours, which means not only a slackening of parental discipline but of general moral restraint. And when both parents are at work all day, as is sometimes the case, the child is completely free. Such facts have their bearing on the morality and crime of the district.

Although a part of the land is the low marsh area that has been filled, this is used largely for factories, and most of the dwellings are on the higher ground. This accounts somewhat for the general soundness of public health here. However, on the streets that skirt the residential section — Bridge, Winter, Vine, Loring, and Gore Streets — there is a prevalence of tuberculosis that should sound a warning. In 1912 there was one case in every hundred people, a very high percentage, and among this number the Irish victims were in great preponderance. Infant mortality is low — a fact for which the educational work of the district nurses, baby-milk agencies, and doctors deserves credit. Two detriments to public health which because of wide abuse stand out as more than personal vices are the drugstore evil and the use of cigarettes by small boys. In the sale of liquor by the drugstores we see a practically unchallenged sin, the seriousness of which is understood only by those who try to repair the damages. The product sold by the pharmacies is nearly always inferior and is therefore much more harmful than the saloon output. Doctors say that their worst cases of alcoholism are those which have resulted from constant use of this product. The difficulties of prosecution have seemed thus far insuperable, for the policemen are more or less under obligation because of their free access to any of the druggist's goods, and witnesses are proverbially hard to secure. In addition to this source of liquid supplies, several express companies — there are over seventy pony express licenses in the whole city — do a very comfortable importing business. Finally, Leverett and Cambridge Streets on the Boston end of both bridges are lined with barrooms that exist principally to serve the Cambridge and Somerville patronage. These facts too have their bearing on the moral health of the place. Even so, however, a majority of the people are supporters of no-license. Since 1880 there have been no saloons here, but it was not until the election in 1911 that both wards gave a majority on the no-license side. Hence it is somewhat of a pity that the people are not given better protection from the virtual poison that the apothecaries dispense so freely.

It would be unjust to the better families to generalize about the home life in East Cambridge. If we could discuss the homes by blocks, a more accurate impression could be given, for conditions vary so greatly. It seems clear, however, that in the movement away from here the less progressive, less capable Irish families have been left — those whose children in consequence have been deprived of the best in parentage and surroundings.

One of the most unfortunate aspects of this is that the children of the immigrants get their schooling in American ways from this lowest American class of poorly born children — a schooling that only aggravates the differences between foreign parents and their American children. The homes of the poorer Irish are not exemplary, and many of the children are at the same time insubordinate and weak morally as well as physically. The general custom among the Poles and Armenians of keeping lodgers also tends to weaken family ties. After all, it is by the human results that the success of the home life is best attested. We are forced to conclude that homes have failed if they have provided no chance for amusement or stimulus for improvement but forthwith leave the children to get their recreation on the street and their improvement in grammar schools that have not as yet been able to provide the job training that will enable the child sent out at fourteen years to be self-supporting.

As we endeavor to see the immediate causes of family debility, several become patent. The most important is drunkenness on the part of either father or mother. Lack of adequate income with all that it entails in various kinds of insufficiency, of which housing and nourishment are the most obvious, looms as either a very direct or a subtly indirect cause wherever a home does not function. Another cause is the lack of a type of education that will turn out children capable of becoming really productive members of society. It is the lament of all who are close to life here that the years from fourteen to seventeen are practically wasted for both boys and girls. About three fourths of the pupils leave school at the end of grammar school, and the process of adjustment in the commercial world is a slow and often demoralizing one. As it has failed to provide healthy homes and suitable education with all that these mean, let the community murmur not that it reaps poor workmen. The conditions of advance for the ambitious still exist, but no one familiar with working-class neighborhoods would dare to say that this upward climb is as easy or as generally accomplished as it was twenty-five years ago, either by families or individuals. For the environment in which life has to be lived today is more crowded and more foreign; the work is less individual and less skilled; and for these reasons the means toward assimilation are not so continually present.

A complete picture of the family life will be gained, however, only as we fill in the background with a sketch of social relations that unite the people. The social life of the older residents is a matter of comparative simplicity. What little there is follows racial and religious lines quite closely. The fraternal societies and lodges have with two exceptions practically stopped taking in new members and are content to work with rapidly diminishing returns. With the exception of these and of special church affairs, the interchange of courtesies is limited to small groups, and to those intimacies which go on over the back fence or a cup of tea.

Among the newer arrivals the social life is necessarily restricted. Important functions like a christening, wedding, or funeral are made the excuse for those out-of-the-order gatherings that do occur. At such occasions, which generally take place on Sunday, the friendships of the old country are renewed and refreshed. Chairs are brought in from all the neighbors; a case or two of beer is bought; and the convivialities, if not over-refined, are essentially human and domestic. Among the Polish especially Sunday weddings, sometimes two or three on the same day, give opportunity for much jubilation. This brings to mind what is so easily forgotten, that these people are neither city-bred nor sophisticated. The newcomers are peasants — country folk to whom the whole industrial, away-from-the-soil life is a bewilderment. Whatever social life and diversions they have been used to are of a very simple sort. The adjustment to confined rooms, factory labor, evenings of leisure is no easy matter. And it is the inevitable lack of resourcefulness of these people under city conditions that leaves their children and young people so largely on the streets.

The St. John's Literary Institute, previously referred to, owns its hall, which being both the largest and most centrally located in the district is rented four or five evenings a week for dances, socials, and political and labor meetings. With its pool tables and bowling alleys it also serves as a rendezvous for the three hundred members among whom at present the literary pretensions are sustained chiefly by the society's name. The Father

Mathew Total Abstinence Society with its woman's auxiliary gives expression to the social instincts of certain groups. The Society also owns a building on Cambridge Street in which it has club rooms. Among the Portuguese the Luso-American Club is the distinctive organization. This is a men's club with rooms, called a "civic center," which are used for a general gathering place. The Portuguese Fraternity, a benefit society to which some six hundred men belong, holds its meetings here, and the club aims in every way to conserve the interests of the Portuguese people. The immigrants from St. Michael's Island have their own fraternal organization numbering about two hundred, and there are two similar societies among the women. The Portuguese church has commanded the loyal and liberal support of many parishioners, but the existence of a small Portuguese mission in the Methodist Church calls attention to the fact that as a people they are by no means the devoted churchmen that the Irish are. In a number of cases they have been content even to be married by Protestant ministers as this is a more economical way.

The Polish Catholic Church is the center of a large and flourishing parish that extends well into the Port and Somerville. Prior to 1905 the only Polish church was in South Boston, and there the people went until a census reveled the presence in Cambridge of nearly 1,500 Polish men, women, and children. The Universalist Church was therefore bought, and the parish began to look after its own. The church basement serves as the meeting place for various organizations. The Polish National Alliance and two other benefit and insurance organizations, two women's societies, and the Polish political club all use these rooms. The last-named gathering was organized about five years ago to familiarize its members with political affairs and to help and encourage them to become naturalized citizens. Its membership approaches 160, of whom nearly half are voters. A Polish young men's society hires rooms on Gore Street. Its purpose is social and educational, and to the latter end, particularly in the teaching of English, it has worked through the Cambridge YMCA in a spirit of remarkably happy cooperation. The same thing may be said of the educational work that has been done at the Portuguese civic center and at an Armenian boarding house. Just enough is accomplished in a personal, human way to show

the shortcomings of the city night schools and to reveal the possibilities of a work more thoroughly and permanently organized
— a work that would be calculated to be in active sympathetic
relations with all newcomers all the time. The older Polish
residents — and this is true of Portuguese and Armenians as well
— make a very gracious and fraternal effort toward adjusting
matters of all sorts for the immigrants, and if merely by way
of supplementing this work more regular and definite instruction
in things American could be given, their confused outlook would
be much clarified.

The Armenian group has for some years centered on one
street where the leaders have lived, where there are several
boarding houses and where there is a small library of both
foreign and American books and newspapers. Whatever church
affiliations they have are brought to light with the monthly visit
of an Armenian priest from Lawrence who holds services in the
Church of the Sacred Heart. These people also have a political
club for mutual civic education, and probably a score of its
members are citizens.

It would appear that the church is the great conserving
influence among these peoples. It looms largest as the old-world
institution that retains its familiar aspects in the new; about it
and through it the ancient sacraments and sociabilities find their
life. It tries, and often without success, to keep alive these former
customs, habits of thought, and national interests as being the
things worth clinging to in the confusion of the new life. Therefore to get a more discriminating picture of the state of mind of
the newcomers, the advent of the I.W.W. must be mentioned.
If this chapter could be written another year from now, the
organization of the unskilled workers would be a matter of less
doubt. The propaganda of industrial unionism is now going on.
Meetings have been held; the idea is in the air; and it is only
a matter of time when such unions will be formed disregarding
craft or racial lines. In particular the rubber and slaughterhouse
workers are striving to create the loyalty and enthusiasm necessary to make a union permanent. In this connection can be stated
also all there is to be said about the trade unions. Their position
in Cambridge as a whole is weak because of the variety of industries and the nearness to Boston. For example, all the team-

sters, of whom a goodly number live and work here, belong to Boston locals, as do the machinists, upholsterers, and woodworkers. The fact that there are less than 1,000 members in the Cambridge unions shows that they have yet far to go in the way of strong aggressive organization.

The more evident social life of East Cambridge is that of the young people. There are nearly twenty young men's clubs, many of which hire a room that they fit up with card tables, chairs, and a few posters. These rooms serve as "hangouts" where the fellows come in the evenings to smoke and amuse themselves. These groups have rather naturally evolved out of corner gangs that wanted some place to gather. Their membership averages between forty and fifty. Two interests serve to perpetuate enthusiasm: the yearly dance and the political contests — and with some clubs the desire to hire a cottage for the summer. The clubs pride themselves on their annual dances, and in general these are well-conducted and pleasant affairs. In fact, the local dances, given both by clubs and individuals, are the chief source of recreation. For until this winter (1912) there have been no other amusement facilities save poolrooms and two bowling alleys. However, the ubiquitous moving-picture theater has now found its way here. The proximity of the lurid lights of Tremont Row has of course something to do with this seeming lack of attractions in the district. Nevertheless, as one sees the large numbers of young fellows and the sprinkling of girls about the streets in the evening, it is impossible not to realize that the problem of the normal and healthy amusements of a working-class population is as yet unsolved and almost unrecognized. The young men's clubs multiply and flourish especially at times of political activity. The importance of forty or fifty votes that can be delivered as per directions is not overlooked by the politicians or minimized by the club. There results oftentimes a form of bribery that is distinctly demoralizing. A club, for example, might suggest its need of some article of furniture, and it has even been known to happen that it has accepted the gifts of opposing candidates. It is largely through the agency of sporadic clubs that the politics of these wards is organized. The constituency is practically all Democratic, and because of this solidarity it has for some time played an important part in city politics. As the Irish control municipal affairs, the interests of the district are by no means ignored.

The Portuguese temperament seems to lend itself not at all to the political game. In the years when the contest between the Republicans and Democratic parties was close, the three hundred solid Portuguese votes held the balance of power. At that time they banded together definitely, but the organization was not held together through the second year and has never been reassembled. Three of their number have become policemen, and one has been in the legislature a couple of terms. But that keen delight in being in the run of things and of accepting and bestowing patronage so characteristic of the Irish is not present among the Portuguese. The advent of the Poles into politics will be viewed with much interest, for they seem to be more eager for the fray than most of the Portuguese, and their ambitions will therefore be a matter of some concern to the present incumbents. However, as the seat of Democratic power has already shifted well up into Cambridgeport, the next ten or fifteen years will undoubtedly show a shift of power in East Cambridge as the numerical ratio of the nationalities changes. It would be untrue to characterize the politics here as really corrupt; it is merely not disinterested. Personal motives and small local considerations are the determining factors, and in this respect the situation is in no way unique; is in fact quite typical.

As we look thus at the social and industrial forces at work, we get a clue to the assimilative influences that are in operation. The workers are thrown into contact with other nationalities in factory, street, and night school. The races are scattered and mingled to a remarkable extent through all the tenements with the inevitable result that suggestion and imitation exert their powerful effects. Most pronounced, however, is the influence of the schools, to which reference will be made later.

The criminal records of the district are distinctly enlightening. The public drunkenness is confined almost entirely to the Irish with the Poles a far-removed second. In the year 1911 there were 110 residents of East Cambridge arrested there because of intoxication, of whom 43 were born in Ireland, 5 in Russia, 3 in Portugal, and the rest in this country. Gambling and disorderly conduct cause the next largest number of arrests, and the figures show that many boys between seventeen and twenty-one come here from out of town to gamble. The matter of petty larceny among the small boys deserves mention, for it again evidences the lack of wholesome influences. The presence of the loaded and unprotected freight cars proves too great an incentive to adventure, and some very clever thefts have been effected by youngsters not twelve years old. Undirected and unorganized energy, if directed and organized, could to a large extent be guided into legitimate, athletic channels. In the last year the playground of the new Thorndike School has been opened, and a much more liberal appropriation for able supervisors and outfit would very probably show a reduction in costs for probation officers, damages, and arrests. The sex delinquencies make a negligible showing in the police records, but this is not an altogether accurate index of the morality. In fact, it is virtually impossible to give such an accurate index. The moral tone of the young people, however, as indicated by corner gangs and testified to by those who are in a position to judge, is low and vulgar or even worse. Nevertheless, taking it by and large, East Cambridge is a remarkably safe and law-abiding place. It offers homes to a large number of hard-working people who during the day leave the streets quiet and serene except when the children issue forth to play — as they do in great numbers. At night, although groups of men gather at the corners in the early evening, the streets are comparatively deserted, save for Cambridge Street, which is the Fifth Avenue and Rialto of this section. Yet even the quiet and serenity rather serve to intensify the pervading atmosphere of drab mediocrity and inertia that hangs over the place with an oppressive weight. At best, life here is constricted and unbeautiful. And now that the reality of this feeling has been expressed, it is only fair in the interests of a balanced impression to make vivid the constructive forces which are at work.

First, last, and all the time, glory and honor are due to the four public schools in which over 2,000 children are, chemically speaking, in solution. The schools are like a mighty rock in a weary land. They are the bottom rungs of a ladder that leads to larger individual life and greater social usefulness. Here we see the only conscious effort to make American life and purpose intelligible to our newcomers. The regret is, as has already been suggested, that the children cannot stay at school longer and get a more practical education and some personal guidance into a worthy vocation. The night school, which all between the ages of fourteen and twenty-one who cannot read and write English must attend, is overcrowded and undermanned because of the large number of young men and girls of recent immigration. The building that has just been finished for the Thorndike School is admirably fitted for the extension of the educational scheme in all directions — recreational and industrial as well as mental, evening as well as day — and it is a pity it should be only partly utilized. A sincere realization of the educational work to be done and an enthusiastic acceptance of the opportunity will have much to do with bringing order out of chaos.

The work of the churches in such a place as this is fraught with great difficulties. There is so much to be done and the technique of the work is so ill-adapted to present efficiency that it reminds one of a person trying to play the piano with his hands tied behind his back. However, when an issue arises, notably the temperance one on which all are clear, its people make a stand, and all credit is due to their energetic attitude on no-license. And inasmuch as over 90 percent of the children are Catholic, a sincere declaration by the church means the eventual influencing of a majority of the inhabitants. Under able leadership the Church of the Sacred Heart, the oldest and strongest Catholic communion, has been a vital force in cherishing a faith in individual piety and a slight sense of social obligation. But the churches have yet to stand on any positive, intelligent basis in a fight to correct broader social abuses or to inspire sound social construction. The Sacred Heart parish supports two parochial schools, the one for boys having been started only this last year, a kindergarten, and a day nursery, and five priests are busy with its ministrations. The work of the Portuguese church includes, in addition to what has been described, a boy's organization, the St. Anthony's Cadets, which prides itself on its band. The Polish church to a marked degree keeps the interests of its people about it. So all in all the churches have and will continue to mean much in the life here, and inasmuch as no one institution could really be expected to meet the needs of the present situation, it is hardly fair to blame the church for not having gone the whole way.

There are, however, several immediate needs that could well be met with profit to the community. Some of these have been suggested, namely more intimate and thoroughgoing educational relationships with all immigrants, together with better-equipped evening schools, the use of the Thorndike School as a neighborhood center, the introduction of industrial education, and more generous and intelligent use of the playground. In addition any supplementary efforts that would help boys and girls from eight to eighteen to find themselves and to assert and value their finer qualities would certainly not be amiss. Also the problem of clean amusements must be more fairly faced. If the young could people provide for themselves, in their school halls or elsewhere, opportunities for social intercourse, dances, athletic games, and dramatics, there would thus appear the beginnings of a capacity for spontaneous self-amusement that is now quite dormant. Another need, perhaps the most searching of all, is that of the sanely directed organization of the factory workers.

In all that has preceded it must have occurred to the reader that perhaps the most interesting thing of all about East Cambridge is the fact that it embodies in miniature all the aspects of the larger industrial world; it is a complete microcosm that because of its comparative unity can be studied more readily and more accurately than would otherwise be possible. The play of forces and the operation of causes and effects in the organized life of today are here illustrated. The upward thrust of immigration, the usurpation of the lower standards of living by new arrivals, their slow emancipation into a more healthy standard, the industrial exploitation of the unskilled, the lack of organized power in this same group, the careless housing and inadequate schooling, the prostitution of politics to petty ends — these are all here. In East Cambridge the hopes and fears of our American progress are met. That the fears are indeed well grounded would seem to be the indication of the preceding analysis. The benumbing effects of an environment where low standards of life, inertia, and lack of skill prevail can be computed only in terms of the human product. It is in the fight for the conservation of this human product that the hope can and must be cherished.

A more conscious effort to understand the forces at work and the results at stake, and a new hope that these fearful tendencies can be checked by intelligent cooperative activity — these are the firm conditions of a better day.

In other words, conditions in East Cambridge are not accidental. They were caused, and a knowledge of these causes should and does lead the way to a comprehension of the present and an insight into the future.

V

ROXBURY AND DORCHESTER

Just south of the inner belt of neighborhoods formed by wards 9, 10, and 11 lies one of the principal parts of the zone of emergence. It includes a strip of land three and a half miles long and four-fifths of a mile wide, extending from the old harbor on the east (part of Ward 16 in what was once Dorchester) to the Fenway border of Brookline on the west. Most of the territory is low land and a considerable portion of it was once a part of that tide water marsh which separated Boston from Dorchester, Roxbury, and Brookline. Although the majority of the land once belonged to Roxbury, it has been built upon very largely since 1850, and the traditions of the community, so far as it has them, are of Boston rather than of Dorchester and Roxbury. The inhabitants of the territory have, therefore, always been strangers in these communities and have not grown up in the older traditions which still so vitally influence the citizens of these once flourishing and influential towns.

Roxbury, originally spelled Rocksborough or Rocksbury, and so named from its uneven, rocky surface, was founded in 1630, a month or two before the settlement of Boston. Like the settlers at "Shawmut," the first comers belonged to the company of John Winthrop, and were among those who left Charlestown because of the supposed lack of good water there. For a number of years Roxbury Street, or Town Street, as it was called originally, comprised the entire town. Through fear of the Indians all persons were ordered to live within half a mile of the meeting house located on what is now Eliot Square. In course of time, however, the population gradually spread toward Dorchester, Cambridge, Dedham, and other neighboring towns.

For more than a century and a half Boston was connected with Roxbury only by a narrow strip of land known as the Neck, the thoroughfare across which, so named after the President's visit in 1789 has become the Washington Street of today. Just north of the Roxbury line, at what is now Hammond Street, was the widest part of the Neck — a full half mile; at what is now

Dedham Street the width was about one third of a mile, or 1,700 feet; and from there it tapered sharply until at Dover Street, the narrowest point, the actual land was only 200 feet. The salt marshes on each side were always covered at high tide, and at times of full tides they overflowed, making the Neck almost impassable. A dike had to be built along the eastern side, which later became Harrison Avenue, while a sea wall was constructed on the west running from Dover to Waltham Streets.

During the first century, very little was done to the Neck beyond keeping it open for absolutely necessary traffic. In winter it was a desolate and dangerous place, travellers lost their way and were sometimes frozen to death on the marshes, and in all seasons it was the scene of frequent robberies. Not until 1723 was it fenced in, and only after 1757 was an attempt made to pave it and keep it in repair. In 1794 it was formally laid out as a street, and at which time there were only eighteen buildings between Dover Street and the Roxbury line.

After the close of the Revolutionary War, when the Neck had become safe and even pleasant for travel, it was quite the fashion for citizens of the two cities to ride, drive, or stroll into the adjacent town. Ladies from Roxbury walked into Boston and brought their purchases home with them. The Neck, indeed, became a boulevard, the Fenway, as it were, of that day. In winter when sleighing was good every vehicle upon runners was in use, from pungs to barges, and the sidewalks were crowded with spectators watching the excitement. Sleighing parties from Boston came out to the Washington House which was on the site of the old George Tavern at the Roxbury line. Early in the century two horse stage-coaches, carrying forty-five passengers, began to run once in two hours; and in 1826 hourly coaches between Roxbury Town House and the Old South Church in Boston were inaugurated. These soon gave place to half-hourlies, which were followed in 1856 by the horse railroad. There was a stage route to New York through Roxbury until 1834, when the Providence Railroad opened with a single track.

In 1818 the Boston and Roxbury Mill Corporation (chartered in 1814) began to build the Mill Dam, or Western Avenue, which established artificial connection between Boston and the mainland, and also, though no one foresaw it then, was the first step toward filling in Back Bay. It took three years to complete the building of this one and one-half miles of road, and for the work of this great undertaking came America's first importation of Irish laborers. It was expected that an enormous amount of water power would result from the construction of this dam, until it was found that there had been gross miscalculation, and the possible power was of little or no value. All attempts to make use of this property failed, and in 1859 the Boston Water Power Company obtained permission through the legislature to turn it into building lots.

A glance at the map shows the stretch under consideration plowed through by a series of roadways leading into Boston. The Old Colony, the Milton Branch and the Providence Division of the New York, New Haven & Hartford, the Elevated to Dudley Street, and a series of avenues including Huntington, Columbus, Tremont, Shawmut, Washington, Harrison, Albany and Dorchester Avenues all lead into the heart of the city. All of them except Albany Street are traversed by street cars. With the single exception of Massachusetts Avenue [and Dudley Street] there are no crosstown car facilities, which makes the wards relatively inaccessible to one another and divides them more or less into water tight compartments. The absence of natural boundaries makes it impossible to say anything definite concerning population before 1895, the date of the last rearrangement of the ward lines. In that year the total population of the four wards was [81,485] in 1905 it had increased to [97,571], a definite indication of its growth. The vertical compartments into which the strip is naturally divided makes it natural to treat the sections separately, and the remainder of the chapter will be divided into three sections, the first of which will deal with Wards 18 and 19; the second with Ward 17; and the third with Ward 16.

Roxbury Crossing

The early historic Roxbury was for the most part to the south and south-east of the wards here considered, although they lay largely within the borders of that town. Their history therefore is of negligible concern until the middle of the last century, especially as much of the land was low and marshy. When it is remembered that Ward 18 extends from Washington Street along Camden Street to the New York, New Haven, and Hartford R.R., and from the tracks again along Linden Park Street to Washington Street, a glance at the map will show that the lower portions of the Ward were liable to tidal overflow. As late as 1867 the maps show Ruggles, Camden and Tremont Streets as the high and dry spots bounded by treacherous bogs. When the Sherwin School on Sterling Street was erected in 1871 no house stood anywhere near it; and there is still a corner lot nearby where no bottom sufficiently trustworthy to build on has yet been reached. On Vernon Street, however, the land rises, and at Eliot Square, Highland Park and Parker Hill, all in Ward 19, the situations are commanding, and in the case of Highland Park, historically significant. The boundary of Ward 19, contiguous to Ward 18 along Linden Park and Bartlett Streets runs irregularly from Highland Street across Minden Street to the Fenway which it follows to near Rogers Avenue and the railroad tracks. However, the section to the west of Huntington Avenue [the Fenway] is not here discussed as it forms no part of the homogeneous unit treated in the study with which we have to deal. We have then a section bounded by two main thoroughfares, Washington Street, and Huntington Avenue; divided by Tremont Street, Columbus and Shawmut Avenues and cut laterally by Ruggles, Dudley, Roxbury and the outer end of Tremont Streets. Although the appearance of their principal streets belies the assertion, these wards are largely residential. The factories, breweries and stores, located, of course, with a view to accessibility, are found hardly at all in the side streets which are closely set with a variety of old one family houses, three deckers and large tenements.

Ward 18 has only two open spaces; one the Columbus Avenue Playground, the other the park in Madison Square. This ward, be it said, is the fifth most congested area in the city. The available land in Ward 19, especially about Parker Hill and along Huntington Avenue is not as yet exhausted. But as the two large estates between which the south side of the hill was formerly divided have been put on the market and are partially built up, it seems likely that eventually the rest of the land will be utilized even though its steepness makes building expensive. It should be noted in this connection that here as in other parts of the zone, improved transit facilities have profoundly modified and altered the growth and character of these sections. Roxbury Crossing, for example, was a thriving local center fifteen years ago. The Boston Elevated Company built the terminal of its road at Dudley Street and the prosperity of the Crossing became a thing of the past. This will undoubtedly prove a deterrent to further building activity on Parker Hill, and also to the upkeep of all the property of the Ward. For the more successful inhabitants will be the first to take advantage of the ease of transportation into more remote suburbs.

There will be a tendency to a reduction of rents and this will draw those with a less satisfactory economic status out of the city proper. This constant enlarging of the area necessarily devoted to housing workers of very moderate means must eventually entail a far greater measure of municipal control and even of municipal enterprise in this sphere than is now dreamed of. No one can witness the physical deterioration which neighborhoods farther and farther from the city have necessarily suffered without seeing the fatuity of it, and becoming convinced that it is quite short-sighted and unnecessary.

The population of these two wards in 1910 totaled 54,449, as against 51,334 in 1905 [Ward 18 22,735, Ward 19 31,714]. Of these the native whites of native parents amount to only 8,220. Native whites of mixed foreign parents number 23,339; and the foreign born whites 17,488. In Ward 18 there are 5,122 Negroes and 218 in Ward 19. Of those foreign born, 7,841 are Irish and approximately 5,000 Canadian, Scotch and English. About 1,100 of Russian birth, almost wholly Jews, live in Ward 18. About 700 of the same nativity, largely Letts, are in Ward 19, which has also about a thousand Germans. Three and a half percent of the population of Ward 18 is illiterate; while in Ward 19 the percentage is not quite 1½ — an interesting side-light on the relative advance and intelligence of these districts. Another significant index of the distinct differences in the character of the wards can be found by comparing the industrial and economic status of the men, as revealed by the police lists [1912]. In Ward 18 about 47% of the men are in unskilled occupations where the wage does not rise over $12 weekly; in Ward 19, this number is not over 37%. The skilled in Ward 18 number about 30% of the men; and in Ward 19 about 34%. Those engaged in various kinds of clerical work are 19% in the one ward and 22% in the other. Too much emphasis cannot be laid upon the figures relative, first, to the large number of foreign born in the wards — about 33%; and second, to the proportion of unskilled, poorly paid workers. Both factors enter enormously into a proper accounting for the quality and character of life as it is here lived.

In addition to these two factors and contributing to them there is the reaction of the local industries upon the wards. Especially as certain of them were on the ground before the influx of population began, their quite considerable determining influence cannot be ignored. The famous Stony Brook, now subterraneously confined, offered opportunity for a large number of tanneries; and a chocolate mill, grist mill and slaughter house were also among the factories of a hundred years ago.

Cordage factories, iron foundries, chemical manufactories, a belting and carpet factory were of later inception. Ward's Rendering Plant was formerly here, as was the famous Prang lithographing establishment. Not a few forlorn and deserted buildings scattered through the district, give evidence to the industrial importance that was Roxbury's. Factories closed or moved to less expensive sites; but others have come in, and the supply of cheap, unskilled labor which is afforded in quantity offers no small inducement to a certain type of manufacturer. The belting, carpet and oil clothing factories are among the older of contemporary industries. These alone employ about 1,200 people, of whom 800 are women and girls. In all three wages have always been meager, the work heavy and sometimes unhealthful, the workers low grade. Over half of the employees live in the district. A suspender factory utilizes about 200, most of whom are young girls of the neighborhood. And a large manufacturer of drug products, employing 1,200 people, 800 of whom are women, also draws largely upon the local population.

The latest addition to the number of industries is a shoe factory which came from Lynn for the obvious reason that it wished to avail itself of less-expensive non-union labor. This concern employs about 650 people of whom nearly a half are girls. Another and much larger shoe maker — brought here by the same reason — has built just beyond the region under discussion, and to some extent draws on the inhabitants of these wards for his labor.

An interesting and significant moral cannot but be drawn from a comparison of all these factories in their attitude and treatment of employees, with a large cigar factory which has recently moved here from downtown. Strongly unionized in all branches of the work, the employees have better wages, shorter hours and far better working conditions than do any of the rest. An admirable spirit of harmony prevails, and what people are pleased to call the "welfare work" which is done is in reality the least that any intelligent interest in industrial efficiency, social well-being and human happiness would dictate. Amid the chaos, waste and squalor, amid the exploitation and short-sighted disregard of young and weak human life; amid the ignorance and stagnancy which are of the very fiber of some parts of this community's life, it is refreshing to see a well-ordered, harmoniously conducted industrial organization treating their workers as self-respecting men and women. As one would naturally expect, the employees in this factory are not residents of lower Roxbury, but come from all over greater Boston — a contingent directly conditional, be it remarked, upon shorter hours and better pay.

The breweries have purposely been left for separate treatment, as their rise, growth and influence have been of unique importance, more especially in Ward 19 where eleven of the eighteen breweries in the city are situated. The business was started by the Germans in the late forties, and large use was originally made of several springs in Stony Brook. Although these soon proved inadequate, the demand increased and a country-wide market was developed by the competing brewers. To so great an extent was the competition pushed that in 1885 when the employees joined in a widespread strike, the competing capitalists consolidated into two large corporations which at once found that the demand could be supplied more economically by closing down several of the plants.

In the end, the strikers compelled recognition of their union and succeeded in getting much better terms as to hours and wages. Before that they had been compelled to work on call at all hours seven days a week, and the wages had been low. Today a nine-hour day is the rule; the closed shop is in force; wages are higher than in other industries of similar skill; employment is steady; a sick leave makes it possible for men to return to work any time within three months; and a discharged employee may take his case to the officials of the company for trial. Roughly speaking the inside work is done by Germans and the teaming by Irish; in fact the whole business throughout the city is in the hands of those two nationalities. Of the Irish employees, at least sixty percent live in the immediate vicinity. But the Germans with their ambition for small homes with gardens have quite largely moved into West Roxbury. Those who remain form a colony in the Minden Street neighborhood.

The breweries themselves are large and extensive plants and are so scattered through the ward that the pungent smell of malt and hops cannot be escaped. The large army of workers which the size and number of the establishments might lead one to expect dwindle in reality to not over nine hundred men in the whole industry. A typical plant turning out between 63,000 and 64,000 barrels a year gives employment to only 13 brewers, a brewmaster, four department foremen, two coopers, seven men in the engine room, a carpenter, twelve drivers with nine team assistants and a foreman with three watchmen. In the bottling department twenty-five men with seven teamsters and a woman to label are needed. The office force amounts to eighteen people. Hence the total number required to run a brewery that covers a block and a half is only one hundred and four.

The connection between the producers and the distributors of these beverages is intimate. Although liquor licenses are not owned by brewers, money is lent for the purpose of procuring licenses. In such event the creditor's brew is especially advertised and sold — not, however, to the exclusion of goods bearing other labels. Of the influence of the breweries on the local community it is difficult to speak with precision. The consumption of liquor is large hereabouts, the number of saloons far too many. The whole industrial and moral shiftlessness acts both as a cause and as an effect of the liquor traffic, and it is undoubtedly true that the advertising which the mere presence of these establishments affords makes for an increased use of their products.

Since a discussion of the character, history and achievements of the people necessitates more particular treatment, the wards will be considered separately in this and some other connections. Ward 18, it will be remembered, is built very largely upon land filled in during the years 1855 to 1870. The rather substantial looking brick blocks on Hammond and Kendall Streets, Shawmut Avenue, and about Madison Square were all erected in anticipation of an influx of that prosperous population which was in some incalculable way soon diverted to the Back Bay. And inasmuch as much of these buildings especially around the Square, had been rushed up on insecure foundations, the owners were only too glad to get out from underneath and make way for the Irish population which was pushing out from the city. By 1885 the district presented much the same appearance as it does today — the only difference being that most of the property has been allowed to go into the most dismal unrepair. Some of the streets — Arnold, Woodburn, Vernon — and isolated houses here and there, still suggest the atmosphere of the prosperous Yankee town of sixty years ago. But from the squalid blocks on Hill and Madison Streets, through the neglected portions of Cabot Street, along Tremont Street — that road of unrealized possibilities — and in the short alleys that connect Columbus Avenue with Tremont Street, the total impression is one of dismal failure, ugliness and neglect so far as the housing of the people goes.

There can be no doubt that the constant movement through this district is a contributing cause to this state of affairs. The Irish and German and English families which moved in among the first are no longer to be found here. For example, the Germans, of thirty years ago lived on and about Ruggles Street, where today scarce one of their families is to be found. Numbers of them are still in Ward 19, but the bulk have gone even farther from the city. The northern end of the ward from Camden to Hammond Street has been entirely surrendered by the Irish to the Negroes who began to settle thereabouts some twenty years ago. Of the Irish it should be reiterated here as has been found true elsewhere in the zone — and for that matter is more or less true of every race — that there are among them those who progress and those who do not. And this sifting process seems to have worked especial hardship among the Irish. For those who are left, who do not move on and up, become the victims of all the maladjustments to which a complicated and inchoate social organism can be heir.

It is this latent germ of unprogressiveness and even degeneracy that taints the air and cripples the social institutions of the ward. A synonym for "eternal vigilance" might well be "surplus energy," and without this liberty and order are purchasable at no price. To revitalize or eliminate these weak strains in the local life is a condition of health, economic advance and social happiness. The relief agencies here are at one in acclaiming unemployment, drunkenness, shiftlessness and poverty as powerful influences in the lives of all too many. Particularly do these causes conspire to make the problem of wife desertion an acute and vexing one. Discouraged by lack of work and impoverished by drink some men have found the easiest escape from family obligations to be in resort to the expedient immortalized by Rip Van Winkle. That there is this absence of virility in portions of the stock here deserves frank recognition, as it explains important deficiencies.

It should be remembered, however, that these preceding statements are drawn from the facts to which attention is being directed at that time [sic], and are not to be widely applied. For in addition to these facts there are others which lead to the assertion that the step outward and upward is continually being taken by families which have obtained a start here. Of sixty families which had moved from one school district in the summer of 1913, thirty had gone to Ward 19, Dorchester, or other parts of Greater Boston, and of this thirty at least twenty were Irish. The other ten were from the Jewish colony which is central in the vicinity of Ruggles Street and Shawmut Avenue. At any rate, for a great number of families this seems to have been the place where they gathered themselves for the grand effort to get out of their cheap surroundings. Possibly the low rents make saving possible, possibly the squalor becomes unbearable. But that many have pulled up stakes is undeniable.

In addition to the colony about Ruggles Street, there is also a scattering of Jewish families on Washington Street and still others on Tremont Street where they are preempting the poorly-built houses which fell into disuse upon the transfer of much of the street railway traffic from the Crossing to Dudley Street.

Thinking that this section was destined to become a large colony, the Jewish leaders bought a huge Baptist church on Shawmut Avenue in the nineties. The increase in the colony was not forthcoming and they were forced to sell the building which is now used by a large Negro congregation. A smaller church on Vernon Street, formerly owned by the German Baptists is now the sanctuary of Judaism in the neighborhood. To see the goodly collection of black-bearded elders sauntering meekly forth from synagogue on Saturday mornings, with their ponderous women in shining black silks clutching at cleanly arrayed infants, is to breathe in a pious atmosphere of far-off things still cherished amid the sorry dilapitude of lower Roxbury.

The Catholic stronghold in this ward is the St. Francis De Sales church, also on Vernon Street. Prior to its erection in 1867, the communicants attended mass at the House of the Angel Guardian, a home for wayward boys on the opposite side of the street. But now they have not only an ample edifice and parish house but are about to open a large parochial school which, although not beautifully situated, gave the opportunity to tear down some very bad tenements. If this building can be put to the uses captioned under "school center work" it will undoubtedly prove of value in providing, insofar as it consistently can, what no other agency has yet offered the ward. To be sure there is a settlement house on Ruggles Street, the Boys' Industrial Institute on Tremont Street, the Young Men and Young Women's Christian Associations, the Cabot Street Gymnasium and Baths, the South End Industrial School, recently installed in Norfolk House. But none of these, with the possible exception of the last, has had in mind to establish a neighborhood center where the recreational and social life of the people might be unified. In a region so predominantly Catholic this opportunity is unique and might well be taken advantage of.

The two Catholic institutions, the House of the Angel Guardian and St. Vincent's Home for Orphaned Children, have extensive establishments on valuable parcels of property. In fact were we to add to these the institutional holdings in Ward

19 there would be represented a value which would approach
$800,000. All of these, however, bear no intrinsic relation to the
life hereabouts.

The municipal gymnasium and baths, just referred to, are
among the best in the city, and it is to be hoped that more
regular usage thereof may soon become a compulsory part of the
school curriculum. The other agencies are doing such work as
their titles would indicate and each in its way is conserving the
better things in life in whatever souls it can reach. But they
fight against unseen powers of darkness — against devitalized
inheritance, weak ambitions, ill-adapted education, low wages,
congested housing and the resultant general spiritual stagnation.
The diseases and the remedies are alike deep seated and far-
reaching, and they await the day of wise and powerful doctors.

The white Protestant churches here, over half a dozen in
number, are patronized very largely by non-residents. The Norwegians, Danes and Swedes have located their buildings here and
in Ward 19, as it is very central to all points accessible by the
Elevated. The Negro churches would add five to the total above
given.

Public school education occupying the place of enormous
importance that it does, serves only to give earnest of what it
might do for the new generation, and what it will do when it
comes into its own. The schools here have been fortunate in
the retention over a long period of years of a remarkably able
and large-hearted group of teachers and principals. The impress
of their work and lives has been one of the strongest influences in
accomplishing a finer transfusion of Celtic and Ethiopian blood
into the American stock.

The first parents' association in Boston schools started at the
Sherwin-Hyde School some years ago, and the work in connection
with vocational placement, school visiting and school nursing
also received early and successful trial here. It should be observed that the school population of the ward is perceptibly decreasing, although there are still about 4,200 children. This is
in line with what has been said about the outward movement;
and there is no reason to believe that it will stop. If in the future
the number of children increases it will indicate not more but
larger families — predominantly Jewish. In Ward 19 the reaction

is felt in terms of a constantly growing school enrollment, there being in the 1913 census 7,511 children.

However, despite the heroic work of the schools it must be said that the problem of "child welfare" has been a very serious one here. Especially from the points of view of recreation, vocation and morality does lower Roxbury have its most serious and obvious short-comings. In fact the distinction for the largest number of arrests for juvenile offenders comes to this part of the city. For the year from October 1, 1910 to the same date in 1911, there were 232 delinquent boys, with 453 cases settled out of court, and 151 delinquent girls. In addition to these, 27 boys and 36 girls were "neglected." If searching for causes we turn now to the recreational assets we find them meagre and ill-adapted. There are 25 saloons; [number omitted] pool rooms; four moving picture shows, three public halls which can be rented for dances, and certain of the philanthropic agencies already named. The Columbus Avenue Playground — incidentally one of the first in the country — is the one definite play space and it is on a far fringe of the ward. Anything like a policy, a well organized and statesmanlike plan for knowing and meeting the real needs for the recreation and refreshment of 23,000 people has apparently never been dreamed of, much less contemplated. That this side of the district's life is inadequate and often coarse in its manifestations — who should wonder at it? Who should be surprised that boys and girls alike run amuck the police so frequently? What cause for consternation that a dance hall has to be closed because of indecent conduct. Here again we meet a circle of causes: inferior amusements degrading the people; degraded people enjoying inferior amusements. And yet it is not all said with that. It cannot be too strongly emphasized that the tone and quality of the recreation of a community find their causes in the kind of life from which that community must needs refresh itself. If life in the home, factory, and street is dull, monotonous, congested, inadequate, the recreation will tend to offset and compensate for it insofar as it can. And this is just what is happening here. The recreational life for its true redemption waits upon the thorough revitalizing of all the rest of the people's living. Much, however, can and should be done

in the way of constructing a wholesome and stimulating organization of local recreation in connection with the school, playground, social center, and the like, in which and through which
something of new, pure, vigorous wellbeing can be imparted.

That such a neighborhood should have its political peculiarities is to be expected; although they are not so much peculiarities
as characteristics of all wards similarly constituted. There is
a strong Democratic Club, which in addition to owning its own
building seem — politically speaking — to have the whole ward
more or less in its pocket. The boss, who dispenses largesse at
Christmas in true Tammany style, is a powerful figure who is by
no means the rascal such bosses are frequently pictured. Here,
as in so much else in life, it is not so much absence of character
as arrested intelligence, which one would criticize. The direction
of such [a] well-knit, close-to-the-people organization into really
far-reaching channels of beneficent influence is bound to come as
leaders come to see the kind of consideration and of legislation
which their constituents need and will demand for their well-
being. Of course, baneful alliances with church, saloon, real
estate dealers, etc., must be offset. But popular discussion of all
kinds of social reform is being simplified and disseminated
through the press in such wise that a public sentiment is created
which the alert boss is coming to heed more readily.

If what has now been said about Ward 18 appears to be a
curious complex of contradictory assertions it will not be altogether misleading. Contending forces, contradictory facts, divergent tendencies are all there and are all at work. If in the
main the life has progressed, has moved out and bettered itself,
it is indeed a tribute to the potencies of human nature, to its
inextinguishable vitality. Urging itself on under such adverse
conditions, what could it not do were it to grow under more
favoring surroundings and were it in its growth consciously to
pattern its life upon a well-conceived elastic plan of avid [?]
adjustment in all the departments of life.

Ward 19 presents a very different front from its neighbor.
Physically hilly, it is historically older and structurally less
dilapidated and crowded. About Eliot Square centered a prosperous colonial colony and the simple dignity of the several
remaining edifices of that day still gives a certain charm to the

adjoining streets. On the Highland Park hill, where the old Cochituate standpipe recalls the days before the metropolitan water system, the houses are single or in blocks with a family to a house. The ownership here is largely individual by residents themselves or by those formerly here, and the neatness of the streets indicates a pride in their good appearance. At the foot of the hill, however, the tenements on both the Marcella and Tremont Street side are cheap and ill-repaired, and in the neighborhood of Parker Street, with its little dwellings across the tracks, the same condition exists. About Minden Street, however, where the Germans are making a last stand, the houses although cheap and small are largely for single families. On the side hill the three decker seems to hold absolute sway, very probably because this is the only paying investment on buildings erected on such a steep slope. Across the hill between Parker Hill Avenue and Tremont Street the three decker again prevails. And on the lower side of Tremont Street through to Rogers Avenue there is a miscellaneous mixture of one, two and three family wooden dwellings, all of them of rather long-standing and many very much in need of paint, plaster and general overhauling. In fact this back eddy of the ward between the railroad and Huntington Avenue partakes quite fully of the already described characteristics of Ward 18. It is inhabited by brewery workers, city employees and factory hands, some of whom are no doubt held here by the proximity of the Mission Church. It is nevertheless one of the most squalid sections of Roxbury; and the facts as to conditions of health, housing, and economic status of its population lend emphasis to the statement.

One of the interesting features of the German colony is the building of one of the fraternal organizations which focuses much of the social life of the neighborhood. Although only the fathers join, the membership is virtually by families as they participate in many of the festal events of the year. In a significant way such a society points the way which neighborhoods must follow in creating a normal recreational life for themselves. The building affords a meeting place for the men where they smoke and talk over their beer. There is a choral class for the children; and socials and entertainments are scattered through the year. Best of all, it is a neighborly local organization of, for, and by the people themselves. And this homelike quality of the German social life lends color to all their activities. Nearly all the men own their homes and cultivate their miniature gardens much to the enhancement of their streets as well as to the satisfaction of their souls.

Religiously the majority of the Germans are Protestants, and more especially Lutherans. This denomination has owned a church on Parker Street since 1872 where in addition to their regular service they also conduct here on Saturday mornings a class in the "mother tongue" to which the none-too-willing youngsters are sent. The German Catholics still return into the city to the church on Shawmut Avenue, opposite which there is also the Boston Turn Hall. Germans from all over the city gather here not only for the use of the gymnasium but for the fellowship afforded by the congenial drinking and meeting place. With a strong sense for organized mutuality of all sorts the Germans also have Kossuth Hall, on Tremont Street in Ward 18, which is used as the meeting place of numerous benefit societies most of whose members, however, live far from that immediate neighborhood. The next fifteen years will in fact find very few Germans in either ward. The younger generation, most of whom have gone through high school, have become bank clerks, draftsmen, and entered commercial houses so that they feel financially able to remove farther from town. But young or old, this people possess certain fine qualities which cannot go unremarked for they bring to the American character those which it sorely needs. Their technical training and industriousness, their artistic sense, their domestic propensities all qualify them to be of those whose days are to be long in the land which has become their heritage.

The type of Irish who live on Parker Hill or Highland Park Hill is naturally different from that found in the other ward. Many government employees, foremen, clerks, policemen, firemen and streetcar men live in quite comfortable circumstances here, accessible to the city yet quite above it. There is a general air of prosperity which receives no mean reflection in the ecclesiastical establishment which this part of the city has had the lion's share in financing, namely the Mission Church.

This unique and powerful Catholic parish is the outgrowth

of a very modest mission started in 1871 by a band of Redemptorist Fathers, an order originally German, who by the sincerity and piety of their lives were quick to draw immense throngs to hear them and to be healed at the Shrine of Our Lady of Perpetual Help. So successful was the mission that in 1878 the present structure was dedicated, and the holdings of the church have been steadily increased until they now occupy a whole block. In 1889 a parochial school with accommodations for 1,500 was opened under the direction of the Sisters of Notre Dame, with the result that today Ward 19 has more children in private schools than any ward in the city, that is 2,886 out of 7,511. No less phenomenal than the growth of this parish — it was so set off in 1883 — has been the social work it has successfully undertaken. It has a large boys' organization, band and choir, a Young Men's Catholic Association which has a well-equipped building, and a similar organization for young women. Every year a Lenten drama is produced. The fathers make extensive missionary tours all over the country. The shrine draws many by virtue of its reputed cures and its dramatic array of crutches. In fact the entire organization is a masterpiece of careful, able leadership. To be sure the whole atmosphere of the institution with the curative waters for sale in nearby stores, with its resounding chimes, with its immense throngs of worshipers, with its great tower so built that, illumined, it reveals by night the outlines of the cross, with its black-frocked, kindly-faced fathers — all is intensely medieval, startlingly unworldly and remote. But it is there — to be reckoned with and evaluated — a mighty influence in the neighborhood.

All Saints' Church on Centre Street, although just beyond the boundaries of the ward, extends its parish lines so as to include a part of the territory under consideration. It was set apart from St. Joseph's parish in 1895 and the church was completed in 1901. There are about 3,700 souls on the roll; sodalities for married and single women; senior and junior Holy Societies for the men and boys; and a Sunday School of nearly 700 boys and girls. The size and prosperity of these churches is a fair index of the surrounding population. And the increase in their constituency in the last twenty years is a clear token of the migratory trend of the second generation Irish. Naturally there are few Protestant churches here, and those that there are, with one or two notable exceptions, hang reluctantly on with little to identify them with the neighborhoods they adorn. A recent addition is a Lettish church which uses the chapel of the Lutheran Church on Parker Street, drawing from a small but increasing colony in the nearby streets.

The problem of recreation calls for solution here with an urgency almost as great as in Ward 18. Although in parts of the ward there is some open land, there is no play space set apart save the Marcella Street Playground across the line in Ward 22. Social clubs are in vogue among the older boys and young men here as elsewhere. In fact these organizations seem to represent the natural medium in which the group instincts assert themselves. Under wise, understanding oversight their potential power might be directed along definitely constructive lines in recreation and politics. But such oversight will depend upon the conscious coordinating of recreational assets through some such agency as a social center. However, it is true that home life with the normal amusements which center therein is a much larger consideration here than in the lower ward. By far the majority of families have sitting rooms and the social graces which attend thereunto. The rub comes with the older boys and girls who are confined in shop and office all day and demand some liberation of body and spirit in the evening; and in the younger adolescent boys who need a strenuous out-of-door or gymnastic outlet for their uprising exuberance.

In all, Ward 19 represents a distinct advance in the general outlook on life over Ward 18, as that in turn means, especially for Jew and Negro, a progression from the West or South Ends. As has been suggested the elusive difficulty of many of the problems here existent is heightened by the unstable fluid nature of the population. This fluidity of personnel weakens the ordinarily intensive effects of the school, lessens the sense of local pride and responsibility, and therefore makes political bossism easy and every sort of spontaneous neighborhood-betterment organization hard. Even so we would not stop this flux if we could. However, it does become apparent that eventually these neighborhoods will assume a more static condition. The question then rises at once as to their proper maintenance and control.

In supervision from city-wide agencies as to uses of land and recreational facilities and in municipal ownership of new houses to replace the poorer tenements the way points for the improvement of the environs of life. The formal educational system must put a new virus into city youth in terms of industriousness, appreciation and morality. The industrial opportunities in the immediate vicinity emphasize to the mind that can put itself behind the bricks and the grated windows that if the work of life offers nothing more than these factories hold out, it is a sorry life, and labor itself has become guilt, since it conduces so little to life. Industry too must modify its demands and its technique that it may elicit and not kill the instinct of workmanship. And home, school, and church must come to a clearer knowledge of the power they can and must exert to permeate the whole mental life of the new generation with respect and reverent awe for their physical bodies and the way they are reproduced, with delight in diligent, creative, useful labor for the common store, with satisfaction in the achievements of the finest minds in book, building, picture, statue and symphony. Our life waits on such children who shall come, and lo, in their coming shall make all things new!

ROXBURY, WARD 17

Neighborhoods like individuals carry stigmata which tell their story plainer than statistical accounting could possibly do. Ward 17 impresses the observer as does a man who has lost confidence in himself. Many of the streets show evidences of fading sufficiency. One is constantly coming upon half improved streets, boarded-up factories, tumble-down buildings, shoddy dwellings inhabited by careless tenants, a dull monotony of tenements broken by certain streets of utterly unindividualized cottage houses. This condition is redeemed to some extent by the fact that there is still vacant land near some of the worst tenement blocks, that many of the cottage houses have yards, and in a few exceptional cases, gardens; and that compared with the downtown wards, the streets are relatively quiet and free from traffic; that the several playgrounds and parks afford generous play space for children; that excellent schools care for the boys and girls. Even at its worst, however, the ward is better than the North or West or South Ends, though this advance is of relatively uncertain tenure. The day is not far off when the vacant land will be built upon, and land and room congestion will come close to duplicating the conditions found in the downtown wards.

Each of the districts in the Zone of Emergence came into that sphere more or less as the result of the breakdown of a higher form of local organization. The process of change, in the case of Ward 17, is so recent that it repays consideration. Pressure of new needs, the movement of population outward, the growth of transportation, such causes as these are constantly producing new tides in city life. It is altogether likely that in the very course of events Ward 17 would have taken on some of its present characteristics even under ideal conditions. But the process of change might doubtless have been delayed, and the inevitable evils lessened, had it not been reinforced by three causes which were working parallel with the main lines of evolution. The first and most serious of these was a decided change in the character of the local industries; the second was the type of building saddled on the ward; and the third was the character of the local political leadership.

The most important cause of the disintegration of ward life was the decided change which came over the character of the local industries about a decade ago. High grade industries located near a desirable residential community automatically attract and build up a high grade of population; conversely, industries employing a low grade of operative tend to call low grade help into the nearby dwellings. The latter class pull down the local life to their own level. Twenty years ago there was a group of industries located in Ward 17 which employed men predominantly on processes which made it possible to pay good wages. In the course of the next fifteen years more than ten high grade factories were discontinued. Several industries were absorbed in great combines and the local plant abolished; others failed in the industrial depression of 1898-1900; others moved on account of labor troubles; and others still found the land too valuable for their purposes and sought out suburban locations. Trusts, labor troubles, and excessive expense of production, comprehend a considerable portion of the causes of industrial disaster.

Naturally enough the loss of so many industries, employing nearly fifteen hundred operatives, left its mark on the community. A failure in the downtown portion of the city is soon covered; whereas a failure in a town or neighborhood leaves scars which are long remembered and talked over. Thus the failure of the New England Piano Company in 1900 was a bitter blow to many people in the ward. In summer the older school boys found jobs in its processes and prepared themselves for regular work. Many young men started their industrial careers in the factory, and were paying for their homes on the strength of the future. When the blow came many lost all their savings and had to seek work of another character. A proportion of the forepeople and skilled workers went to pieces morally and never recovered. Family life was pulled down. In a neighborhood where the local gossip traces out the wreckage of such a failure as this, it becomes possible to see how thoroughly the life of the worker is built into his work.

Perhaps it is only in the Zone of Emergence that the tragic aspects of industrial disorder can be seen and studied. The newly arrived immigrants who work in ditches and clothing factories suffer in times of stress and strain, but there are many agencies of relief open to them. They find it relatively easy to hasten to some other part of the land where their labor is in demand. But the craftsman who gives his youth to the acquisition of a relatively scarce form of skill, and the foremen who build their careers on the basis of faithfulness to a specific organization for production face utter ruin when for any reason the firm employing their skill or faithfulness fails. Many of these workers lose as heavily in comparison as the owners and managers.

The dispersion of a great labor force in a decade entailed serious consequences on the neighborhood in its outer aspect and its inner life. The way was opened for a less capable type of population; and the disintegration of all social life carried off the natural leaders of the people and prepared the way for a decided lessening of moral fibre in the population.

A second cause for deterioration is to be found in a series of land booms and building operations. In the decade between 1890 and 1900 a considerable number of new buildings were erected, one group on Dudley and the adjacent streets, and another group in the region south of Northampton Street and west of Harrison Avenue. The houses erected on Dudley Street were well constructed and have been inhabited by skilled workers and clerks, the true emergence group. (Precincts 2-4-8-9) The tenements in the south end of the ward, however, are of another kind. Many of them were built by a one-time political boss of the ward. At the time of their erection it used jokingly to be said in the neighborhood that a man might contract for a three family tenement on the way to work in the morning, and find his family moving in on his return at night. The structures began to disintegrate before the building was completed. The houses also covered a large proportion of the lot on which they were built, so that the sun never penetrated the back rooms. It hardly seems possible that public opinion could have tolerated such reckless planning. In this neighborhood the streets are still unpaved, the back alleys are damp and uncleanly and unwholesome and the whole atmosphere one of depression.

The houses are frequently acquired by honestly minded people who thought to purchase a home as an investment. But in time their bad condition and undesirable location made them a center for those who moved out from the North and West Ends. These houses therefore became a receiving station and brought in a less desirable type of inhabitant than the ward had heretofore attracted.

The changes which grew out of the failure of industries also threw a considerable number of one family cottage houses on the market, and these were either turned into two or more tenements or allowed to run down through lack of repairs to a point where decreased rent and hence less desirable tenants alone seek them. Some idea of the number of alterations in property can be gained from the fact that between 1899-1908 there were 647 permits for alterations, an average of 64.7 per year. Probably the majority of these permits meant changing single family houses into two or three tenements, though these figures, of course, are no indication of the doubling up that involved nothing more than an extra door bell. It is part of the tragedy of industrial failure in such a district that the inevitable lowering of property values falls heaviest on small holders. Workmen who invested their money in a home, forced to move because they can no longer

find work or because the level of life in the community is below
that in which they desire to rear their children, have to bear the
brunt of the depreciation in the value of their investment. For
some time the value of real property has been decreasing, except
in the northern part of the ward.

A third and potent cause for the falling off in the ward may
be traced to the political situation. It is significant that the two
most notorious politicians which the ward has produced came
into power at the time of its decline. Even before their time,
however, Tim Connelly [Connolly] had "held the ward in his
hand" and exploited it to his own ends. The ward remembers
him by some of the worst tenement property in the community,
so badly planned and constructed that it argues a special dispen-
sation from their building department of that day for its erection. He lost his grip on the ward, partly through business
difficulties, partly through decreasing personal power, partly
through the fickleness of his constituency. For the demos is never
loyal to an individual and takes away with even greater satisfaction than it gives.

For some years past the Curleys have been the nominal
overlords of the ward. They set out definitely to build up an
organization based on the New York democracy, and boldly
labelled their headquarters the Tammany Club. They have built
their power on a regime of political paternalism involving jobs,
Xmas parties, assistance to the sick or afflicted, and to law break-
ers; by acting in short as a kind of big brother to all their
retainers. The leaders once, at least, went to the length of taking
the civil service examinations for the position of letter carrier
in the name of a constituent, were discovered, and sent to Charles
Street Jail for a term. The public spirit of the ward, however,
was with them. While in jail one was re-elected to the city
council and the other to the state legislature, and their release
from prison was turned into a triumphal reception. The sentiment of the ward definitely elevated the function of job getting
by hook or crook as the great and paramount service of the local
politician to his constituency.

Naturally enough the tradition and practice of the ward held
and brought those who had aspirations for municipal or public
corporation jobs. It was the constant tendency for the really

capable and skilled to move away and for the politically dependent to remain. It was equally inevitable that outsiders who
wished to share the benefits of such a regime should immigrate
into the ward. The man with the type of mind that finds satisfaction in political fellowship with others like minded naturally
sought out Ward 17, more especially as that kind of thing tends
increasingly to disappear elsewhere. Of 4,500 voters in the ward,
3,500 are still committed definitely to the machine, and there has
been no real competition in ward matters for some years. A
decade of boss rule has finally rendered democratic self-help
difficult if not impossible. The very foundation of democracy is
undermined and a whole community becomes committed to a
sort of feudal dependence on a leader who fosters the delusion
that he is their chosen representative.

It is against such a background as this that the present life
of the ward has to be outlined. It is of course the tragedy of
Ward 17 that the industries which replace those which have
departed are not of an equal grade. Indeed certain of the old
factories have been turned into storage warehouses, others stand
vacant, one has become a Salvation Army Barracks, perhaps the
last stage of industrial degeneration and degradation.

The most important group in the present industries is that
made up of a series of foundries, factories, and machine shops,
where work on metals is carried on, employing in the aggregate
close to one thousand men. Next in importance is a group of
woodworking establishments employing in the neighborhood of
two hundred and fifty men. Largest in point of numbers is a
series of firms which manufacture, cleanse, or distribute, articles
of immediate service in the necessary business of housekeeping,
such as food, laundry, coal and wood.

It is this last group which seems likely to fix the status of
the ward in the future. For the district is strategically located
to be a center of a vast system of distribution. Sheridan Square
marks one of the geographical centers of Greater Boston, a situation which makes the ward peculiarly well located for industries
which deliver over a wide area. Railroad facilities are also close
at hand and goods can be sent quickly to a large number of
thriving suburbs. Since 1904 the ward has had freight terminal

facilities and the Railroad Commission has removed a discriminatory freight tax, so that car lots are delivered at the same rates as in other districts in the Zone of Emergence.

Unfortunately, however, these industries employ a relatively unskilled grade of worker. Baking, the handling and delivery of coal, ice, and laundering do not call for skill. The laundries especially employ women who are reduced to this last extreme in a female industrial career. These relatively low grade industries are now reinforced by a considerable group of rag and second-hand shops and the ward is facing that extreme danger that comes from the location of such business.

To these industries must be added a considerable number of people employed in the retail shops of the community. In addition to the small shops scattered through the ward there are several department stores on Washington Street near Dudley which employ close to 500 employees, mostly women. These, however, are on the edge of the ward, and affect its life only incidentally.

A portion of the city thick beset with factories quickly empties of the most skilled workers. Only the very poor or the very well-to-do can afford to dwell in the neighborhood. The northern part of Ward 17 is increasingly given over to factories. In the southern portion are pleasant streets and the homes of many types of people. In 1905 the population of the ward numbered 24,313. Of these 7,587 in 1912 were men over twenty years of age (listed by the police officials). Of this male labor force 2,913 were unskilled, 2,409 might be called skilled craftsmen, 1,824 were clerks and small shop keepers, and 176 were professional men. The table given below [table never prepared] shows the population graded by skill and divided by precincts. The skilled craftsmen and clerks are the important group in an emerging community. It will be noticed that they form [number missing] percent of the population and they are found in largest proportion in Precincts 2, 4, 8 and 9 wherein they make up nearly 80 percent of the population.

The better paid operatives in the industries of the ward no longer live there, but take their families out into the districts beyond. As we have found elsewhere the successful craftsman buys a house or establishes himself in some suburb which is convenient to all the industrial portion of Greater Boston. Except for a small portion of the outer part of the ward there is no place that would attract a successful mechanic.

The population is, of course, predominantly Irish. In 1905 71.41 percent of the people of the ward were born of foreign parents (first and second generation). Of those born of foreign parentage 58.07 percent were Irish; 7.17 were English and Scotch; 18.37 were Canadians; 4.99 percent were Germans; 2.01 percent were Swedes, 2.77 percent were Russians and 2.08 percent were Italians. Of the total population born of foreign parents 83.61 percent used English as their native language and were in possession of English traditions.

The Irish are the ranking nationality. A considerable number of the American born are third generation from Irish, and a substantial proportion of the Provincials have Irish ancestry. Locally the Irish are scattered over the ward among Americans and Provincials, though there are colonies with a distinctly national complexion on the streets off the lower portion of Harrison Avenue and on those west of Magazine Street. The majority of the Irish population is made up of the less successful and less skilled, though there is a remnant of better-to-do workers who stay on because they own their homes, or because they cling to old associations, or because it is near their work, or in the case of older people, simply because they dread to try to strike roots in a new community. This nucleus is, in many ways, the very cream of the population and its influence is powerful.

Ward 17 was one of the first suburbs into which Irish came in their movement from Boston. St. Patrick's Church was erected on Northampton Street in 1837 and for many years was an outpost not only for Roxbury but for all the towns beyond. So bitter was Protestant sectarian feeling in that day that loyal members of the church had to be told off to guard the edifice against incendiaries. For a number of years Ward 17 represented a strong, close grained, and generally upward moving Irish community. The people were buying their homes and establishing a strong neighborly and community feeling in the ward. The church with its sodalities, benefit, and recreational organizations, included almost everyone in a round of socializing and moralizing activity.

The tradition of Irish life, with its religious and national loyalties, its regard for a certain type of fundamentals, bred a type of character that is everywhere admitted to be of a more excellent kind than that which is being produced under seemingly more liberal tendencies and the more material abundance of today.

Industrial disintegration and its consequences have brought it about that the more capable Irish have moved away, and their places have been taken by the laggards in the general progress of the main body of the race. Still even for this type, the ward represents an emergence. Two generations of living in America has, at the very least, brought about an American standard of cleanliness. Even the laggards are cleaner than the Jew, or Italian, or the Pole. Though Irish children become soiled with the dust and dirt of the street, they are really clean compared with the newly arrived. The living conditions of the Irish in ward 17 are probably what one would find in any American community where the wages and housing was the same: this much has therefore been accomplished.

The full results of this physical improvement of the third generation is however offset by evils which have arisen through the breakdown of neighborhood structure. Nowhere is this so clearly seen as in the matter of juvenile delinquency. Among young boys between seven and seventeen years, delinquency takes the form of petty stealing and that sort of malicious mischief which leads children to hector inoffensive householders, a situation which is duplicated in other parts of the Zone of Emergence.

Three causes contribute to this state of things. First of all is the fact that the outer wards are more open than the inner downtown districts, and this fact makes it relatively easy for the evil doer to carry on his operations without being seen. Schools or shops are entered, windows broken, destructive mischief devised, often without anyone observing what is going on. This situation in itself might not be serious, were it not reinforced through the breakdown of neighborhood life. Children now commit depredations on those living within sight of their own windows, and are unrecognized. The multiplication of tenements and the fashion of frequent moving has killed the old community spirit. People no longer live among neighbors and friends, and children lose all sense of that common unity of feeling which

under ordinary circumstances would be outraged over the violation of primary ties.

Perhaps even more influential still in promoting lawlessness
is the breakdown of family life. Parents no longer exercise the
same degree of care and control over children that used to
obtain. The father sees little of his sons, the mother is often
away, children are more and more on the street day and night.
The present-day parents no longer teach children to respect
people as such. No child would do the things, nor adopt the
attitude that many children do, had they been taught to respect
human nature as such. This tendency is further reinforced by
the breakdown of neighborhood ties, and the vicious circle
becomes complete.

Fortunately there are two strong Catholic parishes in the
ward, St. Patrick's and St. Philip's. These two churches have the
allegiance of the bulk of the people who are Catholic but for a
small group of Americans and Provincials. The parochial schools
care for girls and the sodalities, clubs, benefit organizations and
other associations affiliated with the church supply spiritual
assistance and recreation. The two churches set the tone of the
community and focus, in large part, its recreational and associa-
tional life.

Though the Irish make up the bulk of the population, there
are, as we have seen, a residium of Provincials, Germans, Swedes,
Jews and Italians. It is in localities such as Ward 17 that it
becomes possible to understand the ease with which a considerable body of people may lose itself. Even when a fourth or
a third of the population is decidedly alien to the main group
it leaves surprisingly little, if any, trace of its presence on the
local life if no church is established and no stores [are] opened.
It becomes easy to discard the old loyalties, to take no part in
the local life, to cut one's self off utterly from one's fellows. This
is the reason why, to some extent, at any rate, characteristic
national institutions, some holding to the past, are sane and
healthy; and explains why, so long as the local community does
not automatically include each resident in a round of friendly
and moralizing activities, the growth of foreign institutional
loyalties ought to be helped and encouraged rather than hin-
dered; why the Irish with their strong religious loyalties and

their efficient church organization will be found in the long run to have accomplished a powerful work in the difficult problem of Americanization.

The Jews have established a colony on Hampden and its side streets which shows the same stench in the houses, the same overcrowding of rooms, the same dirty yards which one finds in the West End. The influx into Ward 17 began about 1898, though the main body of immigrants came about the time of the Chelsea fire, a catastrophe, by the way, which served to unsettle the entire Jewry of Greater Boston. There are now about one hundred families in the ward. The people are mostly small shop keepers and junk dealers, though there is a raincoat factory employing a small number of hands. A congregation, which is not wholly local, however, meets in a hall on Northampton Street, the Rabbi dividing his time between three parishes.

The Poles are settled about Fayerweather Street. So far they have not established any characteristic institutions. They are quiet and orderly except for an occasional brawl. The Italians have also come into the ward lately and are located on Cottage Street and a few other ways, mostly in little colonies of a few families each. They too have no characteristic institutions.

There are a series of institutions, mostly churches, scattered through the ward, which are without any local significance. Among others are a Russian Congregation, a Pentecostal Church, and the Salvation Army. They might as well have been set down in any other neighborhood, the source of attraction being the Dudley Street Elevated which makes the immediate streets convenient to all parts of the city.

The moral tone of the ward is, on the whole, good, especially considering the fact that it edges on Washington Street and Dudley Street. One corner is also given over to a lodging house neighborhood, which unlike certain of those further intown is respectable. Organized and unorganized vice goes downtown. Arrests and violations of the law there are. The Jewish shopkeepers let their customers in the back door on Sundays and junkmen violate the rules governing peddling. The Poles fight when drunk. The Irish indulge in brawls. Liquor forms the great curse of the neighborhood. Perhaps the most serious aspect of this problem is the money taken out of family life through the indulgence of the breadwinner. Large sums are spent on Sunday at the various hotels in the vicinity of Dudley Street, which are heavily patronized by poor men who indulge themselves out of all proportion to their earnings.

Perhaps the most serious element in the situation is the generally lowered tone of the life of the ward; a condition that makes itself evident in the homes of the people with telling force. A study of individual houses all over the ward shows a number of tenements in which bath tubs were used for storing coal or water; a certain amount of evident misuse of [water] closets; decided incapacity or unwillingness to co-operate in the care of halls, closets, cellars, and streets. Even a modest amount of knowledge quickly convinces one that the question of housing is quite as much a question of people as of rooms and accommodations. We need inspection of people. No one [who] has been revolted over vile conditions in a lower tenement, which at first sight seemed to inhere in the rooms, and has afterward entered the tenement above and found it a place in which he might live without hardship, will question the need of providing penalties that will put pressure on criminally careless tenants.

Dorchester, Ward 16

It would be easy but unenlightening to say that the most distinctive thing about Ward 16 is its lack of distinctiveness. Still clinging to a faint suggestion of eighteenth century village life, and having a strong substance of nineteenth century suburbanism, with these two encroached upon and retreating before the twentieth century three-decker, this section of Dorchester requires particular rather than general statements. The quite arbitrary lines of territorial division increase the need of particularity; since little of what may be said of the Polish colony about Andrew Square applies to the section about Edward Everett Square and this in turn bears no likeness to the Mt. Harrison streets [hill crossed by Howard Avenue]. The few general statements which can be made will become apparent as the several districts are described, and will be brought together by way of conclusion. Suffice it to say at the outset that we have to consider a region almost wholly residential, comprising a population of over 25,000 people.

The approximate ward boundaries at present are: Columbia Road from its intersection with Newman Street in South Boston to Quincy Street, across Quincy Street to Blue Hill Avenue, down the Avenue to West Cottage and along through East Cottage Street to the midland division of the New York, New Haven and Hartford Railroad. The line follows these tracks to Massachusetts Avenue and then takes in all the marshland on the South Bay over as far as Southampton and Dorchester Streets whence Newman Street runs to meet Columbia Road again. Topographically, except for the cutting through of streets, the elevating of railroad tracks, and the filling in of the marshes, the ward remains practically unaltered. The building of Columbia Road across the harbor front has been the means of draining much marshy land and the building of Massachusetts Avenue has meant the permanent reclamation of still more. In the not very far future the dump-carts will have done with their dumping and there will be no more sea between Massachusetts Avenue and Southampton Street. When this land as well as that between the Old Colony division of the railroad and Columbia Road is at last made, the ward will have taken on its permanent aspect so far as actual terra firma goes. The distance above sea-level increases very gradually from the Andrew Square (formerly Washington Village) section to Upham's Corner, but beyond Dudley and through to Quincy Street the land is quite hilly and even sightly. It is also important to note the way the ward is crossed by through thoroughfares. Dorchester Avenue, Massachusetts Avenue, Dudley Street, Blue Hill Avenue, all serve to make the place easy of access to the city and serve equally well to take much of the "emergence" beyond the zone altogether into Wards 20 and 24 [central and outer Dorchester].

Ward 16 has shared largely in the historical traditions of "good old Dorchester." A Dorchester writer has summarized the early history of the Five Corners region (now Edward Everett Square) as follows: "General Washington marched with his troops to Dorchester Heights, passing the spot where Edward Everett was born. The first church and the first school house, stood but a moment's walk from here and the first town meeting was held in Town Meeting Square just opposite. This spot where the William E. Russell school now stands, which was once a swamp, was partly filled by slaves belonging to General Oliver who lived in the house in which Edward Everett was born. In this swamp only about 160 years ago a cow got stuck in the mud and the wolves came in the night and devoured her." [from Dorchester Day Celebration, 1913]

The Blake House which dates from 1648 still stands on Pond Street and nearby tablets mark the site of the first free public school in America and of Edward Everett's house, which, however, was not built until 1745. Although the first church early moved and gave the name to Meeting House Hill, the section about the Five Corners continued to hold its own; for the Rev. Richard Mather, the grandfather of Cotton Mather, lived opposite the Blake House during his pastorate at the First Church and other old and prominent families settled on what became Boston Street and thereabouts. Most of the land was apportioned among several large estates; and this colonial country village with its truck gardens, prolific orchards and ample pastures remained intact until long after the Revolution. Indeed the fruit farms of Dorchester were so renowned that the Andrew, Clapp, and Harris families, to mention only a few, gave their names to various rare species of pears which they produced. Grapes, cherries, and blackberries were also largely grown; in fact we are told that as late as 1850 the German women used to come out from Boston to pick and pack this fruit. Today the City of Boston maintains in this same neighborhod very attractive hothouses and a nursery from which bushes, shrubs and flowers are distributed to its parks.

Much of the land on Mt. Harrison apparently remained barren and wooded until the 1830's when several pretentious estates were built and a deer park was fenced off. However, its northwestern slope remained as pasture and orchard until a comparatively recent time. For years a stage coach ran out Dorchester Avenue, formerly a turnpike, to the Lower Mills, but in the 1850's it was superseded by horsecars. The first station out of Boston on the New York and New England Railroad was at Dudley Street and this early made for an influx of people of comfortable means who could commute from their estates in this country suburb. The gradual advent of the electric cars altered all this and was one of the prime causes of the change in population.

There is little to record of the developments hereabout until well into the nineteenth century. There had been more than half a dozen tanneries near the marshes and a glass factory stood between Dorchester Avenue and the Old Harbor. But by 1860 these had all disappeared. The growth in population up to this time was small and was confined almost exclusively to Yankees. It was not until after the Civil War that the real flow of immigration began. The streets on Mt. Harrison began to be broken through after this time and for twenty-five years thereafter a steady growth in substantial one-family houses can be noticed. The families who settled thus were Yankees many of whom still remain. The community life was congenial and an air of smug, suburban complaisance still gives to these few streets that odor of sanctity which brings to mind the fulsome and uncritical eulogies of American family life which we like to roll like sweet morsels on our tongues. If we were at liberty to write a psychological rather than a sociological study nothing would be more interesting than to study the true significance of this standard of life in its reaction on those who enjoy it. For it becomes painfully evident that it does affect their minds and hearts unwholesomely. In the face of the outward march of Hibernian and Jew the Yankees have girt their garments well about them, snatched up their skirts that so much as a hem might not be defiled by contact with "foreigners," and have betaken them elsewhere in a spirit little and shallow, if not mean and snobbish. This unsocial, inhuman and unintelligent attitude of the "native inhabitants" is one of the sad attendant facts which would have to be recorded and explained in a study of the psychology of emergence. The subtle way in which the invading host has heaped coals of fire on the heads of the better-than-thous deserves recognition. In every instance the newcomers have in short order established the foundations of a local life quite as refined and substantial as that which the Yankees had left. And only blindness can make them fail to see that the life of the newcomers is in its own way exactly as human, as ambitious, as loyal to family, God and country as their own. In a broad survey such as this the truth is again brought home that the things which bind are in reality more numerous and more significant than those which keep apart the human family. The only difficulty is to see and appreciate the samenesses through the differences.

On the other hand it is possible that this bearing of hostility unwittingly represents a blind desire to maintain a well-founded standard of living against encroachment and cheap imitation. The more one has to lose the more one has to fear, may be a possible explanation; and it may very well be that the economic status and the cultural background are in some peculiar way rendered more secure by this attitude. Again, humanity has ever spurned the rungs by which it did ascend. The prospering newcomer for some odd reason arouses not an admiring but a resenting emotion in those already successful. If this should prove to be a necessary adjunct of the struggle for a fair economic standard it shows both how intense the struggle is and how narrow the standard.

The other end of the ward from Mt. Harrison has quite a different story to tell. Its nearness to South Boston was a potent factor in determining the nature of the population and of its housing. For in the middle 70's when the streets between Dorchester Avenue and Boston Streets were being cut through many of the lots were bought at the outset by young men from South Boston who refused to live in the wretched "cheese boxes" [small alley 1½ story houses] where their Irish fathers had been content. Some German families also moved in and some Yankees. But from the first opening of these streets the incoming of the more ambitious and prosperous Irish was most pronounced. In the streets nearer Edward Everett Square the development was largely in one- and two-family houses of a modest suburban type — with front lawns, yards with a small garden and fruit trees. Through Howell, Washburn and Rawson, and along Boston Streets, however, the buildings have been erected more recently and are of the three-family type. Some of the families that settled here have by this time moved farther out but most of them remain and constitute a fairly successful class whose children can start life on a normal, hopeful basis.

It may not be amiss to insert at this point the reasons why even in its least attractive streets Ward 16 can never quite approach the dreariness and dilapitude of so much of Ward 17.

In the first place the houses here are largely separate wooden buildings with some inlet for light and air on all four sides. At their worst they have been built closely together with a minimum of yard space in the rear; but at their best they are set back fifteen and eighteen feet from the street, are fifteen feet apart and have decent yards. Probably the majority of three-deckers, especially those built several years ago come somewhere between these two limits. All this contrasts with the brick blocks of Ward 17, where light and air are available on the two ends only, where the buildings are set close up to the sidewalk, where there is no way of painting up or rejuvenating the brick structure to give it an appearance of youth and freshness, and where there are few trees, back yard gardens or front lawns. The fact of the general environmental superiority of Ward 16 stands as both a cause and an effect of the incoming of a decidedly worthy and progressive type of Irish family. The whole life of the district noticeably retains much of its tone and quality because those of this better class have made comfortable homes here and have had some interest in preserving and cultivating the green and fertile areas which they found. Gardens, window boxes and trees, be it said again, have been the means of cherishing to a considerable degree this valuable appearance of out-of-townishness.

Although the origins of a quite new departure in suburban dwellings go back of 1890, the more well-defined development of the three-family wooden house, or three-decker, has come in the last fifteen years. The growth and success of this type of house throughout Dorchester and elsewhere is important to understand. The actual cost of construction becomes the first consideration. It is easy to see that by eliminating the expensive pitched roof of the two-family house, and substituting a flat tar and gravel roof the first substantial reduction is made. One cellar, one water and gas main, one plumbing shaft for three families, divide the cost of these by three for each family. The number of tenants that can be accommodated is of course multiplied by three, and this is what has made possible such a large outpouring from the city proper. At first, as has been said, the three-deckers were packed together and run up to the street in a manner and with a speed calculated to ruin all property values; and as a matter of fact the values do fall before this advent, although in the long run such a result would inevitably follow as the city population moved out. But experience has shown that tenants insist upon privacy from their next door neighbors and upon adequate yard area front and back. Hence the new three-decker is a more rational structure although it will never be able to boast of either beauty or variety. The values which the tenant receives in this modern flat are so little short of luxurious that it is no wonder they are in demand. A flat which rents for from twenty to twenty-five dollars a month includes a parlor, dining room, kitchen with set tubs, cook stove with gas stove and water heater attached, two bedrooms, front and back piazza, hot air furnace, electricity, and hardwood floors. Such a home, so located and so fitted out, is well calculated to appeal to the ambitious clerk, mechanic and the like whose weekly wage averages in the neighborhood of twenty-five dollars. To be sure all three-deckers are not thus equipped and these less up-to-date ones rent for from sixteen to twenty dollars monthly. Admittedly the houses are cheaply constructed of medium grade material and with hurried workmanship. But they do offer and establish a standard of living which is well above what most of their occupants were accustomed to in the more crowded parts of the city. And as it is this class of citizens, in ancestry Irish, German, Swedish and British, which predominates in the ward, these apartments have supplied a very urgent demand. The police polling lists for 1912 show 2,800 clerks and business men, and 2,853 skilled workmen as residents here, with only 2,112 unskilled and 251 professional men. As the type of dwelling just described becomes more popular the tendency is for the one-family houses to go out of business altogether. The impression derived from walking through the Mt. Harrison district is that well nigh a third of the single-family houses are white elephants on the hands of their owners. It is probable however that here the property will simply be bought by prosperous Jews and not be remodelled in any way.

The three-decker has, of course, attracted both the builder and the small investor as a money-making proposition. For the builder the advantages are in large scale production inasmuch as the profit on a single house is small; but if a man builds thirty three-deckers a year and gets only three hundred dollars out of each, he has no need to complain of business. About half of these houses the builders unload as soon as possible on to families who live in one apartment and rent the other two. If a house is kept full all the time and the owner does not expect to live on his rentals the investment is a reasonably good one. But that the houses are expensive for the average man without capital to try to pay off mortgages on is undeniable. Yet be that as it may, the actual number of *bona fide* foreclosures on three-deckers is no more in proportion to their numbers than in other types of buildings — in fact it is actually less.

The pros and cons of the fire hazard of these structures are many and devious. It is admitted that the loss by fire in these sections has been less in the last few years than ever before and less than in the parts of the city where second-class construction prevails. It is admitted that the three-deckers are over-insured. It is admitted that with stairways and piazzas on two ends of the house it would be practically impossible for people to be burned alive — and thus far losses of life in three-decker fires have been infinitesimal. Furthermore it is generally agreed that if a big fire ever did get started its path of destruction would be wide. It is a fact that so far as certain parts of Dorchester are concerned the water supply and pressure are inadequate. It is a fact too that whereas the fire department here included six engines in 1880, today there are only seven — and that with a population which has increased in that time from 16,600 to about 130,000 at present. Numerous commissions have in view of these considerations, recommended the extension of the [first and second class] building limits to coincide with the city boundary — thus making the erection of any house with a wooden exterior or a shingle roof illegal in the city of Boston. Naturally opposition to this has been great and the matter stands today about where it has for several years. There are two factions each with strong convictions either for or against the three-decker. Bills are regularly introduced to extend the building limits but sufficient hostile public sentiment has thus far been abroad to kill them in committee. Meanwhile the building in wood goes on; more people are moving out from the city; Dorchester is becoming more thickly settled, and the end is not yet.

Finally, it seems to be reasonably fair to say that if third-class construction were made illegal, dwellings in more attractive kinds of brick and in some form of concrete or hollow tile would become in a very few years quite as cheap as the wooden house today. The argument has always been advanced that if second-class construction were made obligatory, brick blocks which occupy about 90 percent of the lot will be erected, and the North and West End type of dwelling will prevail. But it is a fact that the price of three-deckers is climbing because of the increased cost of labor, and it may well result with the reputable builder that the place where either kind of construction is in the long run equally cheap will soon be reached. When that time comes, if not before, because of possible legislation, the thought and care which now go into the three-decker will be directed toward devising a desirable type in brick or other substance. The question is a complex one; it is a problem in housing as well as in fire hazard. More and more, however, it will become a problem in transportation and when it is at last considered on that basis a more extensive and thoroughgoing solution may be in sight.

A further aspect of the building extension is seen in the rise of the family hotels, for the most part along Dudley Street. A few of these were built over twenty-five years ago to supply the demand of wealthy businessmen for apartment hotels near the city. The accessibility of the Dudley Street railroad station has already been mentioned; and the kind of building now going on in certain parts of Brookline was at that time promised for this section. These hotels however are not on the increase. Those that there are provide for tradesmen and physicians who have to live in *res medias* and for traveling salesmen with small families.

Having outlined the way in which the several types of homes have grown up to supply the demand of varied kinds of people, it is now possible to look at the dwellers themselves more directly. Solely for the sake of convenience, and not at all because the life is capable of such definite division, the people will be considered in their ancestral groups. The Yankees we have said reigned practically supreme from the days when the pastor of the flock was paid out of the town treasury down to the second quarter of the nineteenth century when Irish and German women used to work in truck farms and orchards. The impress of this life is still strong in Dorchester and in a tangible way it is being artificially preserved through the observance of Dorchester Day every seventh of June. This celebration, originally a humble affair of the Dorchester Historical Society, has of late been made to include the many civic, social, political and educational bodies of the city. An attempt is made to exalt local tradition and foster pride, and in this the older ones who speak tenderly of "dear old Dorchester" are joined by all who for any reason are anxious that the locality may appear well in the eyes of men. There is no doubt that this feeling of pride in its fair name has been taken up and cherished by the Irish and Jews who have now entered so largely into this goodly heritage. However the life of the city so far as it is distinctly Yankee focuses above Ward 16. There are but four Protestant churches actually in the ward. The club and secret orders are likewise centered elsewhere, although two strong Masonic lodges meet at the Masonic Building at Upham's Corner. [Note: According to the 1905 census: 45% had Irish parents, 20% had Provincial, English and Scotch, 6% German, 4% Italian and a scattering of Scandinavian, Russian and Polish. These proportions have since altered in favor of the Jews, Italians and Poles.]

The preponderant element here is, of course, of Irish descent. The advance of this nationality from Washington Village to Edward Everett Square has already been spoken of. In the middle of the century the Village was filled with Irish families, the men of which worked in the iron, boiler and glass factories thereabout. The opening of the streets from Dorchester Avenue to Boston Street in the 70's brought a movement of population which still goes on. The Willow Court region was early given over to the Irish and the land about East and West Cottage Streets was rapidly built over in the 80's. The streets off Blue Hill Avenue, however, do not present the same appearance of thrift as do those on the Dorchester side — the [cause of] which can be in part accounted for by the early introduction of three and six-family houses built with no restrictions on the distance from sidewalks or between dwellings. Along Quincy Street also the Irish have lived, and here likewise the apartment houses were built some time ago. Of late, however, this part of the ward has been preempted in favor of the Jews.

The history of the Roman Catholic Church in Dorchester reflects closely the movements of the Irish population. St. Peter's Church on Bowdoin St. in Ward 20 established in 1872 was the first parish in this part of Boston. Its chapels which have in the course of time become parishes, portions of which lie in this ward, include St. Monica's just out of Andrew Square, St. Margaret's on Columbia Road and St. Paul's on Woodward Park Street. St. John's Church on Blue Hill Avenue was set off from St. Joseph's in Roxbury. The expansion of St. Margaret's offers a typical example of a parish among a thriving body of Irish Americans. Organized in 1893 with 1,500 souls, housed first in a wooden chapel since used as a hall and now in a fine brick church built in 1899, having added a parish house and, in 1909, a large parochial school which already contains four hundred children in the first few grades, this church today counts 6,000 souls as under its ministrations. It has the usual church societies with a flourishing organization of the Society of the Holy Name. Here as throughout the city the Knights of Columbus are prominent.

St. Paul's Church began as a Mission Chapel in 1896 and became a separate parish in 1908. Something over 4,000 souls are enrolled in the church, as compared with 1,500 when it opened its doors. Its rectory was formerly the mansion of the Hooper estate which for years occupied a large part of Mt. Harrison. The use of this beautiful location for the church itself is anticipated in the course of time; and if the prosperity of its parishioners counts for aught this should be a noble edifice. St. John's Church was built in 1895 and is the center of a large parish. Its parochial school taught by the Sisters of Charity who live near-by is attended by 600 children. It is significant to note that over 500 souls have moved from the parish in the past year or two on account of the incoming of the Jews. The streets immediately about the church will no doubt be held for many years by faithful families, but large numbers will inevitably move on in the next few years. But a superficial statement such as this of the facts about the Church gives no adequate clue to the secret of its power. The loyalty of its people and the personnel of its priesthood have both been large factors in bringing it the wealth and the influence now existent. Dorchester has been fortunate in having enlisted among its priests men of fine character, broad outlook, and marked ability. And of this, the success of their work and the esteem in which they are held are sufficient proof.

We see then so far as the Irish are concerned a consistent and progressive rise in economic and social stability as they move through this part of Dorchester and go up, as many are already doing, into upper Dorchester, West Roxbury and Hyde Park. Ever followed by their church which they loyally support and creating social ties both there, in labor and in neighborhood organization, the Americans in Ward 16 who feel the Celtic blood in their veins have every reason to be proud of their descent and hopeful of their future.

In point of numbers the race that claims next consideration is the Jews. The police listing of 1912 reveals 568 Jewish men, which would mean a total of between two and three thousand individuals. The inflow has followed the lines of Blue Hill Avenue and Quincy Street. In the streets in this southwestern corner of the ward the Irish are being rapidly displaced. From Ward 21 where they first settled the Jews have extended their colony in every direction. The first movement brought those of German and English nativity of a more assimilated type; but the Chelsea Fire marked the beginning of an immigration of Russian Jews which has yet to cease. Where the newcomers have been content to buy and maintain the single houses the result has been a clear and noticeable gain from every point of view but that of the disturbed Yankees. These houses have in the main been well kept up with attractive gardens and good lawns. And the property is used to its full. All the relatives are apparently brought in to create a happy family gathering and the ménage overflows to piazzas and yards with an evident thorough enjoyment of these new advantages. But where the Jews have built or have gone into the more tenement-like houses, the evidences of cleanliness and good order are farther to seek. It is here that the danger lies. The Jewish property holders do not hesitate to build cheap brick blocks or poorly constructed three-deckers, and in the event of this [building of cheap brick blocks] a type of family lower in the economic scale is attracted and the richer families go farther out. It should be a matter of no little concern to the present inhabitants of this section to see that there do not come more people than can be educated into a decent sense of community welfare and interest. If the streets are to be kept clean, the houses repaired and the general air of orderliness maintained, the traditions which have made for such conditions must not be swamped by an inrush of those who still conform to West and North End or even Russian standards.

There is little distinctive to be said of the Jewish life here. The men folk are mainly shopkeepers, tailors and cigar makers. The younger generation stay longer in school and the number of those who finish High School is large. These find their livelihood in mercantile and clerical occupations. The sense of social grada-tion among their own people is very strong and often puzzling although in the main it depends, as always and everywhere, upon economic status. This is particularly noticeable in the synagogues in Ward 21 [Roxbury highlands] where the levels of the several congregations seem to be adjusted by a sort of pecuniary barom-eter. Here, as elsewhere among this people, the younger genera-tion finds the faith of their fathers inadequate and unintelligible. But be that as it may, the feeling for the ethical values inculcated in the Jewish home-life and hallowed for some at least by the religious observances, is very strong and permanent. The most casual glimpse of candles burning in frequent windows on Fri-day evening with the family groups gathered about cannot but impress one with the strange power of a religion which has exalted purity, fertility, and an obedience which promised that "Thy days shall be long in the land which the Lord thy God giveth thee."

The Italians in this part of Dorchester, although they do not represent as advanced a standard as the other groups, have shown energy, common sense and intelligence enough to get away from the North End. Around Quincy, Dacia and Dove Streets, along Norfolk Avenue and through Willow Court on the opposite side of the ward there are settled some five or six hundred of this nationality. Their settlement in these streets has been of rather long standing although the individuals come and go as their place of work changes. The men are day laborers, stone cutters, masons, marble and mosaic workers and the like. Especially about Willow Court and Norfolk Avenue their colony presents a most refreshing appearance of thrift and prosperity. Each house has its vegetable garden in front or side yard and the profusion of brilliant flowers shows what Italy could transplant to our shores would we but give her half a chance. The great majority of this group are foreign born and many speak no English. Here again we look to their children to make a marked advance as they come up into the schools. Yet even as we watch for this "marked advance" we cannot be sure that the change from simplicity in home, amusements, and outlook to sophistication and crude, superficial American mannerisms is at all to be desired. The preservation of all the particles of genuine gold in this refining process is truly a difficult and subtle task — and its fulfillment is rather in the hands of the capricious gods than of us prejudiced humans.

The Polish population centers about Andrew Square. In fact the ward line runs through the streets which they occupy and thus the polling lists show only 214 men in the ward in 1912. In the entire neighborhood however there are over 1,000 Poles. The arrival of the first few families antedates the inception of their parish in 1893 by several years. Under able leadership they at once set about the erection of an attractive church and parish house on Dorchester Avenue, and a parochial school accommodating over 200 children has lately been added. The parish numbers more than 2,000 souls but since it is one of only three Polish communions about Boston it draws largely on the outlying district. Brought here by the industrial opportunities in foundries and woodworking concerns the Poles have prospered as only a thrifty folk can. In the iron-working and boiler factories and as machinists their strength has stood them in good stead. Today the property on these streets is gradually coming into their hands. The difficulty which the English language presents has figured largely in the reasons for the seeming isolation of the Polish colony. Thrown back upon itself it has created social ties which are as numerous and diverse as they are valuable. Its clubs, mutual benefit fraternities, patriotic societies and political organizations are legion. All belong to several insurance societies to which they pay fifty cents a week. The National Alliance, the Young Men's Society and the Polish Citizen's Club — practically all the men belong to one or the other of these, and especially the last which offers every encouragement to naturalization to the end of attaining citizenship. There are two Socialist Clubs among them if not more; but most of the Poles are too loyal churchmen to make possible the introduction of new ideas as successfully as has been possible among the Lithuanians. Taken all in all, their twenty years here have brought decided progress. The second generation is now at school and it has proved to be as educable and as ambitious as could be desired. The sturdy qualities which made this people the champions of liberty and freedom in Europe find an opportunity for expression here which should enrich their lives and bring new vigor to our national spirit.

We have now considered the racial groups that stand out as such in the community. As a matter of fact, however, there are about as many people of German as of Italian parentage. There are certainly 500 Scandinavians and many from the Provinces. But as all of these are scattered and absorbed into the American atmosphere it leaves little or nothing to be said concerning them. The tie which binds the family to its native church is often the only index of its ancestry. And Sunday finds the German and Swedish churches in Roxbury and the South End each receiving back members who now live here. The Norwegians and Danes (Methodists) have in the past four years bought the church on Howard Avenue formerly occupied by the Baker Memorial Church, but only about a fourth of the congregation is in residence hereabouts. For the rest, these people are to all intents and purposes already merged into that "American race" for the amalgamation of which "the fires of God are burning."

The character of most of Ward 16 is such that the search for amusement does not present quite the acute problem that it does in some parts of the zone. Much of the life has reached the point where except for occasional trips to the theatre or movies or a social party, dance or church affair, the desire for recreation can vent itself in more quiet, homelike and normal ways. The possession of a parlor and of a piano — these two assure an almost immediate simplification of the whole problem; and these two are found almost universally throughout the ward. The movies have not as yet become numerous. Blue Hill Avenue and Columbia Road have the only two theatres. One more, seating 700 people is about to be built on Dudley Street near Upham's Corner. The virtual exclusion of the saloon speaks well for the local morale although it must be admitted that the vote is about two to one in favor of license. The explanation of this lies in the fact that the vote is on the question of license for the city and not for the ward. Excepting drug stores there are at present five places where liquor can be bought, of which only three are barrooms. The city provides a playground adjacent to the John Winthrop School; and another small ball field is being temporarily used on Massachusetts Avenue. There is a field and locker building on Columbia Road at the foot of Preble Street. A development of this whole waterfront in such a manner as to make it a more attractive breathing place should soon become the concern of the residents of South Boston and Dorchester. At present it is a shadeless, almost barren place, emphasizing too much the fact that it is a recently covered dump. In consequence the park area is used more by automobiles in haste and such as would sleep off a drunk unmolested at leisure, than by the people of the neighboring streets. The bathing place known as McKenzie's Beach is much patronized in summer although it is entirely inadequate in point of size; in winter the Municipal Building on Columbia Road above Upham's Corner is available. This building contains not only public shower baths but a swimming tank, large gymnasium and branch of the Public Library. The attendance at the gymnasium and baths average nearly 2,000 a week. But even so, little in the way of healthy recreation is provided when it is remembered that there are over 5,000 children growing up here. That there are still open lots which serve for baseball and football is not much consolation when building is going on as fast as it is. The question of the provision of playgrounds presents itself as a very real concern of the near future. As far as the less Americanized groups go the social and recreational life is quite simple, spontaneous and homely in its character. Taking the ward as a whole, therefore, one cannot but reflect upon the importance of this oft mentioned standard of living in solving almost automatically divers and sundry problems of which that of amusement is one.

The industries here demand a word which must be more prophetic than actually descriptive; for at present they are on almost negligible quantity. They include three laundries, a boiler, refrigerator and showcase manufactory none of which are large, and an ice factory. All of these are on the edge of the residential sections. The recent building of a large plant for one of the public utilities corporations just inside the district is an earnest of what may well be expected to follow on the outskirts of the ward where more land is found to be available for manufacturing sites within a few years. The tendency will then be for many of the unskilled to live about these factories while the better paid workers move farther out. In this connection it should be said that the [rapid transit] tunnel about to be dug from the South Station to Andrew Square will mean that a still wider zone will be accessible with no corresponding increase in the running time into the city; and this again will tend to push many residents onward and upward.

It will now be readily seen that if the growth of Dorchester has meant anything it has meant a well-marked advance in the standard of living for a large number of people. Irish, Swedes, Germans, Poles, Jews and Italians — all have come to make up this ward; and for all life here has revealed itself as more abundant and interesting than it could possibly have shown itself elsewhere. These gains in the character and quality of life must now be held fast. Values both objective and subjective must be retained. For example, the dwellings erected on the twenty percent of still vacant land must be of sufficiently desirable type to assure tenants of a worthy grade. The houses many of them already in their second and third decade must be kept in repair; for the three-decker is notoriously short-lived if no outlay is ever made for up-keep. Much of the building on the water side of Dorchester Avenue is already badly deteriorated, and more on the Cottage Avenue side is about to duplicate it. Only a constant expenditure will keep much of the property from something far worse than shabbiness in the next fifteen years. Property owners and tenants should see that it is a matter of self-protection to have houses well painted, yards and lawns green, and clean streets.

On its subjective side the life of the established must be protected from such an inrush of the unestablished as is likely to occur in the Jewish quarter. If the present rate of growth should keep up for another ten years there will be real danger of congestion — moral and spiritual if not physical. To be lived well life cannot always be passed in crowds. Dorchester can afford to prize and cherish its disappearing relics of leisurely, ample village life. But if its proud traditions are to remain unsullied there must be self-knowledge, vigilance and organized effort. Yet only as this is carried on in a spirit which values the whole of life — its environment as well as its soul — will it be effectual. And lastly only a spirit of widest human understanding and of respect for divers peoples and creeds is adequate for the conservation of the best in the old loyalties and for the creation of new ones which shall be finer and more worthful. Anything less than this choice spirit augurs ill for the common weal.

VI

SOUTH BOSTON

South Boston must always have been a conspicuous item in the landscape of Boston Harbor. We are told that in the early days its high bare fields attracted the eyes of a newly arriving band of farmer colonists and helped to determine their settlement of Dorchester within access to these upland pastures. One of the hilltops proved the strategic point for Washington's discomfiture of the British and the eyrie from which were watched their departing vessels.

Except for this battle of Dorchester Heights the history of the peninsula covers a period of a little more than a hundred years. In 1800 its fields were still at the disposal of the Dorchester farmers for pasturage, save for a few farms which were actually within its bounds. The narrow south bay of the harbor, however, alone separates it from the most populated district of Boston. Again its hills rising from the flat lands along the water attracted the eye, this time as a promising outlet for the growing population of the town. In 1803 four well-to-do citizens purchased a tract of 600 acres on the western slope and immediately petitioned for the annexation to Boston of the whole peninsula. This took place in 1804 in spite of the remonstrance of Dorchester whose traditional rights were thus abruptly taken away. At the time there were but 19 men of voting age in the region and the only enterprise besides the farms to the southeast were some chemical works in that portion near the mouth of the south bay now one of the busiest industrial sections of Boston.

In 1805 the city surveyed and partially laid out broad thoroughfares through the property of the four speculators, which was thus divided into ample building lots. Judge Tudor, one of the four, began at once the erection of a handsome house on the corner of what is now A Street and Broadway. At the same time a soap factory was established at a point most accessible to the city whence its workmen could row across the channel of the bay.

The period from 1823 to 1845 seems to have been one of active normal growth in population. Those who moved to the peninsula came to make homes and in considerable measure to own them. The hills, the water, the broad streets, the laying out of which had received a setback in the first of the enterprise but which was now continued, attracted many who desired substantial homes. By 1845 it was second only to Ward 11 [sic], Beacon Hill, in the number of those who lived in their own houses. To a reasonable extent therefore the expectations of the men who opened the property had been justified.

INDUSTRIAL SOUTH BOSTON

South Boston has two industrial sections connected by the Dorchester Avenue thoroughfare. The larger and more important lies along the waters of the South Bay and the Harbor, and is, by use of bridges, in close relation to the main business district of the city. The other extends out toward Dorchester bounded on one side by the railroad tracks which lie between Dorchester Avenue and the South Bay and surrounded otherwise by the tenement house regions of the lower part of the peninsula and of Washington Village. It is intersected by the tracks of the New Haven R.R. freight route, the warehouses for which lie between the extensions of Summer and Congress Streets.

The early industrial story of South Boston is continued with the march of time along much the same line as in the beginning. Business develops there as the pressure for space is felt in the city. New manufactures are established because of the opportunity for abundant room. Industries remove but others come and the district preserves its importance as one of the largest manufacturing portions of the city. There is still a considerable amount of land available for such purposes. If Boston grows in the direction of manufacture it would seem inevitable that this section would prove a valuable outlet for such growth both because of its docking facilities and its accessibility to all the downtown region of the city. From the head of Summer Street at Washington Street to its end at the Electric Light Plant at K Street is not more than a half hour's leisurely walk. The electric cars from South Boston to the North Station take about fifteen minutes from Summer Street and Dorcheser Avenue. In spite of the great changes which the past thirty years have seen in the manufacture of iron and steel the machine shop and the foundry have been able to persist in South Boston. There has been, however, of necessity specialization in this industry and newer manufactures are almost as various in product as they are numerous. The older industries were such naturally as to employ almost wholly men. Among those more recently established the character of the work allows for the employment of women in large numbers. In two of the more recent establishments there is an opportunity for young women to earn as good wages as are current in factories. These industries present all the most modern conditions of machine management. In the American Can Company's plant labor-saving devices of the most advanced type set the pace for the workers. There and at the Gillette Razor factory extreme manual accuracy and rapidity of motion are required in order to protect the workers from serious injury from the material handled. A significant element in work done in South Boston is the large amount of teaming which it involves. This and the laboring work at the docks are the only occupations employing any number of persons which require residence in proximity. The freight yards, coal, wharves, sugar cargoes and warehouses depend upon the teamster, the laborer or the longshoreman, and especially in the first two classifications are to be found large numbers of the South Boston residents.

But both industrial sections draw as readily upon other parts of the city as upon South Boston for both men and women workers. The North End is scarcely more remote from the Summer Street extension than is much of the peninsula itself. For the other portion Dorchester Avenue forms the direct route to and from the tenement-house region of Dorchester. Yet these parts of the city are so wholly industrial that it is chiefly those whose duties take them there who know them. The ordinary citizen whom some unusual errand takes across the Summer Street Extension bridge will think himself in another city although behind him scarcely five minutes away lies the South Station, a part of his daily coming and going. The street on the South Boston side is generous in its width and on either side for some

[67] rods it is built up in handsome warehouses. These represent the largest trade in wool in this country. Other wholesale business has quarters there. Familiar names and signs under new circumstance would greet his eye if he were to penetrate the streets which run on the grade below Summer Street. The New England Confectionery Company would be no longer an advertisement, but a sizable building where some 400 or 500 people are employed. The Metropolitan Coal Company would figure in his mind not as a series of coal carts but as a great repository of fuel supplied by laden barges. The sugar refinery would suggest a city remote from his own well-known Boston. At the American Can Company might be found all the familiar household tins, the well-known packages of the "Educator" crackers and many other modern tin forms for a great variety of commodities, but chiefly in the right season it would be supplying the sardine business of New England. Various large buildings without significant titles would add a feeling of some inscrutable purpose standing as they seem to do during working hours silent and self-absorbed. Entrance and inquiry discovers that they are leased to different industries by floors with light and power supplied from a general plant. Each floor is a separate factory. If curiosity prompts a further acquaintance with these parts the visitor may extend his journey far enough in one direction to find the source of the well-known Gillette Razor. At the far end of Summer Street the attractive grounds of the Edison Electric Light plant are to be found.

The character of the South Boston residence district was determined by 1850. Pressure on the part of business for more adequate space brought about radical changes in that part of Boston known as Fort Hill. The height was cut down and a considerable population of working people had to seek new homes. As we look back the logic of events is so clear it is difficult to forgive the blindness of our predecessors of that period. The eye of wisdom noted the advantages of the locality for residence purposes. The nearness to the business area combined with all the attractions of open land and access to the sea made it particularly desirable for people engaged in the industrial life of the city. How much might have been saved in terms of human life and happiness, and better citizenship, if the location and its building up could have been intelligently adapted to the needs of its population and its values safeguarded for the future we may not here compute. In the light, however, of our present failures to treat with new building conditions we must condone those of an earlier date. It is not, however, too late to prevent the worst results from a similar situation just developing in a section of Boston that has for years been the high hope of the speculative investor in real estate. For that reason if for no other the story of South Boston is worthy of study.

Previous to the changes in the Fort Hill region the quality of the demand for real estate in South Boston has proved disappointing. It had not the seal of fashion. The generous width of the city lots along Broadway failed to attract as they deserved. Speculation was forced to cover its disappointment by adaptation to the real demand. This came in the end from the people dislodged from Fort Hill who wanted small houses on small lots. Only the crudest conception of city planning had existed forty years previous when the land was opened. It consisted in laying down a series of parallel lines with another series at right angles on any piece of land that looked promising to the real estate promoter. In the process of adaptation to the new demand no added intelligence was used. The depth of the lots was reduced by cutting through them narrow streets [alleys twenty feet wide] parallel to the broad avenues already built. These new streets and the small lots thus made available were alike too narrow for a constantly growing population. It was like creating the environment in which contagious disease could flourish. South Boston still suffers heavily from the disease of congestion. The trail of the white plague lies over Ward 13 [lower South Boston].[7]

The district as we know it today naturally divides itself into two general parts. That nearest the city which is on the level ground we shall speak of as the lower section. The two hills and

_____
[7] The South Boston wards (1896-1913) 13, 14, and 15 divided the peninsula as follows: Ward 13, lower South Boston, roughly all the land north and west of E Street; the upper section was divided into two parts, roughly the region west and south of Broadway, East Sixth, and K Streets was Ward 15; the outer tip of the peninsula to the east and north was Ward 14.

the intervening space together with the City Point area we shall refer to as the upper section. It is the lower part which forms the congested quarter, and the upper part which gives to South Boston its unusual advantages.

The main thoroughfare, Broadway, runs from one end to the other of the peninsular dividing each section. A local distinction exists whereby Broadway and all parallel streets are west up to the intersection of Dorchester Street on the rise of the first hill, and east thereafter, the numbering however being continuous. The first impression of unexampled unattractiveness which the lower section makes upon the visitor is accentuated by the monotony of its numbered and lettered streets. The hand of man has indeed dealt unkindly with the promised grandeur of the first speculators. The lower part of Broadway is a dreary array of structures devoted partly to dwellings but in large measure to small stores and saloons. A number of the buildings were originally used for church purposes and in their conversion to trade still retain in their upper windows suggestions of a dignified but today unrelated past. The Church of St. Peter and St. Paul alone relieves the monotony by its fine grey stone structure and pointed spire.

As one reaches the higher level, prosperous looking stores suggestive of an independent city mitigate the earlier impression. With the ascent of the first hill the spirits rise and when the Avenue has topped the second the visitor feels that he has discovered a part of Boston not hitherto known and deserving greater fame. The whole of Boston Harbor lies open to the view with its active shipping life. Below at the foot of the hill the City Point park forms the terminus of one of Massachusetts' beautiful parkway systems. Following a car route around the hill the famous L Street Bath House is to be found and when at last at Q Street the alphabet is finally vanquished by the sea one remembers its beginning at A and B Streets like an unpleasant dream.

South Boston is now divided into three wards covering an area of something over one thousand acres and housing slightly more than one-tenth of the population of the city or 64,091 persons as shown by the 1905 census. This proportion has changed very little since the enlargement of the district by the addition of Washington Village fifty years ago. At that time the number of voters was greater than in any other ward, though Ward 6 [Beacon Hill] exceeds it in population.

There are altogether about 7,068 dwelling houses to accommodate this tenth of the people of Boston. In Wards 14 and 15 [upper section] a high proportion of resident owners are to be found, a significant characteristic which the peninsula has maintained in spite of much change since the early days and one in which it compares favorably with such a suburban region as West Roxbury. Even in the section most open to immigration and least desirable for residence, Ward 13, over half of those assessed for property are residing upon it. The percentage of those who go to South Boston strictly as immigrants is small. It is not the approach to the making of the American but rather the home itself of those who know themselves citizens.

The three wards divide the population fairly evenly between them in spite of differences in area. Ward 13 presents conditions, however, which should make it the shining mark for housing reform. It contains 2,148 dwellings and about 385 buildings devoted to industry. Seventy acres in the ward are not built over, since the flats along the harbor are included. The result is that in an area equal to the Common there would be found from fifty to sixty factory or other industrial buildings and from 350 to 450 dwelling houses or 1,000 families [who] number 5,000 persons. Between 1895 to 1905 industry so far encroached as to almost wholly wipe out the gains to population from natural causes and immigration, without mitigating the prevalence of disease. For in Ward 13 babies die in greater numbers than in more heavily populated districts and there are more victims of consumption than in any other quarter of Boston. South Boston has 10.77 percent of the population of the city, 11.41 percent of its deaths and 14.25 percent of all the babies that die. These proportions are a third higher than for the whole state and are only exceeded by Ward 6 [the North End] where congestion is a notorious fact, Ward 7 [the Downtown] where a bad sanitary past still casts its shadow and Ward 5 [Charlestown]. These with Ward 13 practically double the death rate of more favored districts such as Brighton, Dorchester and Jamaica Plain.

Yet in many respects South Boston taken as a whole would seem a favored region in the possession of wide open areas which the harbor and flats afford, a fine park at one end — good playgrounds and a birth rate larger than the average for the city as a whole. Its best friends have hoped that industrial changes, since no other agency seems available, might wipe out the shame attached to the housing conditions of the lower section. From year to year this has grown a more and more forlorn hope, but recent legislation covering three family houses will give to the Board of Health the weapon required to fight this veritable battle of the slums and South Boston as a whole should have pride enough to insist upon radical action.

A large part of South Boston is built up in wooden houses. The lower section of E Street from Second to Ninth Streets presents the congested tenement house area. It is true that it is bounded on two sides by wide open spaces, one the South Bay, the other the Commonwealth Flats. The advantages of these are in a measure lost by reason of the industrial district lying along First Street, occupying the corner of the tract along the Bay and the Harbor.

Along Broadway and here and there in the rest of the section there remain the structures of the earliest houses. For the most part, however, the buildings are those which were from the first erected to house the ever increasing number of working people who sought homes there. On Silver and Gold Streets, two of the narrowest passageways, are to be found numbers of small cottages which seem to indicate the home intentions of the earlier wage-earning residents. There, and elsewhere also, single houses of two and a half stories have been converted into tenement usage. On the north of Broadway the narrow streets have been built up somewhat more recently in a type of tenement familiar throughout the industrial centers of New England. Every vestige of design is carefully avoided. The structure is a high rectangular box, the narrow side to the front which contains three openings to a floor for door and window spaces. Built in the block along each side of a twenty-foot street and painted a curious dirty drab they present an uncomprising and dreary spectacle. The doorway is sometimes inserted into the house with three or four steps under cover of the next floor. This cuts off what light there might be for the hall but serves as an escape from the apology for a sidewalk which is too narrow for two to pass each other unless one steps into the gutter. The blocks are long between A and B and C and D Streets. On one corner of D and Bolton Streets stands the high blank wall of a brewery. Along the opposite side of Bolton Street is an unbroken series of these wooden tenements. The houses face north and south. Those on the north side receive the shadow of the opposite row to shorten the day at both ends. Down this cavernous passageway, the street mongers drive their wagons. The pedestrian walks wary of a sudden exit from some doorway or the opening of a first floor window or blind, the curb being the most available space for his feet. He has unpleasant visions of what such a defile would mean in case of conflagration to the hundreds of people living within it. A recent report of a fire on another narrow street in South Boston says the fire spread across the street which was not wide enough to provide any check to the flames. The access to the rear between Bolton and Third is by gates and passageways from the street. The houses on Third Street have yard space but for Bolton Street houses there is a clutter of sheds and other wooden structures. If fire apparatus had to enter the block the only exit might thus easily become entangled and a panic stricken crowd would find itself caught between flames and trampling feet.

In studying the housing conditions it is well to bear in mind the period of service which the lower section has seen. About sixty years will cover its existence as a residence district for the working man. Here we may learn if we will what is the working life of city houses where no effort has been made to prolong it by proper sustenance and care. Most of the houses belonging to the first half of the period are no longer suitable for dwellings. They are stale with the dirt of the past. They are insufficiently equipped with sanitary conveniences. They are forlorn in appearance and invite careless, unwholesome living. We are in the habit of assuming that a house once erected must remain indefinitely a monument to its builder, whether wood or stone, however well or ill-constructed it remains excepting only within the march of business almost a sacred thing. In these haunts of disease human life is sacrificed to the fetish of property. Within the past few years conservative action on the part of the Board of Health has weeded out a few of the poorest houses along the narrow streets. Much however remains to be done. In striking contrast in neatness of appearance and attractive exterior are the small houses and cottages which have been kindly cared for and allowed to bear the insignia of family dignity. It is extremely regrettable that the whole housing experience of the lower South Boston area could not have served as an object lesson for other districts which have since been built up into compact residence quarters. Its early history as a speculative enterprise, the unforeseeing adjustment made of its rapid increase and change in population, the ruthless usage of its houses by both landlord and tenant have combined to present to our observation the most menacing conditions which are to be found for human beings in city life.

Particularly is it to be regretted that the builders on the upper area of South Boston itself should not have taken warning by the conditions from which many of their tenants have been removing to the new houses on the hill slopes above the old homes. The upper section still has much open space within its limits besides park and playground areas. But ominously the long lines of closely built wooden houses are creeping up and over the hill-side. Rear tenements are not unknown, foreshadowing future evils which even the breezes from off the harbor waters will not overcome. In twenty-five years cheap buildings will establish a city slum. In fifty years with hard usage even good houses will become unspeakable.

Fortunately the narrowest streets come to an end against the sharp rise of Dorchester Heights. From there on, while there is a large and increasing number of small tenements, the proportion of single family dwellings increase and still forms a conspicuous fact in the general physiognomy of South Boston. In spite, however, of the fact that in some parts of the upper section there is scarcely any market for the substantial residences there is a dearth of clean well-equipped apartments and not unfrequently new families who would gladly remain on the peninsula are forced to seek quarters in other parts of the city.

The Jewish real estate dealer has only very recently made his appearance. He has begun to buy and renovate some of the

older brick buildings. A well-known landmark has thus recently
come into his hands and has been greatly improved in appearance. It is a large block of brick which bore the name of one of
the early Irish residents. His heirs failed for some years to agree
and property and tenants alike suffered from a divided and un-
discharged responsibility. The vicissitudes which houses undergo
under the conditions of inheritance and transfer are a frequent
handicap to the proper enforcement of such control as the community at present possesses.

For that part of the population which must be near the
center of commerce and industry no more desirable location could
be found. In addition to its great physical advantages South
Boston has maintained in spite of the modern unsocial impersonal
city customs a local identity and loyalty. Our brief survey of the
distribution and movement of population there has indicated
that it has a substantial permanent element which is resident
there by choice and not merely by force of circumstance.

The community of interest in religious matters and in racial
inheritance makes a people which understands itself. With such
a combination of fortunate conditions the social development of
the peninsula ought to add an important and vital element to
the life of the city as a whole.

Ward 13, today the most crowded part of the lower section
of the peninsula, ranks next to the North End and South Cove
districts as a foreigners' quarter. While Irish descent remains
predominant there as in the other wards, an increasing number of
the peoples of Russia are coming in and buying homes. The
most numerous are the Lithuanians, for whom South Boston has
become social headquarters. The total number of Russians among
whom they count is, however, still less than a tenth of the foreign
born in the ward and about one seventeenth of the whole population.

A few more people live in Ward 14 than in Ward 13, and
more of them are of native birth. Here live a good many English
and Canadians, making a little more than an eighth of the residents born out of the country. This ward is perhaps somewhat
less Irish in its inheritance than the others. In Wards 14
and 15 is to be found a small settlement of Dutch and Belgians
numbering about 500. In Ward 15 the Germans increase over

their numbers in the other two wards and hold place second to the Irish, who nevertheless remain there nearly half of the total number of foreign born. In the three wards there are about 1,000 Italians and somewhat fewer Swedes. In the whole of South Boston about 15,000 people belong to a generation two or more removes from their immigrant progenitors.

In spite of the fact that the increase in new nationalities is now noticeable even to the more casual observer the additions coming directly from Europe are small. It seems more usual that the newcomers have already made a trial of the country in some other city or state and have latterly been drawn through friends or good report to South Boston. Less than ten years ago the Jewish people were scarcely to be found in the whole district. Their number is still inconsiderable, not sufficient to call for a local synagogue. A few scattered Italian families were then coming in. Today they are in possession of some courts and small sections of streets. The Portuguese belong to a much earlier time than any of the other races save the Irish but are now only a scattering remnant. For a score of years or more the Bohemian colony has had its headquarters in South Boston, but the members have lived in Dorchester and elsewhere. It remained for the Lithuanians to become the first considerable new element in the population. Eleven years ago they built their church on Fifth Street and have steadily increased in numbers buying property and forming small neighboring groups chiefly in Ward 13.

Any very considerable increase in this new colony means that the older inhabitants must find other homes, for as the district is today the housing facilities are neither adequate in kind or quantity. Already the process of removal is under way but just where and why they go it is difficult to say. There seems to be no serious antipathy to the newcomers and indeed there are good indications that the population as a whole even in Ward 13 is disposed to be fairly stable. Lack of any standard of permanence for city population forbids satisfactory comparisons. We know, however, from ordinary experience that shifting abode is less a matter of comment to many city dwellers than the fact of remaining a term of years in one house. In the light of such standards South Boston people manifest a distinct local attachment. In one of the largest precincts of Ward 14 where there is the greatest variety in occupations, out of 1,098 men 21 years of age and over; 431 had been at one address at least 3 years; 201 had not moved for at least one year; and 239 had moved within a year but had continued residents of South Boston. The remaining 124 were almost equally divided between those who had come from other districts of Greater Boston, those from some other part of the United States and those immigrants from Europe within the year. Nor are such figures exceptional — even in the precinct of Ward 13 where the newcomers are most numerous the older residents still hold their own. Out of 759 men in precinct 3, 171 have lived at one address at least three years, and 237 have been at least one year in one house. Within a year 197 moved but from some other South Boston residence. Of the remaining 150, 63 came from Europe within the year while the balance had moved either from some other section of Boston or from some other part of the country.

With some exceptions the names indicate that the Irish are maintaining their old addresses. But on the other hand the newer elements are already being made permanent through the possession of property and are sifting in through a variety of channels being numbered in each of the numerical classifications just given.

It is evident that where there is a movement of population away from the lower section of South Boston it is instigated by something more than racial clannishness. The movement there within South Boston bounds and the ward limits is greater than in Ward 14. A reasonable explanation of this is to be found in the housing conditions. Two general movements are to be found, one stimulated by an increasing capacity to satisfy the taste for pleasant surroundings, and natural social ambitions. Poverty and discomfort likewise produce a search for better things in the way of decent living conditions. The more restless and shifting, the greater the lack of resource and quality of the dwellings from which they have to choose. The newcomers who purchase property make some superficial improvements. The Lithuanian women too have habits of cleanliness and are not unmindful of the pleasantness of well-scrubbed stairs and halls. They live for the most part to the north of Broadway and chiefly in Ward 13.

They are scattered in groups up and down Bolton, Third and Athens Streets, making about 450 families. The single men board as a rule in families and do not form a separate lodging house contingent. It is not easy to say how many of them there are. Some of their own people estimate about 4,000 as the total of the Lithuanian colony in South Boston with something over 1,000 in the Cambridge colony (?). The State census in 1905 found in the three South Boston wards less than 3,000 people from Russia and Poland combined, among whom are to be counted the Lithuanians. In the five years from 1903 to 1908 the number of families counted in their Catholic parish increased by 100 and with the continued augmenting of the colony by young men it is reasonable to suppose their numerical strength somewhere near the 4,000 mark.

Their oldest inhabitant counts twenty years or more to the credit of American residence. The earliest immigration was to Pennsylvania even as early as 1868 or '69, but there was not then the distinction now so emphasized between themselves and the Poles. With the increasing number of immigrants of the last ten years has come the propaganda of a nationality movement active in the old country which is marked by the building of separate Catholic churches where they hear their ancestral tongue in distinction from the Polish language which for generations they have been required to use at home. In addition to this new sense of racial distinction, there is a strong Socialistic sentiment prevalent among the young men. They come to this country already absorbed with a conception of a political life and affected by the enthusiasm for their own people, and in the complicated and haphazard condition of our local politics, they are, unaided, scarcely likely to find very shortly the normal point of approach from it to our political institutions. It may well be, however, that the training in an ideal of national unity which seems to have been reborn to them after long submission to a conquering people, will by slow degrees of assimilation make of them the stauncher citizens.

While many of them come here from their native farms, a very large proportion of them are tailors by trade. There are eighteen shops managed and manned by Lithuanians, three of which are in South Boston. The number has doubled in ten years . They go also into the factories of South Boston and may be found in the iron industry, the sugar refinery, in the manufacture of brushes, in restaurants and increasingly among longshoremen. The girls prefer city factory life to living out, and may be found also in hotel work, living together to the number of thirty in one instance outside of the hotel in a separate house.

The South Boston colony is supplied by its own local tradespeople, there being eight or ten groceries and meat markets, two saloons, two dry goods stores, one milliner, four custom tailors, two shoe stores, one furniture store, one drug store. There are besides a lawyer, a physician, a midwife, three printing offices, a photographer, two newspapers and five pool tables.

They have a unique system of boarding among them which bears some resemblance to the English plan of lodgings. A boarder pays to the housewife a stated sum for his room, washing, table incidentals and service. For everything beyond these items agreed upon he pays additional what they cost and they are entered in his separate book. When the housewife goes to market she carries with her as many books as she has boarders and pays for them individually, with a careful reckoning put down to each account. When the meal is served the book appears and it may be left to the imagination whether the comparison of items with the food prepared is always received without comment and to the advantage of the housewife.

A further expression of their strong individuality as a people is found in their numerous social organizations. The combination of benefit and amusement society is well developed among them as it is elsewhere among all nationalities in the industrial ranks. Two national Lithuanian alliances covering the whole of the United States serve at once as benefit societies, local, social opportunities and bonds to their racial unity.

The paper of the Lithuanian alliance of America is printed in South Boston though its headquarters are in Connecticut. This organization pays both sick and death benefit and offers means of some special assistance to students and immigrants.

Other societies numbering about six are more in the nature of lodges and have memberships varying from 300 to 80. There is one especially for women. There is also a literary society as well as an orchestra. A citizens' Society for encouragement to assume their rights of suffrage exists but is not supported with any enthusiasm at present. The organization numbers about thirty(?).

The combination of business and pleasure enters as well into the typical Lithuanian feast as into the societies. The fun which the wedding provides the guests is worth some expense to them and the universal custom of dowering the new couple is frankly recognized in a collection of money taken from the guests. From $300 to $500 is not infrequently raised in this manner. The fun, however, does sometimes get too uproarious, the police occasionally have to interfere and a newspaper account of a Lithuanian wedding gives a notoriety which the more sober-minded greatly deprecate and do not deserve. The trouble is usually due to turbulence resulting from too much drinking.

Were there not the barrier of language the differences between these people from the heart of Europe and the fairer types of English-speaking people would not be marked. They do not suggest any unusual contribution to the making of Americans. Physical sturdiness, industrious habits and definite tastes for sociability on the other hand are all qualities of merit which enhance the value of their religious and new-found racial loyalties. Like children of a slow but normal growth their present seemingly backward development may well be to their advantage in a more rapid assimilation later when new incentives arise. For the present they form only an incident in the typical local life of South Boston. To them has passed from the Irish that Yankee term of scorn "the Greenhorn" which they have ingenuously adopted for their own use, thus divesting it of its opprobrious character.

The main current of South Boston life carries one into the story of the assimilation of the Irish people to the particular social, industrial and commercial conditions of Boston and New England during the past fifty odd years. It is the story of the Celt adapting himself to a situation dominated by Anglo Saxon habits of mind and Puritan reserve of feeling. Large numbers of them who had already established themselves as citizens moved to South Boston from Fort Hill. They purchased homes where they could, and in some instances added other property as certain estates in the lower section today testify.

The leading residents of an earlier day were self-made men who had come from the country districts of New England trained by the district school and the farm to win a fortune if they could out of the expanding industries of a country just beginning to realize its own resources and powers.

South Boston remains the home of self-made men. The Yankee today shares the honors with the Irishman as first citizen. Conditions of business in the city have as we have seen undergone marked changes. Commercial occupations have grown beyond the manufacturies. Population greatly increasing, combined with these facts, serves to reduce the opportunities of generous returns to enterprise, and the reward is given only to the more resourceful.

The Irish met throughout New England a serious obstacle in the prejudice against them felt by the bulk of the Yankee people. It has taken more than fifty years for them to overcome the feeling against their entrance into professional callings and the best business openings.

They had to choose between the heaviest of manual labor or the long road to fortune in commercial pursuits open to such qualifications as only a fairly good education could bestow. Where the father could not himeslf achieve he might hope to lay the foundations for better things for his children.

In order to truly depict the life of this great city district one should make his narrative a family story book, the annals of many families covering some fifty years more or less. The separate tales would be bound together by one main thread of a purpose common to each household.

They would reiterate the story of how the intrenchments between the immigrant and the opportunities of the city are daily being won or lost. The unit in this struggle is not the individual but the family. Sometimes indeed it means the sacrifice of the best chance for one member that the whole family group may win to the particular standard of success which is the goal. There may be much of the sordidness of bare existence in these family histories. Empty larders, the unshod feet of little children, brutal fathers and husbands, ill-natured loud scolding mothers and wives, wages of youthful workers to protect lazy men from hunger. But likewise there will be found the lives crowned not by the sordid care of the struggle against the empty larder but by the loyalty and devotion of children whose youthful resource and ambition take up the task anew as they reach working years. Their joint efforts and filial pride succeed in producing a home for themselves and their parents of better equipment and higher social standard than the early circumstances of the growing family permitted. It is perhaps the most conspicuous fact to be observed of the generation now in its maturity that it has been brought up in large numbers to the modern American standard of comfort through the cooperative opportunity afforded by a close family bond. There has been a comparatively small amount of distinguished achievement on the part of individuals. The strength and protection of a united home have made mediocre capacity count to its full extent. The wages of a somewhat barren field of opportunity have served as a presure upon the natural family affections to hold the group together. Were large rewards to individuals of average ability more conspicuous in the present New England world of business and industry the home tie would be less important and more easily set aside. Yet bound up with these more necessitous considerations are the loyalties of true affection which make possible acts of abnegation that hardship endured by older members of the family may be softened to the younger ones through better preparation. One is lead to the observation of these facts by a circumstance peculiarly noticeable in the material at hand as to the life today of the people of South Boston. It is not unusual to find several men between the ages of twenty and forty-five living at home. In some such cases the father is still living or it may be assumed that the mother continues to provide the reason for holding together. Unfortunately there is no material available which would indicate how many daughters to a family are also failing to establish themselves in homes of their own.

The general cause for such acts may be found as we have tried to indicate in the failure of industrial and commercial or even professional wages to cover the expense of individual earners in the satisfaction of their ideas of comfort and social requirements except as they are part of an earning group which shares in necessities and leaves a liberal margin for personal use. The particular motives in each family, however, are sufficiently various. Conditions of health often place a peculiarly imperative mandate upon the stronger members to remain at home. The early struggles of parents sometimes so affect the imagination of the children who have shared in them that they are unwilling to hazard a second period of poverty with the chance of subjecting children of another generation to an experience similar to that of their own early years. In some families the early working life of the older children has taught them the value of better equipment for work and has shown them the opportunities which education commands. They are then in many cases able to save the younger brothers and sisters for better things by remaining at home and thus increasing the common family purse sufficiently to carry them through the high school and even through college. Under such circumstances is manifested the finest kind of family loyalty and of individual self-sacrifice. On the other hand, however, where the gratification of personal pleasures keeps young men and women from risking anything, one sees one of the cruelest effects of poverty which in so many instances takes away the natural courage of its victims and makes them either sordid or timid. A young man with a trade or a good clerical position if he remain single and pays his mother six or seven dollars a week board can dress well, maintain a small yacht and belong to the Yacht Club. He has some of the appurtenances of life which the ranking members of society by reason of large means have established as necessary parts of a comfortable existence. A young woman who has by hard work made herself skillful as a stenographer or teacher and finds herself at last able to earn fifteen dollars a week, to have some choice as to clothes, to take a reasonable amount of amusement and a pleasant vacation each year will not easily give up this freedom which has been won so hardly to bring up a family of children on the man's earnings which are little more than her own. He on the other hand may not be willing to ask her to make what seems to them both so serious a sacrifice. Either by mutual agreement they wait, or one keeps the other in suspense pending some expected or unexpected change in conditions. The discrepancy between the tastes and the earning powers of the present generation may be to a large degree attributable to our

educational system which cultivates the capacity to consume
without equally training the powers of expert production. The
rising cost of living and the failure of the school to hold the
ambition of the pupil combine to send boys early to work. The
sacrifice thus made to immediate earnings may be noted in the
family groups of men at home. The supply of unskilled labor
is not coming only from the recent immigrants, the second generation furnishes more than its share since in some instances
where the father holds a trade the sons must be rated as unskilled. This does not, as we have seen necessarily mean that
the general living conditions of the family have not improved.
There has been indeed always a movement of population from
the lower to the upper section of South Boston and more recently
outward to Dorchester. An essential factor in this change has
been the increase in family wants and a corresponding capacity
to supply them. In many instances it means careful savings put
into property which saves rent and affords some income at one
and the same time. The three-floor tenement with the owner
using one flat and renting the others is a familiar aspect of the
wage-earner's residence district. Other changes in population
which bring about a lowering in real estate values, the cost of
fashion, place one-family houses in the market within the reach
of thrifty working people who thereby establish themselves on a
higher social standing both as to locality and manner of living.
Here again the cooperation of the family group is necessary to
maintain the new establishment with the possibility that it will
defer the creation of new homes on the part of the children. The
physical advantages of South Boston and the compact social and
religious organization of a large part of its population have
combined to hold its people as their resources have developed
within its boundaries. At the present time the movement away
from the peninsula is quite as much due to inadequacy in the
supply and equipment of housing facilities there as to the pressure of social advantages to be found elsewhere.

In 1833 the presence in South Boston of about one hundred
Catholic families brought about the opening as a church the
chapel established some fifteen years previously. In the past
seventy-six years by division and redivision the territory of
South Boston has been made by the Catholic Church into seven

parishes. During the last ten years three new parishes have been established. Much of the social life of the locality has more or less connection with church affiliations. In addition there are many organizations of a social and benefit character which involve their members in activities in the nature of festivities though there is usually some financial purpose to be fulfilled. Except for the general dancing halls, managed as a business, it is customary for parties of any size to be in the interest of some cause or the special festivity of some organization with a more serious purpose. Besides the more local interests, contiguity to the city and the associations of business bring both young men and young women into organizations of like character with a membership from all parts of the city. For music and dramatic entertainment of a professional nature they practically depend entirely on the city. The various forms of entertainment conducted by the church societies and other organizations make a liberal demand on all forms of amateur talent. A great deal of organizing ability is cultivated by those who become the responsible members of these various associations. An opportunity especially attractive for men in South Boston is provided by the excellent facilities of the Yacht Club. While by power of invitation the social activities are enjoyed in common by young men and women, the organizations are usually limited to one or the other so that part of the time the women are hostesses or otherwise guests of some special friend among the men. As a rule even people who have to live in very humble fashion have many relatives and friends with whom they are in frequent intercourse and unless circumstances are so severe as to preclude hospitality, there is a great deal of informal entertaining of friends. Such sociability is an essential part of the neighborhood life of South Boston and often continues to hold people with easy reach of early associations. There is a special bond between Dorchester and South Boston due to the removals from the latter and these ties are based if not upon church affiliations of early days, or relationship, upon school or neighborhood association. Between Cambridge and South Boston also there is much interchange of which the Sunday car traffic is an interesting witness.

There is no leisure group to direct social activities in such a district, and for the most part it is the younger element which takes the lead, plans and carries out its own forms of entertainment. There are always those who have special aptitude for such undertakings and others whose occupation allow more time for the preparation for amusement. These come forward by a process of natural selection and become the social leaders of their day. As household cares multiply with the women, as they marry, they drop from the more active participation, though if circumstances permit some are able to keep up their interests. The older women have certain church societies which bring them together for charitable and religious purposes. The sodalities in the Catholic Churches are arranged according to ages and meet under the guidance of the priest. In the Protestant churches much the same sort of social intercourse goes on as is familiar in all parts of New England, the women taking important parts in this direction. For them the church forms one of the chief opportunities for social interchange.

The lines of demarcation which society makes in the district are based most of all on similarity in race and religion, next on special occupational interests and on political views. Differences in fortune and education also make dividing lines which intersect the others. Such distinctions do not make for any sort of general society. The risk of being socially misplaced in the eyes of observant acquaintances places upon the choice of associates an importance seriously affecting one's opportunities for getting on with business or the more worldly ambitions. Among the good things of life which are pursued both for themselves and for what is in them as means of acquiring social prestige is the higher education. In the old days most of the men identified with the first growth of South Boston were not college bred. Out of the second generation of the Fort Hill settlers there were a few young men who went through college. Since then there has been a growing number of students leaving the high school for the various higher institutions of New England.

The South Boston High School is not quite ten years old. It is a fine building situated on a commanding spot near the hill top of Dorchester Heights facing toward City Point and the outer harbor and in view of the hundreds of children who live on the streets ascending the hill. A large proportion of the children of that section go to the high school, though not necessarily in South Boston. The tradition of the English High School of the city and the advantages of the college preparation at the Boston Latin Schools attract them as well as pupils from all districts of the city. Many feel the value of the acquaintance formed at the intown schools an important advantage. There is also an attraction in attending school where there are only boys or only girls as the case may be.

There are parochial schools connected with [names left out] parishes. In St. Augustine parish the girls are carried through the high school. There is also a German parochial school for the children of German parentage.

An old resident of South Boston is remembered by a variety of bequests but particularly by the Hawes Art School which has given for many years opportunities in the study of drawing and of industrial arts. The School for the Blind while having no special local significance has been for many years a conspicuous feature both of the landscape and of the general public knowledge of South Boston. Charles Dickens in his American notes describes the view of Boston Harbor from the site of this school.

VII

EAST BOSTON

When the need for additional space began to press on the city the difficulty was met, as we have seen, by annexing near-by towns on the one hand, and by developing a series of suburbs on the other. Charlestown, and Roxbury represent the first method, Cambridgeport, East Cambridge, South Boston and East Boston the latter. East Boston is the last of a great series of land developments which created the city's present characteristic outline.

For two centuries the [East Boston] Island was chiefly a picnic ground, though at one period it served as a meeting place for a small Baptist congregation which was more or less in conflict with the dominant ecclesiastical machine of the day. About 1833 General William H. Sumner undertook to develop the island, and with the assistance of [a] company which he organized, laid out the portion nearest Boston into streets, and erected a few houses. Perhaps no land development was ever conducted more fairly than under the high-minded leadership of the General.

The decade between 1835 and 1845 was a period of slow physical development. A primary school was opened in January 1836. By 1845 there were four hundred and forty-two inhabited houses, and wharves, lumber yards, a sugar refinery, a malleable iron company, and a rolling mill were in operation. Naturally the crafts connected with the erection of houses flourished. The population increased from 1,607 to 5,018.

The period between 1845 and 1860 was one of rapid expansion. In 1845 Donald McKay established a shipyard and began the construction of the clipper ships for which he was justly famous, and other builders soon after established themselves. The statement of a contemporary writer that there was "no place in the United States or New England where there were so many requisites and provisions for shipbuilding" was literally true. The shipyards; floating docks; marine railway; spar makers, sail makers, and riggers lofts, combined with the fact that a considerable body of ship's officers chose the island as a living place, reinforced the air imparted by the industries.

In this period another characteristic industry developed, namely, that having to do with transportation. The island was selected as the terminal of the Cunard packets and steamships, which in itself naturally called for terminal freight facilities. For a time also the Boston and Northern Railroad made the island its passenger terminal. Although the terminal was later abandoned for an all-land entrance to the city, it was influential in the early development of the island. Other industries, however, were established such as that of the manufacture of earthenware and firebrick, linseed oil, cast and rolled iron, saleratus [baking soda], pottery, and engines.

The population grew to 18,356 [in 1860]; and the number of inhabited houses increased from four hundred to nearly two thousand. The island increasingly began to take on the characteristic of a great working class section in the very best sense of the term, and thus early became a district of emergence. The people were chiefly skilled crafts-men and commercial operatives and wages were sufficient to permit operatives to live in separate houses and bring up their families in some degree of comfort.

Thus early the population was highly cosmopolitan. Of 437 children born on the island in 1849, 202 had native parents; 175 were born to Irish fathers and mothers and 60 to English, German, Scotch, and Provincial parents. It is significant that even in 1850 the Irish were holding their own with the native-born population in the matter of increase through birth, a state of affairs which naturally insured the ultimate elimination of the Americans.

The quarter century between 1860 and 1885 was a period of merely nominal growth. The population increased from 18,000 to 25,000. During the period, however, the shipbuilding and several important industries declined, and while new forms of manufactures came in, and certain among the early established industries grew, industrially the island little more than held its own. The Irish and others of the less resourceful population took the place of the American families who increasingly began to seek out other portions of the city. The period from 1885 to the present constitutes another time of rapid expansion, based primarily on incoming Jews and Italians and the establishment of new industries. This growth has been accelerated since 1905 by the construction of the East Boston [subway] Tunnel. The population increased from 29,000 in 1885 to 58,488 in 1910.

In East Boston, as everywhere, the industries make the community. Until very recently, the manufacturing establishments on the island employed only men. The great Atlantic Works, devoted to the overhauling and repairing of vessels of every sort, is the largest industry. Foundries, boiler-making and machine shops, shipwrights and outfitters, wood yards, dredging companies, the handling of freight from ships and railways, were the ranking industries. Within the last few years, however, warehouses have been erected, garment and shoe-making started, and the weaving of cotton begun.

These new industries are of great significance, humanly speaking, for the future of the district. They definitely mark a change in the character of the industry. The old industries called almost wholly for skilled male operators, or for unskilled workers with a sufficient degree of physical stamina to compensate for lack of skill. The women of the island stayed at home or worked in Boston. The very fact that there were no factories which employed women in some measure drove the young girl to prepare herself for and to seek out a more skilled type of occupation than she might otherwise have aimed for. The new industries employ women, and call for a less forceful and sturdy type of male worker.

In East Boston as in other localities similarly placed there has been much local rejoicing over the establishment of new industries. Before rejoicing it might be wise to inquire into the human results of such growth. Under present conditions a highclass locality ought to send out invitations for a plague about as quickly as a cotton mill. Landowners, retail shop keepers, and the low grade politicians, perhaps have something to gain from an influx of poorly paid and helpless operatives. The very fact that a factory offers an easy opening to children, young women, and unskilled immigrants, puts in jeopardy the whole working population. A community with a proper regard for its own well-being will discourage low-grade industries and offer every inducement for the establishment of factories of a superior sort, that a type of life based on a living wage may be assured. With the coming of the new industries East Boston is leaving behind its early high level and committing itself to a perilous way. There can be no doubt that the present tendency, if continued, will leave the island a slum from which neither civic change nor private philanthropy will be able to release it.

An analysis of the industrial make-up of the people of the island is instructive in specifically confirming what we have found to be true in a general way. In 1912 there were 15,927 men of twenty years or more registered on the police lists. Of this number 6,255 may be called unskilled workers; 6,156 are skilled craftsmen; 2,897 are clerks; and 168 are professional or business men; 433 are without occupation or retired. Among the unskilled is a large force of longshoremen and freight workers. Judging from facts in the possession of union officials it is fair to judge that something more than 1,000 men so engaged reside on the island. This body of workers is made up of Provincials, Irish, Swedes, and Portuguese, in about the order named. The Provincials have taken a predominant place since 1895 before which Irish, Swedes, and Portuguese predominated. This is interesting confirmation of the decided falling off in the quality of male Provincial immigration which we note in another place [chapter on the Canadians]. Another very sizeable group of unskilled workers is composed of Italians and other building laborers. A percentage of teamsters and a proportion of Jews engaged in the garment trades must be counted in this group. Among the somewhat skilled is a very large group of men, who, by reason of great physical strength and the power to stand nerve-racking strain, receive pay nearly equal to that of skilled workers. In this group may be listed boiler makers, firemen, and other occupations of like nature.

Very characteristic of East Boston also, is a considerable body of skilled and unskilled workers who are engaged in various water-faring occupations; fishermen, mariners, repairers of ships and boats, marine engineers, and officers. In all, this class of the population amounts to something over 3,000 men.

The mechanical trades naturally include a very considerable number of men who are employed as skilled workers both in the island trades and in neighboring localities. These are boiler-

makers, iron workers, machinists, pattern makers, skilled woodworkers and like occupations, totaling in all somewhat over 1,200
men. A third very considerable group are engaged in the building
trades and include carpenters, painters, plumbers, bricklayers and
masons, and other kindred occupations. This group totals something over 1,300 men.

This analysis shows that about 4,012 men are devoting themselves to the virile occupations connected with skilled manual
work; that several thousand more are engaged as laborers, freight
handlers, longshoremen, firemen, stable men, teamsters; and that
a final proportion are streetcar operatives, watchmen, waiters,
peddlers, garment workers, etc., etc. Although the majority of
the men on the island are engaged in essentially virile occupations, there are 2,897 clerks of all sorts, inside and outside salesmen, floorwalkers, bookkeepers, office workers, collectors and
small machinists of a variety of kinds, and 250 city and govern-
mental employees. A fourth group is composed of 433 persons
engaged in the professions, clergymen, doctors, lawyers, school
teachers, and a limited number of persons in charge of business;
a group, however, which is rapidly diminishing.

Against this background of the industrial composition we may
now project the story of the life of the island. As a place to live
in East Boston has much in its favor. Perhaps foremost is the
fact that traffic on the streets is light, and the district is out of the
rush and hurly-burly of the city. Very important also is the fact
that the community is not blanketed in grime and dust. The air
comes in directly from the harbor, and is purer in summer and
one or two degrees cooler than in the city. Though there are
complaints over the too eager and nipping winds of winter this
disadvantage is amply compensated for by clean air and better
summer atmosphere.

In that often unappreciated, though nevertheless vital good
gift of outlook, East Boston is fortunate indeed. The natural
qualities which made the island a summer resort of distinction
in 1835 remain, and have been reinforced in some measure by the
human interests of the years. From almost any part of the island
where vision is not obstructed there is a view over water. From
a multitude of points one sees the neighboring towns Chelsea
and Revere and the ocean. The contribution of an outlook to the
balance of life is not likely to be over-estimated.

There is a charm of its own in the physical character of the island. The waterfront streets have that indefinable tinge of romance that goes with the presence of business from overseas. The marine railways on the beached vessels at the Atlantic Works, the various ship chandlery and riggings lofts, the abandoned shipyards, the hulks resting on the flats, the wood yards, the storage houses, the public bath floats, combine to give the waterside something of that inevitable charm which Whistler has so feelingly portrayed in certain of his etchings. Any locality which has the flavor of seafaring about it, whose shops and productive enterprises take on that virile type of ship-shapeness — an expression of the unbreakable gospel of those who handle vessels — can never become commonplace.

The streets on the island are broad, fairly well kept, and bordered in the main by small dwellings. To the outer eye at least East Boston still retains much of that village quality that distinguished it in its prime. Numbers of cheaply built tenements are going up, but fortunately these have not yet been wholly able to destroy the essential character of the community. There is a little compensation in the fact that the tenements erected by the Italians, though patterned all too often on the crassest of American models do break out into occasional efflorescence that separate them from the more dreary Anglo Saxon productions and the crude and flamboyant monstrosities of the Jewish builders.

The physical isolation of the island also preserves a kind of local spirit which is at once more intense and sustaining than one finds in most other districts. The passage across water furnishes a barrier, real though light, to intermingling. The ferries and the long stretch of tunnel make vivid and symbolize, as it were, the actual isolation and aloofness. The fact too that a major portion of the industries have been long enough located so that their operatives have settled on the island, that men working in the same shops know one another, and that a considerable number own their own houses, has resulted in a more developed neighborhood spirit than would otherwise obtain.

This gives the island a peculiar value as a place in which to bring up children. The relatively small amount of traffic on many resident thoroughfares makes them possible play space for children, and promotes that acquaintance among the young which is so vital a means of promoting neighborliness among adults. The barrier to getting into town, slight as it is, brings it about that children are generally home-keeping. Their parents take them to Boston only infrequently, and the trip is in the nature of a great event.

One of the most real causes of local autonomy may be traced to the establishment of various immigrant colonies. These adventurers in East Boston have come together in sufficient numbers to build up a community of their own. We shall study the colonies later but it is interesting at this point to emphasize the fact that such national groupings are of the greatest service in promoting the progress of true Americanization. Common traditions and loyalties keep the individual in touch with the moral traditions of his race or nation while he is becoming socially acclimated and he does not become that most helpless of all beings, a man without friends or country. These colonies also give force to the first outreachings of the newcomers toward participation in community life. In the trying experience of integrating themselves in a new community, especially before the good will of the neighborhood and city as a whole can possibly be expressed to the newcomers, these national loyalties perform a function whose importance cannot be overestimated. The insuperable grievance in the situation lies in the failure of the city as a whole to make such connections with these local colonies, that, in their institutional life, they shall begin at once definitely to include the city and the nation among their other loyalties.

Backed by this sense of strength which comes from the assurance that others of one's natural group understand and agree, the immigrant pushes into business, politics, and education. In his relations with the public schools, parents' associations, and the settlements, he learns to take a few steps in leading strings, as it were, and gains strength for later participation in the political affairs of the community. But until the city both comprehends and includes immigrant colonies as such in its scheme of life, we must be thankful that simple people so adequately build up a social structure of their own through which are preserved those community values which America itself neglects.

Despite the number of immigrants which very early settled on the island, until very recently East Boston has always been the home of a sizeable and influential group of American citizens. Its early character as a residential suburb, and its rank in industry naturally shaped the type of its population. It first attracted those who wished to be just out of Boston, and yet within easy reach. The earliest householders were bankers, businessmen, leaders in the East Boston industries, and retired seafarers. So exclusive was the attitude of the members that the chief street was long known among the disrespectful as "Pucker Row." The early industries also brought in a considerable number of American craftsmen; especially ships carpenters came from all over the New England states. A very sizeable group of young men, though a proportion also left their families at home, came from towns on the South Shore, especially from Duxbury. Both classes lived in boarding houses, of which there were a number in the second section. In time, especially after the establishment of North Ferry, an increasing number of clerks and small businessmen from Boston made their homes on the island. They lived in comfortable cottage houses and gave a distinctive suburban tone to the community as a whole.

Hardly had the island been settled, however, before the better-to-do among the American population began to move away. The development of the waterfront for transatlantic vessels, the growth of the railroad yards, the decay of shipbuilding, and the influx of immigrants, led to the migration of the colony in the first section.[8] The constant rough work called for in

---

[8] East Boston was often spoken of as being composed of four sections. Section one was the inner western part of the island between Chelsea Street, Porter Street and the harbor. Section two was the corresponding eastern section of the island, south of Porter Street. Section three was the middle part of the island from Porter to Neptune Road (formerly Island Street). Section four was the outer part of the island north of Neptune Road. Robert H. Lord, John E. Sexton, Edward T. Harrington, *History of the Archdiocese of Boston* (New York, 1944), III, 263-4.

In addition to these approximate divisions, during the years 1896-1913, East Boston was split into two wards. Ward One was the outer island north of Marion Street (sections three and four); and Ward Two was the inner remainder of the island.

building up a community *de novo* and the demand for immigrants in certain island industries, made it easily possible for the workers to own homes, and led to the building up of the low-lying land on the edge of Webster Street Hill. The first Irish acquired a footing by purchasing locations in this swampy ground. They soon built up a community of their own, bought the church of an American congregation which was moving into the more roomy third section, and thus hastened the evacuation of the American quarter. Here again we see the workingman's demand for convenience to his work and recreation governing the movements of people. The well-to-do necessarily acquiesce, and move back before it.

Since 1895 the American remnant of population has decreased with great rapidity. The schools have become more and more immigrant in constituency and teaching force. Politics have come into the hands of the second generation of Irish. The distinctly formal and informal social life of the earlier days has disappeared except for a single woman's club and a few gatherings of the Protestant churches.

The latter, which one might expect to be centers of light and leading, have as a matter of fact, difficulty in keeping body and soul together. In East Boston as elsewhere the Protestant churches mark the last stand of the departing American population. But instead of being active in sustaining the new order they are generally among the most conservative and reactionary, for it is the least successful and broad spirited of the population which remains, once the movement outward is started. This remnant, unsure of itself and with insufficient impetus to get away, cherishes its isolation and keeps apart from the new and seething life about it. Hardly able to keep its organization alive, dependent often on mission aid, such churches are practically negligible in the active constructive life of the community. Not infrequently their influence is destructive because they cherish a spirit of intense and bitter sectarianism, national, and religious.

The Irish are the ranking national group on the island and in reality they preceded all others as residents. The work of leveling the hills, filling the lowland, laying out streets, building docks, excavating foundations, and erecting dwellings called for the energy of large numbers of laborers. A number of these building laborers settled on the island and bought land upon which to erect cottages. The first settlers lived in houses on Everett, Sumner, Porter and Marginal Streets, on the low-lying land on the edge of the marshes. The first child of Irish parents was born on Saratoga Street on November 17, 1833; and several Irish children died in 1838 and 1834 [sic].

The Irish population increased rapidly and the inconvenience of attending church in Boston soon led to the establishment of the church of St. Nicholas, which was opened on February 25, 1844. The building was bought from the Maverick Congregational Society when it abandoned its house of worship to erect a larger structure on Central Square. During the decade follow-ing the Irish increased both by accession from Boston and by births. In 1844 there were 58 baptisms; in 1849 of 435 children born on the island, 175 or 40 percent had Irish fathers and mothers. The rate of birth, five years later was fifty a thousand, a high rate even for those days of large families. In 1854 there were 338 baptisms at St. Nicholas. The census of 1855 returned 3,498 persons born in Ireland, or 23 percent of the total popula-tion. And the opening of the North Ferry in 1854 increased the immigration from the North End.

During the years between 1855 to 1895 the island was truly a place of emergence for the Irish. They bought land, took on those houses of the better-to-do which came on the market, and erected new buildings of their own. When the shipbuilders moved away, and the supervisors of industry began to seek resi-dence in more eligible localities, the Irish moved into their homes. Since 1895 the Irish in their turn are being driven out by Italians.

The second section remains the stronghold of the old Irish families. Here the first Catholic church was established, and the first Catholic school. At one time the ranking portion of East Boston, as seen in its type of housing, and the fact that the churches and hotels were located there, it was gradually given over to the Irish, and is now in its turn being captured by the Jew. Those streets closest the church, however, still remain Irish. But the older population is on the decrease; only those remain whose work keeps them; or those who cannot bring themselves to sell the houses into which through long habitation they have grown. It is the older generation which remains, the children as they marry moving out into the fourth Section or on to Dorchester.

The third section is now the Irish stronghold of East Boston, though it too is on the downgrade. The parish church was established in 1873 and the parochial school in 1883; in 1910 there were 7,000 persons in the parish and 1,200 children in the parochial school. But here, too, the more successful people are moving away, pressed ahead of the Jews. Many of the families of the parish are on the upgrade, however, the son and daughter working in Boston in offices and shops and helping to support the parents and young children.

The fourth section was very early settled by Irish, and the second parish church was located there. [A census of members taken in 1865 showed 145 families, 50 young men and women (unmarried) and 200 children and infants.] It is now the ranking Irish portion of the island; the church has 4,000 members, and there are 500 children in the parochial school. A considerable proportion are those who have moved up from the first, second and third sections, and they make up the solid front of the emerging group, the hard working, moral, careful, saving type of the second generation that lives within its income, lays by a little money, is not particularly venturesome, is less given to show than many who move into Dorchester and Roxbury, and forms the backbone of sturdy, conservative, loyal, people.

The Irish passed through identically the same conditions of crowding and exploitation that all immigrant people encounter. Limited to rough work at the start, the pioneers had to make headway on relatively small wages. They lived on the flats and the water frequently came up about their houses and flooded the cellars. There was much overcrowding. Many of the newcomers were unused to city conditions and tried to duplicate a country regime. During the epidemic of cholera which attacked the island about the middle of the century it was discovered that a number of attics were used as chicken yards, and that in one case a great pig has been raised under the eaves, and could only be removed by being killed and quartered *in situ*.

The most successful of the early contractors also made their money, as others before and since, by exploiting their countrymen.

While immigration lasts the strong are likely to capitalize their knowledge of the manners, ways of thinking, and national feeling of their countrymen. And in a limited measure it must be granted that the service rendered by the immigrant enterpriser who stands between the newcomer and the industrial situation, and organizes the work in such a way as to provide a certain allowance of national fellowship, etc., is performing a service that the bewildered and lonely immigrant is willing to pay for. Little by little the range of industrial opportunity open to the newcomers was enlarged, they found places alongshore, in the iron industry, and in positions of more or less responsibility and trust. As in many other sections of the city certain industries for long numbered these immigrants of the fifties as among their most useful laborers.

It is, however, the social, rather than the industrial life of the Irish which we are to consider in this section. Perhaps even more than in other Boston districts, the Irish Catholics of the island have developed a life of their own, parallel and more or less apart from that of the rest of the community. Their exceptionally adequate and strategically located churches; their parochial schools capable of caring for practically all the girls and many of the boys; their sodalities, societies, and boys clubs; and their possession of a fairly well defined and powerful community sentiment; gives them a singularly complete communal life of their own.

The reasons for this state of affairs are twofold. On the one hand must be mentioned the religious statesmanship of Father Fitton, for thirty years priest of the Church of the Most Holy Redeemer; and on the other the hostile sentiment of the American community. The Reverend James Fitton was born in his father's house at the corner of Milk and Devonshire Streets in Boston, April 10, 1805 [died Sept. 15, 1881]. Among the earliest Catholic students for the ministry he was for many years a devoted missionary priest, and he took up the work in East Boston in 1855 as a result of the dying request of his predecessor. He finished the stone Church of the Redeemer which had been started by Father Wiley and within twenty-five years projected and built the three additional churches which together with his own made up the four parishes on the island proper. The establishment of a church in each of the four "sections" at the earliest possible moment the population justified had much to do in attracting people and in furnishing that stable social organization that both attracts and holds a population, though these "dreams" at the outset were carried out against the opposition of many conservative people.

Next in importance to the work in establishing churches must be mentioned Father Fitton's activity in building up the parochial schools, the first of which was opened in 1859. One by one schools were erected in the various parishes, until the teaching force has increased from three to ninety-one and the children from one hundred to thirty-six hundred. Sodalities and clubs have been multiplied to minister to the recreational and intellectual life of the people, and the great church picnics and social occasions easily furnish the ranking recreational events of the community.

The impetus toward a separate society given by the development of church institutionalism was further accented by the economic and religious antagonism of the Protestant community. In a small locality the success of the immigrant is not viewed with pleasure. The all-too-evident social shortcomings of those who acquire property excite the derision and furnish a subtle but real source of irritation of spirit to the rank and file of less successful native population. The fact that after fifty years the story of the well-to-do contractor who paid one hundred dollars to be taught his signature, and his wife's attempt to halt a ferry boat because her husband was a stockholder, still pass current shows how deep the irritation must have been.

Religious antagonism was also a source of misunderstanding. During many years East Boston was peculiarly a stronghold of Protestant Evangelicalism, and the common intolerance was perhaps more than usually reinforced by the appreciable proportion of Provincials in the population. The effects of this lack of sympathy remain in the tradition of the island. Children were taught to fear nuns and priests; and at one time it was claimed that there were cells in the cellar of the Church of the Most Holy Redeemer which were used to incarcerate Protestants. Children at play on the streets separated according to their religious affiliations. Criticism of the Catholic community was minute and carping, as over the height of the stone steps of the parochial school. In the public schools certain among the teachers tried to proselytize and at least one over-zealous instructress seated her pupils on the basis of religion. This feeling, of course, made Catholics bitter and uncooperative, and they retaliated by despising their persecutors. This unfortunately, as in the case of the Protestants, reacted unfavorably on themselves. Catholic children, feeling that Protestants were without the pale of sympathy, carried the logic of sectarianism to its bitter conclusion and indulged in malicious mischief. The same cause led to the tradition that Catholic children were untruthful. It became difficult for school teachers to secure the best kind of cooperation with the parents of Catholic children.

Within the past ten years, however, a change has been taking place. A more general spirit of good will has developed all over the city, and this includes all immigrants within its scope. There is a widespread willingness to recognize the good in men and institutions. Catholic co-operation in all efforts for community up-building grows; individual Catholics have been and are leaders in certain forms of district improvement; and some of them, among whom may be mentioned Thomas J. Lane, have been very influential. The second generation has now become the clergy, teachers, doctors, and lawyers of the community, and its members are naturally widening their influence to include people of every sort. Many of them reach across all class and religious lines into that larger life which is above sectarianism as such.

It may very well appear in time that this period of stress was necessary and fruitful in its own way. Perhaps only by forming themselves into a forceful community where the best that is in them might be given expression and receive the reinforcement of the likeminded; where the strong racial and national craving for some compelling and enfolding loyalty might receive satisfaction; and where the people might work out their peculiar group contribution to our life, whatever it shall prove to be; could a proper Americanization have been accomplished.

The Provincials were among the early settlers in East Boston, having been attracted first of all by the work offered in the shipyards. Since 1870 a considerable number have become freight handlers and stevedores and many of these live in the first section. Today they work in the building trades, in the machine shops, are clerks in Boston, and engage as pile drivers, dock and bridge builders and other occupations of like type. In the years before 1870 a number built houses in the third section. They have affiliated themselves with the Protestant Evangelical churches. The general attitude of the Provincial to the community at large is considered in another chapter.

The Italians in East Boston are of more than usual interest because the two colonies show the race in its first considerable accomplishment. These communities answer the question as to what kind of citizens the Italians are turning out to be in no uncertain fashion. No other body of immigrants of similar quality has made greater and sounder progress within a limited time. For the Italian is a newcomer: in 1855 there were but eight of him in East Boston, and in 1875 the number had only increased to twelve. And the bulk of the growth has come since 1895.

The larger of the colonies is located in Ward 2 and centers about Cottage, Sumner, Havre, and Decatur Streets. The smaller and finer grained colony is situated in Orient Heights. For the sake of accuracy we may note two pocket colonies found on Lexington and Princeton Streets respectively. It is interesting to say the least, that the Italians should have preempted two of the most sightly locations on the island for their own. Both colonies have charming waterfront views, are easily accessible to open land and parks, and are assured the basis of specially good physical environments upon which to rear their community edifice. The Ward 2 colony is strategically close to two fine playgrounds; the Orient Heights colony is located on the finest hill about Boston.

The larger colony in Ward 2 began to take definite form about 1895, though its period of greatest growth dates from 1904. It now numbers close to 1,400 families, which include something more than 10,000 people. The first comers came from the North End, and for these pioneers the move represented a good deal of an adventure. The Italian does not like to dwell among strangers — so much is this the case that the presence of one Italian family in a house usually means other families in the same house or close at hand. But the more open conditions on the island, the opportunity to buy property, rent as cheap or cheaper than in the North End, and yet within walking distance (except for a penny ferry toll) proved a strong attraction. As the colony grew, and relatives and friends were sent for in generous Italian fashion, more and more newcomers found the way directly to the island.

Almost without exception the people are originally from Sicily, or Calabria; there are few if any north Italians. In the matter of education they are typically southern, hardworking, plodding, dull, formed on years of hard conditions of living. Most of the men are laborers of one sort or another, though they are found in a wide range of occupations. The bulk are pick and shovel laborers, although a few work on the truck farms near the city. A percentage are saloon keepers, bartenders, barbers, tailors, shoe workers, polishers, musicians. They are good workmen — sober, quiet, and within limits, efficient. Though they lack the strength and the practical intelligence which the unskilled Irish laborer contributed to his task, they are steady, easily handled, and reasonably effective. They conduct themselves satisfactorily as factory operatives.

Many of them seem to have a lust for employment; and are always willing to work overtime for extra pay. The case of a night laborer who agreed to work four hours a day in a garden, on the ground that five hours sleep was enough for anyone, is typical. This intense interest in work has for its end the hope of owning a house. The south Italian has the peasant's lust for land. All his energies are devoted to securing property, and no sacrifice is too severe for the accomplishment of this end. Perhaps one of the most costly evils which the future will chalk up against the present increased cost of living is the lowered scale of the already more than frugal living among Italian laborers. The struggle for a house often puts so severe a strain on the physical and social aspects of family life that it brings on injury to bodies and danger to the souls of the second generation.

As a property holder the Italian deserves the highest praise. In the first place he builds his house of brick rather than of wood. In Italy dwellings are of masonry and the Italian is therefore suspicious of wood, which seems a peculiarly unpermanent material. This feeling for the material of building is reinforced by the fact that Italian contractors depend on the labor of their countrymen who are acquainted with the use of masonry and know little of building with wood. The saving in labor cost over what would be required to pay union wages to American or Nova Scotian carpenters probably more than makes up for the expense of building material. A further saving is effected by the use of second-hand brick and stone. Italians frequently take the work of tearing down old buildings, and they sell the used material to their countrymen. Such brick is cheaply cleaned and is probably every whit as solid as new material would be.

Some idea of the extent of Italian occupation, and of the land hunger of the people, may be gained from a glance at the figures concerning ownership of property. Of approximately 2,400 polls registered on the police lists there are 687 property holders, controlling land assessed for $275,000 and buildings valued at $1,809,500. The owners secure the money to purchase through building and loan associations, banks, a credit union, and private persons. Italian mortgages are regarded favorably by moneyed institutions, because the Italian keeps up his payments and meets obligations faithfully and on time.

Most Italian buildings are either three, or more often six family, dwellings of the type of American tenements. Usually, however, they show distinctive Italian touches. One notices inlaid mosaic pavements, colored glass in the windows, a more elaborate cornice, a bit of carved stone about the doorways or windows, a touch of color to curtains. Though the massed effect of rows of tenements is dull, the individual houses do not show that dullness of pure discouragement which characterizes certain Irish communities, nor the riotous crudeness which is typical of Jewish neighborhoods. The interior of the Italian-built houses is as carefully constructed as the exterior. Though the rooms are small and the suites include but few rooms, the construction is good and the plumbing is acceded to be excellent. In all the newer houses, also, one finds the rooms disposed so that they receive strong light, and may be adequately ventilated.

Housing introduces the question of the order of family life. The small suites and small rooms naturally tend to cumber living quarters, and family congestion is increased by the inevitable habit of taking boarders. Perhaps Italians feel this overcrowding less than other races. They are habituated to meagre interior accommodations and to outdoor living; a tradition which should be seized upon by Americans and used not only in promoting community life among Italians, but of other races as well. The decreased size of tenements and rooms everywhere makes it evident that the life not only of the laborers, but of the middle class as well, must find an increasing part of its expression outside the home. Recreation from now on will be a public function. We may, in cities, be able to save the home for sleeping, eating, and for such intimacies as our increasing democracy leaves us.

The Italian has dwelt in towns for centuries and has worked out a technique of living under urban conditions. He has learned to take his pleasure in an orderly and delightful fashion on the public squares. We should provide increasing opportunity for this wholesome democratic meeting which would satisfy him, and reinforce our own backward adaptation of the town man's way of life. So far our people have tried to live a country life in the city with ill success. At this point the immigrant may well be our teacher. The Italian has already added many touches of color to American life. We shall doubtless be in his debt for this additional one.

So far as he can, the Italian endeavors to duplicate the fare to which he was accustomed at home. A number of Italian provision stores dispense typical articles of diet. In the fall one sees wagon loads of grapes delivered at the doors of tenements, to be made into the wine which is an indispensable part of the menu. There is an impression that the Italian dietary is lighter than it should be for our climate, especially during the winter. Yet the universal testimony of all observers is to the effect that Italian women are better cooks than the women of any other working class group, and prepare a savory as well as a balanced ration.

Parents are passionately devoted to their children, though they are not always quick to seize and apply the results of new knowledge in the care of children. The possibility of sickness is thought of and prepared against. There is always a store of clean linen against emergency, and many families reserve a fund to pay physicians' fees. The average Italian manifests better judgment in this respect than most other immigrant nationalities.

Social life naturally centers about the church, which however, is no such power as in the case of the Irish Catholics. Perhaps the chief cause is to be found in the condition from which the people have come, never having been in the habit of contributing directly for the maintenance of religion, and religious loyalty not being, as in the case of the Irish, powerfully reinforced by national loyalty as well. Children are not sent to the parochial school, partly because the parents do not think it worthwhile to assume the additional expense and partly because there is not the same feeling as to the need of continuous religious instruction. Italians do not make sacrifices for the church. It will doubtless be several decades before the people can be educated to that financial loyalty which is so striking a feature of the Irish Catholic congregations. The church, however, is a great sustaining force in the Italian community. Its services, its festas and its sodalities afford solace and recreation alike to the plain people. It is greatly to be desired that the Italian Catholic will see the necessity of contributing generously in the future so that a strong parish organization of a type analogous to the Irish churches can be built up.

In the matter of convenience to public recreation facilities the Italians are well placed. The colony is situated directly on one playground, is within easy reach of Wood Island Park, and is relatively close to the public gymnasium, public library, and the evening recreation center. An Improvement Association made up of Italian businessmen represents the colony before the city. There are lodges (The Foresters and the Bruno Society) and several provincial benefit organizations. Naturally much social life still centers in the North End.

The people of the community are orderly despite the warm temper of the inhabitants. Such difficulties as arise are mainly caused by drink. Unfortunately the Italian is consuming more and more beer, and there is a tendency for "speak easies" to be established. The most discouraging trait about the colony is found in the number of grown boys who live suspiciously idle lives: a class that is coming to be more and more looked up in cases of thievery or gambling.

It is, of course, the second generation that holds the key to the future. The children are bright and quick and compare with the average child of other races in capacity and responsiveness. On the whole they are more tractable. Very few, however, go on to high school. It is the general impression among teachers that the girls take education better than the boys. They are more willing, more impressionable, more likely to make as much of themselves as they can. Even when they go to work they try to improve themselves. American conditions on the whole, have a tendency to bring out the Italian girl, and there are many fine spirits among them. The boys on the other hand are slower witted, less given to improving their opportunities, and more quick to settle back. Neither mentally nor morally are they the equal of the girl. Until the present, girls continue to marry at the direction of the parents, and doubtless many fine personalities are thus condemned to be wasted. It may well come about that as under American conditions the girls secure greater freedom of choice, they will marry into other racial groups, and this tendency will inspire the men to a higher standard of life. As in the case of other immigrant groups, the second generation girl is often ill prepared when she comes to establish a home of her own. She is not usually as good a cook as her mother, having spent her time in school and at work, and her home and children are the sufferers.

There is coming to be a vital interest in politics, especially among the young. A Mazzini Club has been organized and has twenty members who meet to study economics, American political institutions, and the lives of the Italian and American patriots. Certain among the younger set are considering politics as a career. They point out the fact that several wards of the city will in time be predominantly Italian and they look forward to the time when growth in numbers will give them a degree of numerical strength comparable to that of the Irish of today. Whatever may be the attitude of a small proportion of the population which dreams of an old age in Italy, the second generation regards itself as here for good and is making its plans "to take possession of the land."

The colony in Orient Heights is of a much higher grade than the one in Ward 2, and is a shining example of what the north Italian is capable of accomplishing. Physically the colony is ideally located on high land from which one gains a noble view

of the harbor. The means of transportation are good. Here again
the observer is impressed by the houses which have been erected
by Italians. Many of them are of brick, decorated with carving,
mosaic, or fresco. The rooms are fairly large and there are more
of them than in the houses in Ward 2. Many of the people have
also bought cottages and two-family houses. Apartments and
cottages alike are fitted with sanitary appliances, and there is a
sense of sufficiency of room and the beginnings of generous living
about all the houses. Within the houses are well furnished. There
is much plush furniture and a decided tendency toward gaily
colored rugs; both legitimate and worthy ways of celebrating real
accomplishment. Very distinctive and charming are the frequent
gardens, even about the tenements, the space being in some
cases divided into three plots.

The inhabitants of this colony are largely from the north
of Italy, though there is a proportion of southerners. The population numbers between 1,500 and 2,000 people; of which number
454 are men over 20 years of age. A large proportion of the workers are small merchant[s], saloon keepers, bartenders, skilled
craftsmen, and a small proportion of laborers. There are 185
property holders with land valued at $193,000 and buildings
worth $426,000.

The colony has developed a community sentiment of the best
kind. Some years ago it was made evident in no uncertain way
that the householders would not tolerate disturbance of any kind,
and troublesome settlers have ever since been warned away.
There is practically no crime here. An Improvement Association
organized twenty-five years ago included Italians as they came,
and the Association secured a number of local improvements,
and seconded the East Boston Association in its efforts to obtain
the tunnel and other large benefits. The more intelligent Italians
of the Heights are manifesting a real interest in politics and are
a force in the local precinct.

A church was organized in 1893, and a resident pastor
secured ten years later. It is now a strong congregation with
sodalities and a boys' club. A convent of Franciscan sisters is
located on the top of the hill. A branch of the public library is
much used by children and young people. There is a great deal
of visiting back and forth among the people. The men go into

Boston to lodges, benefit orders, and large social events, but on
the whole it is a homestaying community.

The outlook is much better for the children of the families
in this colony than is the case with those in Ward 2. Some of the
young people have gone to college and entered professions, others
are in high schools in East Boston and in the city. Yet on the
whole a relatively small number are given the opportunity of
higher education, and many bright young people fail of their
larger possibilities. What was said about the relative difference
between women and young men in Ward 2 is even more true
of Orient Heights. It will doubtless prove a great help to the
second generation of Italian young people should the bill to prolong compulsory education through the fifteenth year be passed.[9]

Within the past decade the Jewish population has increased
with great rapidity. The first Jews came on the island in 1872
when the Jewish Cemetery was founded. The first synagogue,
established in 1892, marks the beginning of Jewish community
life. It was not until 1900, however, that the Jewish invasion of
East Boston assumed any proportions. Until the last few years
the type of population has always been a little higher than that
of Chelsea, the island standing between that suburb and the
North and West Ends on the one hand, and Roxbury and Dorchester on the other, in the upward climb of the race.

The Jewish Colony now numbers about [4,645], [?][10] of

[9] In 1913 the compulsory education laws required all children between
the ages of seven and fourteen, inclusive, to attend school. *Mass. Acts and
Resolves of 1913*, Ch. 779, sec. 1. The resolution Mr. Kennedy refers to
was not passed; indeed the age limit was not raised until 1939 when it
was placed at the sixteenth birthday where it now stands. *Mass. Acts and
Resolves of 1939*, Ch. 461, sec. 3.

[10] The numbers of Jews and Jewish men over twenty was omitted in
the original manuscript. Using the South End House method of approxi-
mation by counting all the Russians and half the Germans as Jews, the
East Boston Jewish population in 1905 was 4,645. *Mass. Census of 1905*
(Boston, 1909), I, xcv-xcvi; Frederick A. Bushee, "Population," *The City
Wilderness* (Robert A. Woods *et al.*, Boston, 1898), 56.

whom are men over twenty. The table below gives the facts regarding the various occupations. There are more skilled laborers and artisans than one might expect though naturally enough the favorite occupation is the clothing trade. Most of the tailors are employed in Boston, though there is a certain amount of infringement of the tenement house sweating law amongst the Jews, which may mean that some of the tailors are employed with their families in East Boston homes. The skilled laborers are for the most part employed in Boston and their trades are widely varied.

Tailors 166
Small storekeepers 76
Junk dealers 41
Carpenters 41
Salesmen and clerks 40
Industrial Workers 145
Laborers 40
Pedlars 47
Painters and paper hangers 28
Teamsters, shoemakers, and printers — each 20-30
Express men, cigar makers, butchers, plumbers,
    machinists and blacksmiths — each 10-15
Total number of occupations mentioned in the police lists
about 125.

The Jew naturally sets up as an independent trader. The small storekeepers comprise the third largest group in the industrial population. It is a favorite device among the charitable to advance $50 or $75 to the poverty-stricken for the purpose of stocking up a small basement store in which the family clears the necessary $5 to $8 a week which keeps life together. Many Jews, however, have advanced from the basement store up and into broader fields. The junk-dealers and peddlers number ninety or more. Jewish women are now employed in the Maverick Mills and in several small clothing factories. Every Jew is a born real estate speculator. Even the poorest among them manage somehow to obtain a house. Having secured title by load[ing] on all the mortgages that the property will stand, the equity is used as a basis for trade. Houses are traded somewhat as the Gypsies swap horses.

In comparison with the two Italian districts the Jewish colony seems peculiarly dirty and dismal. The location is not as good as those of the Italians; the people have bought old houses rather than built new ones; and the environment is the dirtiest and most noisome on the island. The passage ways of the tenements are dark, filthy, and permeated with fetid odors, while the litter on the floors, the torn wall-paper, and the kicked-out bannisters bear witness to the presence of parents and tenants carelessly content with squalor. While the Jews are unwilling to give up the five-room tenement for the more sanitary three- and four-room tenements the Italians are building, they belie their racial thrift from the little use they make of the additional rooms. As a rule the apartments are decked out with well worn-out old furniture, and colored advertisements of local dealers. A distinctive touch is furnished by the symbols of orthodoxy, or a fine old brass samovar or mortar well covered with dust.

Acquaintance with the people gives the impression that they are most concerned with the things of the spirit. Almost any adult Jew grows quite animated in telling of the prowess of his children in High School, or the brilliance of the near relative which he invariably has in Harvard. The one aim of parents is to give their childen an education with one of the professions as a goal. Even the poorest will keep young people in school beyond the age limit if they show any degree of ability.

The Jews are perhaps the chief patrons of the municipal recreation facilities. Attendance on the evening school center has been predominantly Jewish. The library is also heavily used. A proportion of Jews attend the municipal gymnasium though the baths are much more used than the apparatus. The local moving picture shows are well patronized by the Jews, the women in their shawls forming a "family circle" in the center of the house, while the boys scramble with the other races for the seats of vantage in the front and vigorously applaud all heroic parts, and join vociferously in the songs. The desire to improve their time is ever present here, and the boys frequently moralize in loud stage whispers to the disgust of their neighbors.

The Jew is beginning to be much interested in local politics, although as yet very few participate actively. Little has been accomplished because of the tendency to split into factions. The older Jews, who speak English with difficulty, have not been sufficiently aroused to look beyond the narrow confines of business though many of them are posted on the political situation, read the papers carefully, and have opinions on everything. When not involved, however, the Jew votes for the best man, one reason for the fact that Jews with political tendencies find it hard to build up a strong constituency. The Young Men's Hebrew Union is preparing young men for citizenship, the East Boston chapter having one hundred and seventy-five members. Its meeting is modeled on the national legislative bodies, the members follow the Congressional Record carefully, debating the important questions. Jewish boys are the most active in the East Boston Civic Association, and monopolize the debating interests at the school center.

Four synagogues minister to the religious life of the people. The oldest and largest owns a large, though ugly, edifice on Paris Street which was once a Protestant church. The membership numbers two hundred and seventy-five, and is made up of more successful Jews. The other synagogues are small, and their rabbis speak little English. Like Christian churches, the congregations are constantly forced to face difficulties caused by unsocial and reactionary members. Many Jews keep up their synagogue affiliations because it is the thing to do, rather than because they are genuinely interested in religion. Aside from the fact that certain chafe under the restraints of orthodoxy, the chief obstacle to religious life is the inability of the young to understand Hebrew prayers, the fact that the synagogue exercises deal little with present problems, and the conflict of Saturday's business with religious observances. The attempt of the people to remedy the situation is comparable to some of the efforts of Christians to bolster up certain of their activities. The more progressive among the rabbis are dealing with present-day subjects; the Young Men's Hebrew Union has adopted the plan of having chapters of the Bible read in English at their meetings; and there is a very slight desire, at present more felt than expressed, in favor of moving the Sabbath forward one day.

One impression gained from studying the people is that the

old are living for the young, and the young for themselves. Not that the former are actuated by any unusual spirit of altruism, or that the latter are necessarily selfish; but both realize that this is the best method of putting themselves ahead in America. Many girls secure a good high school education and their position is much exalted over that of women in Europe. Those girls that must go to work, enter clothing shops because of the stigma attached to domestic service; a small proportion are trained at the home and a dowry prepared for the husband. The boys are advanced over the girls because they can carry the race upwards faster. Many of them have been to Harvard; those that have not have spent a great deal of time in study. They are energetic, appreciative of the best motives, and may be expected to occupy a far from unimportant place among the citizens of the future.

An interesting development of the past few years is the growth of the Portuguese population. The first comers date back as early as 1875 though for half a century their numbers were negligible. Within the past few years Portuguese have begun to move over from the North and West Ends. The bulk of the men work in Boston, and they are cigar makers, fishermen, woodworkers, barbers, and longshoremen. In 1912 a priest was brought from Lawrence, and a congregation established. A lot for a church had been secured on Princeton Street, and a building is being erected. Of the approximately two hundred and fifty families on the island one hundred and twenty-five are on the parish roll. In addition there is a social organization with a membership of nearly 300, the people are rapidly buying homes, and Portuguese holdings to the amount of $175,000 in locations scattered all over the Island are registered in the assessors office.

Until within very recent years the island was decidedly a sociable place. Most of the people owned their own homes, attending near-by churches, and met at various gatherings in the homes of friends and neighbors: there was real neighborship up and down the streets. This local life was fostered by the isolation of the community and by the ferry which offered greater opportunity for sociability than the street cars. Local shops were prosperous, and furnished social centers of a certain degree of significance. While there was some feeling between the Irish Catholic and the American and British Protestant, yet within these two large groups there was much unity of feeling and real neighborliness.

The growth of the population, the gradual incoming of various immigrant nationalities and the changed character of industrial life has sapped the strength of the American population and made the first and second generation Irish the ranking social group. It is this portion of the population which fixes the tone of the island as a whole. The striking events, the really impressive aspects of local life are second generation Irish. Just as in the case of the American population, however, the Irish are now beginning to find themselves pushed. The Italians and the Jews are making portions of the community undeniably their own, and marking it by the myriad undeniable signs of their definite peculiar type of civilization. The island will never again give quite [the] unity of impression which has obtained until the past few years because it will never again be possible for the local life to be organized by a clearly unified racial group.

Each of these various bodies of citizens, whether old or recent, center their social life in a little group of well tried communal organizations. Most in evidence and most important of all is the church. Even though in each case a considerable body of people have given up church attendance, the subtle values associated with religion retain their power and affect the average man both for good and evil. Deep rooted feelings based on religion, half unreasoning prejudice and half loyalty, tinge the individual's point of view toward his neighbor and the community as a whole. The great, strongly organized, well administered, and effective parish churches of the Irish Roman Catholics, and the struggling congregations of the newest immigrant groups, offer a simple nucleus about which the sanest and most wholesome elements of family life in some degree, at any rate, center. Certain of the stronger churches manage social events that assume a fairly community character, such as the Irish Catholic picnics, the Italian *festas* on the Saints' days, and the fairs of the Protestant churches. But it is only the Catholic church that has had the vision to see that the very fact of neighborhood organization offers a re-enforcement to every sort of communal effort which is at once unique and compelling.

Perhaps, next to the churches, the lodges exert the strongest influence on the social life of the community. At the very least there are forty of these organizations meeting on the island. Organized primarily to hold together loyalties of race, nation, and religion, and to provide death and sick benefits, they offer opportunity for meeting among the like-minded, direct the good will of members in cases of illness or disease, carry on educational functions of a real sort through their larger affiliations, and give simple people an inspiriting sense of "belonging" that is of high moral value. The secret character of most of these organizations make it very difficult to come closely into touch with their work, but so far as an outsider may go, he discovers powerful reserves of good will and strength finding more or less adequate expression.

In addition to the lodges and the guilds and clubs organized in connection wiith churches there are a dozen more or less purely recreational clubs. A few of these latter are in possession of rooms and pose as athletic or political organizations. Others are simply groups of young men who combine together to manage a dance, the proceeds of which are divided among the participants or used to provide summer outings.

East Boston is now in possession of a group of municipal agencies of public recreation which is an increasing factor in the lives of the people. Chief among these are the playgrounds. Wood Island Park comprises a tract of 56 acres jutting out from the mainland into the Bay. It is provided with an athletic field, a bathing beach, and has good walks with fine vistas. It is laid out with real individuality and charm, and constitutes a great asset. It is not, of course, a merely local institution. By its very situation it is hardly possible that it should become a neighborhood park, though on the other hand it is within easier reach of the whole island than are most other localities of the zone under consideration of recreational facilities of equal importance. As in the case of so many other municipal agencies, the park is sadly in need of better lighting at night, more resourceful policing, enlightened publicity, and recreational leadership of a superior grade. The island is already in possession of several small local areas, parks and playgrounds. Those at Maverick, Central and Belmont Squares are breathing and lounging spaces. The Cottage

Street Playground is in the center of the Italian colony in the first section and ministers to a large number of young people in a variety of ways. The playground on Paris Street in the second section is in course of establishment and will be a center for an increasing Jewish population. A movement is under way to secure a water-front playground, and this should be accomplished shortly. It would indeed be a pity that a community which in so large a part draws its revenue from ships and shipping should not reserve a breathing space with an outlook on the water side. Play spaces should now be secured in the third section, and there should be two at least in the fourth section. The inevitable growth of population in the future is already bringing the problem of additional playgrounds before the leaders of the community, and these will doubtless be provided.

Indoor recreation is provided for by the municipal gymnasium, the public library and its branches, and within the last two years by the recreation center established in the high school. It is an interesting and significant fact that a number of experiments in the direction of public recreation had been tried out in East Boston. The first municipal gymnasium, established in 1896, was the gift of a one-time resident, and the experience of the city in managing this venture offered a basis for the further extension. A splendid new-municipal gymnasium now replaces the old building. In 1911 the Woman's Municipal League secured the use of the East Boston High School and established a municipal recreation center for young working people over fourteen. This venture was so successful that after the first year the plan was made part of the educational system of the city. An orchestra, a band, a choral club, debating societies, dramatic clubs, classes in folk dancing, athletics and sewing, games, lectures and entertainments offered opportunity for young people of all tastes. As was expected the complexion of the center has been predominantly Jewish. A small settlement on Webster Street affords a meeting place for Italian children and young people of the first section. The municipal concerts given in the public schools bring out a considerable number of persons regularly. The parents' associations of the various grammar schools are well kept up and maintained, and in several instances have become

an influential part in the recreational and civic life of the
mothers of school children.

The striking thing about this group of municipal agencies
in East Boston is the fact that they are considerable in number,
well used, and capable of almost indefinite extension and development. As we have seen in so many cases, the very isolation and
provincialism of the island has turned out to be a source of
strength. In no other portion of the city will one find anything
like so well knit and humanized a population and one so fitted
to participate in local affairs. Not only is it easier to stay in
East Boston than to cross the channel, but there is a decided local
tradition which favors this provincialism. A number of these
municipal agencies have begun to have real neighborhood significance. Thus the stations in the Public Library, the parents
associations, all the varied sodalities of the Catholic Church, and
the playgrounds, are all endeavoring to build up and reinforce
local public spirit. A few more playgrounds, additional recreation centers in the grammar school, a slight increase in the number of municipal concerts, somewhat better advertising of the
city's resources, and a few local agents to devote their time
specifically to the work of fostering and building up neighborhood life, would do wonders in crystallizing the prevalent neighborliness and good will of the people in democratically organized
channels of community upbuilding.

The commercial agencies of recreation are not numerous.
First, and foremost, however, are the saloons, of which there
are something over [number omitted]. These are centered on a
few public streets and along the waterfront. Their social function
is most real in this latter situation, inasmuch as longshoremen and
sailors off duty congregate in them for warmth and recreation.
Though the steamship company has provided a shelter for its
longshoremen awaiting work, this does not seem to take the place
of the better appearing and more humanly organized saloon system. There are two moving picture shows, no better and no
worse than those elsewhere, which provide recreation for a
considerable number of children and women. Eighteen pool
rooms, two bowling alleys, and a penny arcade and shooting
alley complete the list.

The public spirit of the island is, while not overstrong, yet real, and it is built on a long tradition which goes back to the early history of the island. In 1851 the East Boston Ornamental Tree Association was organized. Its efforts secured the planting and care of a number of fine trees which grace certain streets. There are at present two improvement associations, one known as the East Boston Association, and the other as the Orient Heights Association. The former has had a very real part in securing the erection of a long series of municipal buildings and new schoolhouses, and a number of other local betterments such as pavements, a public landing at Jeffries Point, improved car service, the removal of the gate at the Devonshire Street Station of the tunnel and the subway, the laying out of a good roadway and sidewalk from East Boston proper to Wood Island Park. The Association, like others of its kind, has times of unusual activity alternating with periods of comparative quiet. The Orient Heights Association has obtained an appropriation for a playground, secured the extension of the local street car system, brought about the acceptance of certain streets by the city, obtained electric lamps for all the streets at the Heights, and has taken charge of the safe and sane Fourth celebration.

The island supports two weekly newspapers which interpret the local life, one devoted to the remnant of the Americans and Protestants and the other to the Irish Catholics. The several columns of personals that appear in each paper demonstrates the reality of the local interest.

There are, of course, as in other communities, all sorts of agencies for the assistance and solace of those in need. The Associated Charities, the Hebrew Charities, and certain among the churches relieve the unfortunate and those in want. East Boston has comparatively little abject poverty. There are, of course, widows with children, the occasional destitution that goes with sickness of the wage earner with small resources, and a small percentage of ne'er-do-wells, but these are no more characteristic of East Boston than any other locality. An Emergency Hospital looks after cases of industrial and other accidents and renders first aid. Before the city built this hospital, it used to be necessary in cases of accident to obtain a local physician or to take the injured person across the ferry. The dispensary is not used to its full capacity, and it is to be hoped that an out-department will in time be established. The Maverick Dispensary, one outgrowth of the discontinued East Boston settlement, is located on Chelsea Street. It has a capable staff of physicians who are rendering excellent service of the highest grade, and it should receive the support of citizens on both sides of the channel. A small Italian dispensary on Webster Street carried on by a trained nurse with occasional assistance, is devoted to the Italians living in the first section. The district physician and the nurse of the Milk and Baby Hygiene Association, public schools and tuberculosis assistants all contribute their skill toward the upbuilding of the community. A day nursery on Princeton Street cares for a small number of children.

The floating population of the island is looked after by several characteristic agencies. St. Mary's for sailors maintains a recreation center on the waterfront. The Seafarers Federation is conducted as a mission from Trinity Church. There are two or three homes which look after newly-arrived immigrants.

Compared with other districts within the zone, the moral tone of East Boston is high. The fact that it is still essentially a residential district, that is not a thoroughfare into Boston, and the public sentiment is really opposed to lawless recreation causes it to be avoided by the vagabond and the drunkard. The local spirit and the real though diminishing feeling for neighborliness also keeps down evil. Having made these general statements we may proceed to give the figures. In the year 1909 there were 230 arrests for offenses against the person, of which 200 were assault and battery; 67 offenses against property committed with violence; 25 offenses against license laws; 49 offenses against chastity; 1,130 arrests for drunkenness; in all 2,417 cases. The arrests for drunkenness in proportion to population are not as large as many other portions of Boston. Of those arrested, 1,199 were born in the United States, 291 in the British provinces, 289 in Ireland, 70 in England, 153 in Italy, 93 in Russia, 44 in Sweden, 34 in Norway, 20 in Scotland. It is very evident that a most considerable portion of delinquency is bred at home. The Irish and the Italians engage in assaults, the Jews break the city ordinances, the Irish, Provincials and British furnish the arrests for drunkenness.

There is little if any organized prostitution on the island. Public sentiment would not tolerate it, and those who support such places go to Boston. Occasional cases of extreme sexual depravity come to light, especially among some of the more recent immigrants, but in no numbers. The sorest point in the East Boston situation is the prevalence of juvenile lawlessness. 321 children were arrested in 1909, but these arrests are, of course, only a most infinitesimal index of annoyance suffered. The average citizen is driven to action only when conditions become insupportable. Loitering on the street, congregating in the front of dwellings, scaling back fences are common. A public holiday, or a strike, offer opportunities for lawlessness and violence. The causes of this condition may be put down primarily to the lack of a proper outlet for the pent-up energies in the children for whom the present provision of usable public play space is entirely inadequate; to defective home training; insufficient vigilance of the police; a need for more compelling penalties in the case of real crime; and in the fact that there is a certain percentage of young men who are supported by their families in idleness at the expense of sisters or younger children. The chief sources of improvement must come from better organized home life and the building up of neighborhood spirit. The growth of juvenile lawlessness in every case seems to run parallel with the decay of neighborliness on the one hand and the incoming of families without ties on the other.

The island until twenty years ago was Republican in its political affiliations. When East Boston was divided into two wards, the new second ward had a chance to give effect to its convictions, and since 1890 has been consecutively Democratic. Ward 1 continued Republican until a year or two ago, when it became Democratic. This complete vote largely registers the disappearance of the old American leaders and the emergence into the community of the leadership of young Irish Americans. As we have already seen, however, the sway of the second generation Irish will not be long undisputed. Both the Italian and the Jew will shortly demand a share of the prizes and offices and may be depended upon to add interest and complication to the struggle for representation.